Great Escape Forger

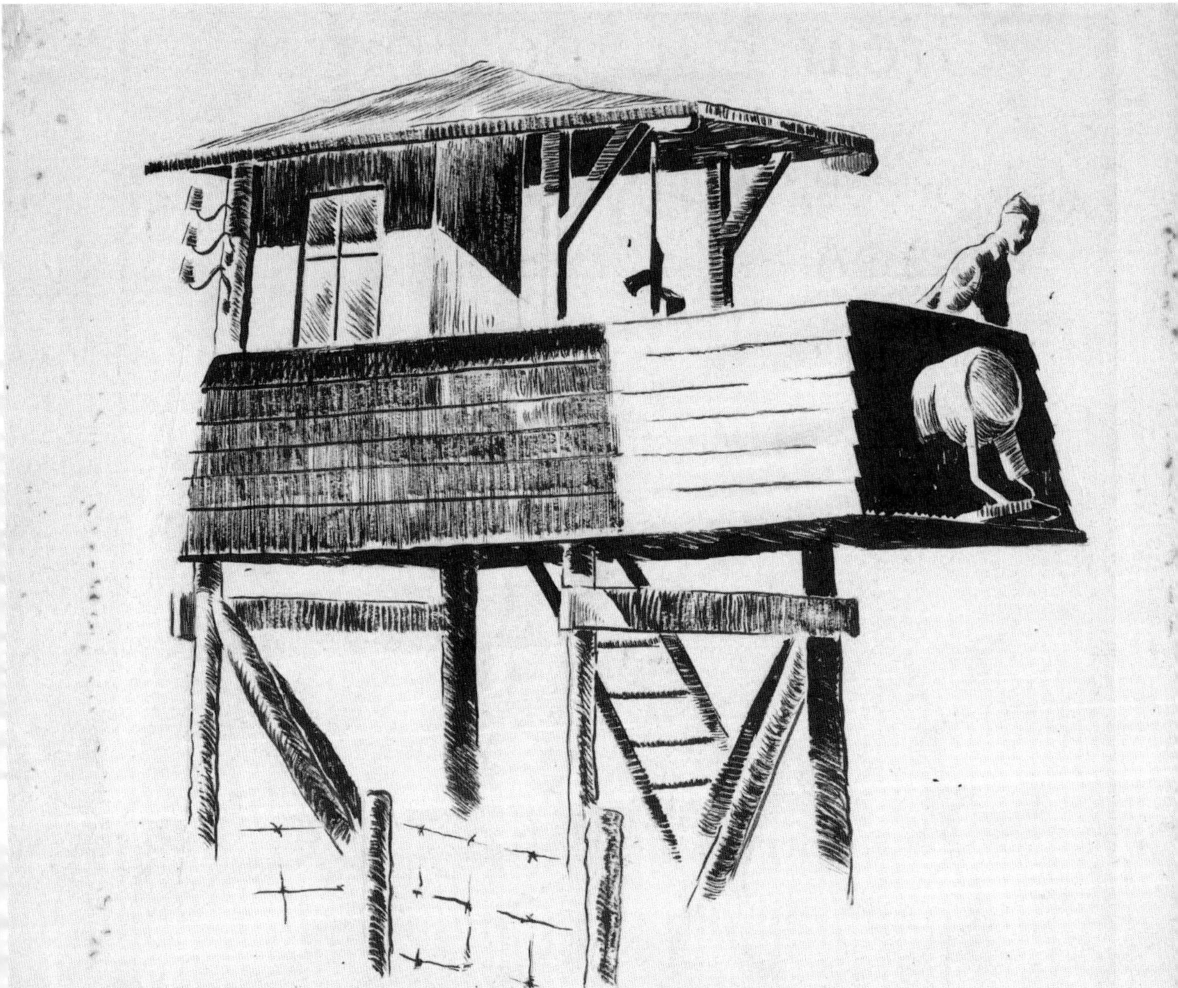

Great Escape Forger

The Work of Carl Holmstrom – POW#221
An Artist in Stalag Luft III

Susan Holmstrom Kohnowich

Assistance with manuscript preparation by Marilyn Jeffers Walton

Pen & Sword
MILITARY

First published in Great Britain in 2022 by
Pen & Sword Military
An imprint of
Pen & Sword Books Ltd
Yorkshire – Philadelphia

ISBN 978 1 52676 798 1

A CIP catalogue record for this book is available from the British Library.

Typeset by Mac Style
Printed and bound in the UK by CPI Group (UK) Ltd, Croydon, CR0 4YY.

MIX
Paper from responsible sources
FSC® C013604

Pen & Sword Books Limited incorporates the imprints of Atlas, Archaeology, Aviation, Discovery, Family History, Fiction, History, Maritime, Military, Military Classics, Politics, Select, Transport, True Crime, Air World, Frontline Publishing, Leo Cooper, Remember When, Seaforth Publishing, The Praetorian Press, Wharncliffe Local History, Wharncliffe Transport, Wharncliffe True Crime and White Owl.

For a complete list of Pen & Sword titles please contact

PEN & SWORD BOOKS LIMITED
47 Church Street, Barnsley, South Yorkshire, S70 2AS, England
E-mail: enquiries@pen-and-sword.co.uk
Website: www.pen-and-sword.co.uk

Or

PEN AND SWORD BOOKS
1950 Lawrence Rd, Havertown, PA 19083, USA
E-mail: Uspen-and-sword@casematepublishers.com
Website: www.penandswordbooks.com

'Everyone here in this room is living on borrowed time. By rights, we should all be …dead!

The only reason that God allowed us this extra ration of life is so we can make life hell for the enemy! Three bloody deep, bloody long tunnels will be dug: Tom, Dick and Harry. One will succeed!'

Quote of Mastermind of *The Great Escape*, Squadron Leader Roger Bushell

Contents

Acknowledgements

The inspiration for this updated version of my father's original PoW sketchbook was my father's great talent and love of art. The quality and detail of the drawings he created as a PoW with limited materials provides an historic visual image that precisely portrays the life he lived while in captivity. My quest was to save and preserve this remarkable artwork that he carried through war-torn Germany on his eventual road to freedom so that it was not lost to time. My family and I feel that the drawings are his best work.

I would like to thank my brother John Holmstrom, and my sisters Elizabeth Holmstrom and Anne Shumate. This book could not have been done without their support and contributions.

I would also like to acknowledge the help I received from Marilyn Jeffers Walton, whose father was also a PoW at Stalag Luft III and a friend of my father. She and I have spent countless hours over the past five years exchanging emails and working on the narratives for each picture. With her many connections to veterans groups, I was able to create the biographies of most of the men in my father's portraits. Their backgrounds help the reader understand what an extraordinary group of men they were.

This book could not have been completed without the help of Jim McNally, Army Art Curator, and Michael A. Mira, Registrar, at the US Army Heritage and Education Center, and Tom Ahearn, a family friend. My family and I shall always be very grateful for their help with the preservation of my father's over 70-year-old drawings and their expertise in the creation of high quality images of the drawings used in this book.

Introduction: 'For You the War is Over'

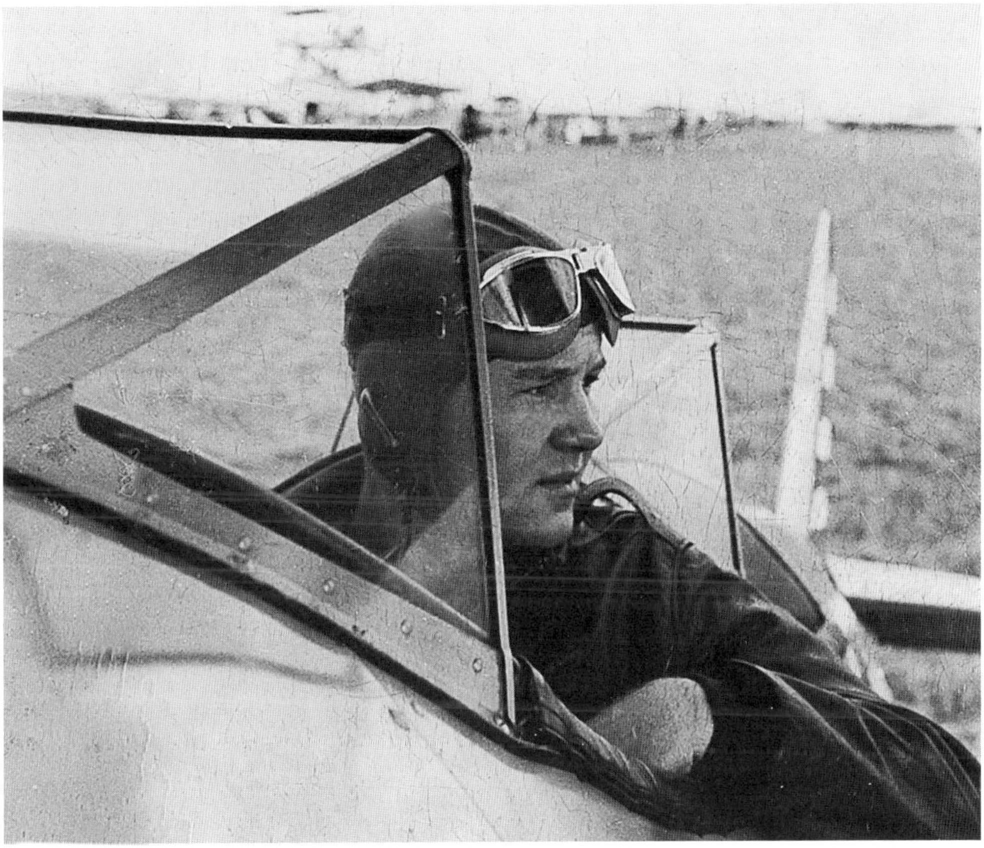

With this commonly used phrase, the downed airman met his German captor. Dazed by his capture and unfamiliar locale and the speed with which a strange new life of lost freedom confronted him, the realization came gradually. The ugly truth that complete mental, physical and emotional readjustment was necessary became a stark fact.

The first ordeal to overcome was interrogation in Oberursel, near Frankfurt, Germany. He found himself searched, with many of his possessions taken from him. Then he went to solitary confinement which lasted normally from three days to three weeks or longer, depending on when a man was captured and the amount of information that the Germans thought they could obtain from him, particularly if he had been in intelligence work.

During interrogation, the prisoner lived in a U-shaped building that held 240 cells measuring 4ft by 8ft. Each room had for its only furniture a dilapidated bed, a chair and a small table. A high opaque window blocked daylight. Food given to the prisoner was an indigestible small amount. For breakfast, there were two pieces of heavy, sour German black bread with sawdust mixed in, with ersatz (imitation) jam and ersatz tea. For lunch, there were a few small potatoes and a weak cabbage soup. In the evening, the prisoner received the same unappetizing meal as at breakfast.

Questioning was done by a German officer who often spoke excellent English (usually because he had lived in the United States) and who had a plentiful supply of American cigarettes. Some Kriegies accepted the cigarettes, but others stubbornly refused them.

The PoWs were stunned by how much the Germans knew about them, even their parents' names.

After enquiring how the senior officer of their group was, referring to him by name and asking how they liked their new base, naming its location, the German Intelligence Officer would get down to the business of asking about the specifics of each mission: the bomb load, the target or hopefully information on the new Norden bombsight. Some interrogators specialized in interrogating only fighter pilots.

Name, rank and serial number were the only bits of information the men were allowed to release. Some interrogators, falsely identifying themselves as Red Cross workers, tried to obtain more information, asking for a Red Cross form to be filled out, but usually failed.

Prisoners were soon released from 'solitary' and sent to a compound where they would transition to their permanent camps. Here they could shave, shower and eat full meals with others. When the number of men held there reached a certain number, they were given Red Cross cardboard valises with necessary toilet articles and some clothing to take with them and released together to take trains or trucks to their new location. Officers and enlisted men were segregated and sent to different Luftwaffe camps. American officers who had been forced down early in the war were billeted with RAF officers in the British compound of Stalag Luft III. Some officers were sent to Stalag Luft I in Barth, Germany, the only other officers' camp.

Upon entering the barbed wire enclosure of the permanent camp, the new Kriegie found a community with its own language, customs and code of ethics. Being captive on enemy soil created a unique bond that held the men together and was strengthened by a common cause. Tolerance and consideration for others grew from the confinement and restricted life style.

Since the British officers were the first prisoners to be captured, they originated most of the rules. Some Kriegies, especially the Americans, were slow to adapt to the social conditions established by fellow British prisoners who had been in captivity for two years or more, but compliance came in time.

To all Prisoners of War!

The escape from prison camps is no longer a sport!

Germany has always kept to the Hague Convention and only punished recaptured prisoners of war with minor disciplinary punishment.

Germany will still maintain these principles of international law.

But England has besides fighting at the front in an honest manner instituted an illegal warfare in non combat zones in the form of gangster commandos, terror bandits and sabotage troops even up to the frontiers of Germany.

They say in a captured secret and confidential English military pamphlet,

THE HANDBOOK OF MODERN IRREGULAR WARFARE:

". . . the days when we could practise the rules of sportsmanship are over. For the time being, every soldier must be a potential gangster and must be prepared to adopt their methods whenever necessary."

"The sphere of operations should always include the enemy's own country, any occupied territory, and in certain circumstances, such neutral countries as he is using as a source of supply."

England has with these instructions opened up a non military form of gangster war!

Germany is determined to safeguard her homeland, and especially her war industry and provisional centres for the fighting fronts. Therefore it has become necessary to create strictly forbidden zones, called death zones, in which all unauthorised trespassers will be immediately shot on sight.

Escaping prisoners of war, entering such death zones, will certainly lose their lives. They are therefore in constant danger of being mistaken for enemy agents or sabotage groups.

Urgent warning is given against making future escapes!

In plain English: Stay in the camp where you will be safe! Breaking out of it is now a damned dangerous act.

The chances of preserving your life are almost nil!

All police and military guards have been given the most strict orders to shoot on sight all suspected persons.

Escaping from prison camps has ceased to be a sport!

Second Lieutenant Carl Henry Holmstrom, POW #221

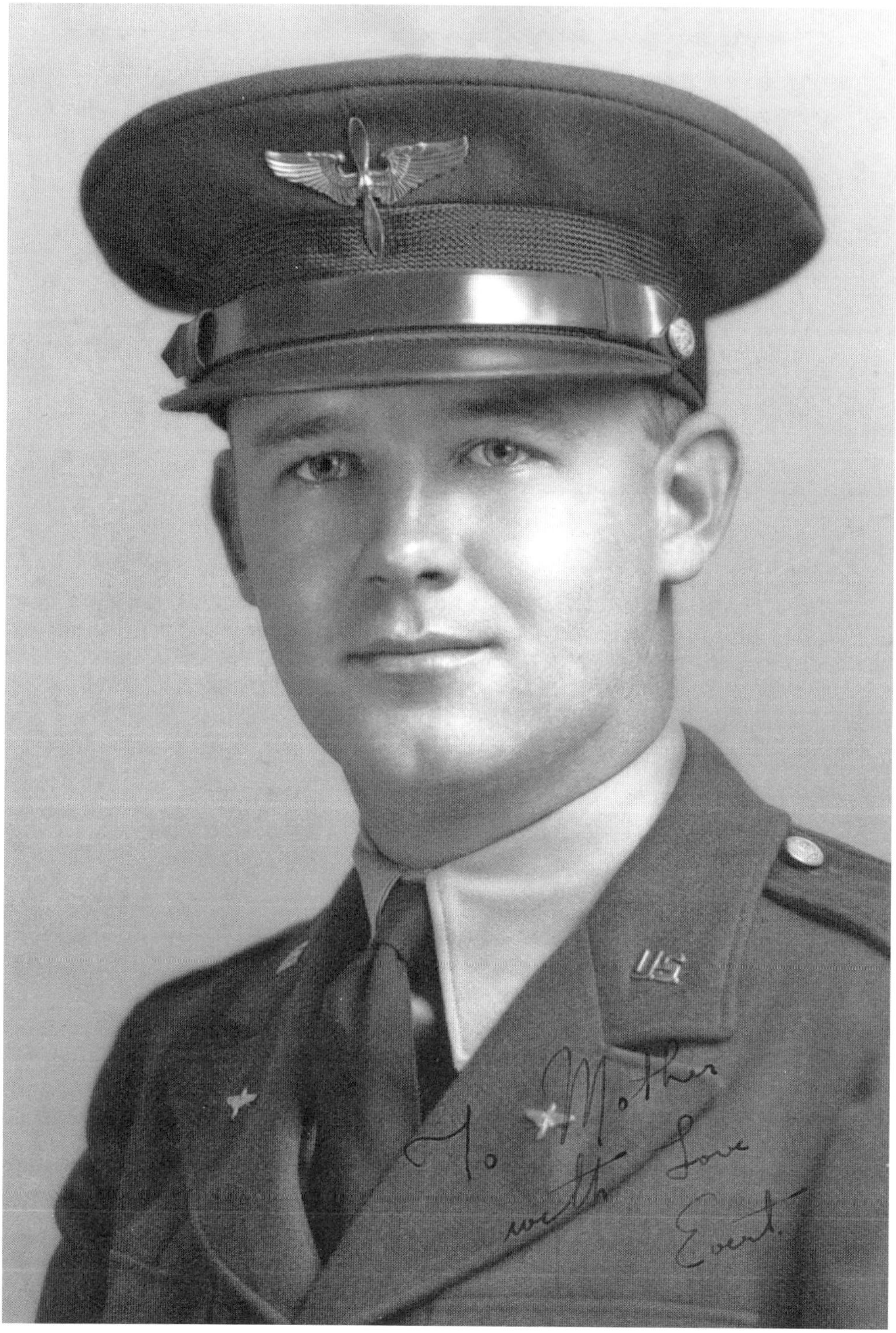

'The Bill Mauldin of the prison camps in Europe was Second Lieutenant Carl Henry Holmstrom of Branford, Connecticut. Now home, Carl, who was captured early in 1943, won wide fame among "Kriegies" for his powerful sketches of prison life.' (*Coast to Coast* by Walter Winchell, 1946)

Foreword: 'The Life of a Kriegie'

In so many ways, Carl Henry Holmstrom's life will forever be defined by the twenty-eight months he spent in captivity during the Second World War. However, that wasn't his whole life, and it certainly wasn't his dream.

Carl was the son of Anna and Fred Holmstrom, two Swedish immigrants who met on the ship that carried them to America. He grew up in Branford, a small seaside town on the coast of central Connecticut in the 1920s to 1930s. Then he moved to Brooklyn, New York, where he finished a three-year course at Pratt Art Institute with a major in calligraphy, graduating in 1940.

Carl enlisted in the Army Air Corps in March 1941, nine months before Pearl Harbor. There was no Air Force as such then. The Air Corps was a part of the regular army. He received his commission as a second lieutenant in 1942 after bombardier training in Midland, Texas, and was sent to Tunisia. Carl had been trained as a bombardier on a Boeing B-17 'Flying Fortress' bomber. His commanding officers were impressed by his ability and tried to talk him into training pilots and bombardiers, but Carl wanted action. He wanted to go to the front and fight for his country.

On 3 January 1943, he became one of the first Americans taken as a PoW in the North African European Theatre of Operations when his plane crash-landed 30 miles north-west of Gabes in the Tunisian desert. German paratroopers, riding small motorcycles, surrounded his B-17. Carl grabbed his pistol, ready to shoot it out. His senior officer barked at him: 'What are you, nuts? You want to get us all killed?' and ordered him to drop the gun. The point was that they were behind enemy lines, in the middle of the desert, and had no chance of survival if they tried to shoot it out with the Nazis.

The flight crew was taken to the Tunis airport and flown to Naples, Italy, where they spent the night in jail. The next day they were sent to a prison in Rome and from there travelled by train via Frankfurt, Germany, to Dulag Luft which was composed of three installations: Auswertestelle West, which was the interrogation and evaluation centre in the town of Oberursel; the hospital at Hohemark; and the transit camp at that time also located in Oberursel. The transit camp was moved after being bombed later in the war to Wetzlar, where PoWs would be processed to a permanent camp after interrogation. 'There were some civilians on the train, and it was incredible to them that we were Americans. We were the first to be taken,' Carl Holmstrom said in an interview with the *Waterbury Republican* after the war. 'Interrogation meant solitary confinement, very little food and the "heat treatment".' The heat treatment that Carl mentioned was the overheating of the cells to 'soften them up' for interrogation. After the war, several Germans were put on trial for overheating the cells and were convicted.

During the interrogations, Carl was told more about himself and his crew members than expected. Much of the information was very personal in nature, information that was gleaned from careful examination of newspaper articles and from seemingly innocent comments dropped by other prisoners. The Germans had a massive file system called BUNA where clipped articles, recovered maps, captured pictures, theatre tickets, personal letters, and anything else that came out of prisoners' pockets or planes was kept for further use.

After interrogation, Carl Holmstrom was sent to Oflag XXI-B in Schubin, Poland and was transferred to Hohemark Hospital having been diagnosed with yellow jaundice. This was a PoW camp for officers and enlisted men, located 15 miles south-west of Bromberg, where he stayed for two months recuperating from his injuries. Ironically, this was a converted boys' school which was first occupied by the Germans in 1939. The camp was later renamed and became Oflag 64 on 6 June 1943, four months after Carl arrived in Schubin.

Although later in the war the Germans attempted to keep different nationalities apart, in the early stages of the war they saw no need to do so. The camp went through several transitions; at one point, as Oflag XXI-B, housing Americans with air crew of the Commonwealth forces. These were PoWs from England, Scotland, Australia, New Zealand, Canada, South Africa and a few other nations such as France, Poland and Denmark. Some had been captured at Dunkirk. Many PoWs later came through that camp first before going to Stalag Luft I and Stalag Luft III.

It was at Oflag XXI-B that Carl started sketching and drawing the details of the prison camp and his everyday life. 'The drawings were made during imprisonment,' he told a newspaper reporter after the war, 'and represent a sincere effort to portray to the American people and especially to the relatives of the prisoners intimate glimpses of "Kriegie Life".'

At the end of six months, Carl was moved to Stalag Luft III in Sagan, Germany, and placed in South Compound, barrack 135, room 14. The camp was specifically constructed to prevent escapes of Allied air officers, who were generally treated better than other non-flying American PoWs because *Reichsmarschall* Hermann Göring, a highly-decorated First World War Luftwaffe pilot who administered the Luftwaffe PoW camps, still upheld the tradition of honour among airmen.

Out of the hundreds of German camps that imprisoned American soldiers and airmen, Stalag Luft III is definitely the best known because of what later became called 'the Great Escape' when seventy-six PoWs tunnelled out of the camp, fifty of whom were later murdered by the Gestapo. At that time Carl, as an inmate of the prison camp, looked at it as just another escape until the deadly consequences became evident.

As a professional artist, Carl was assigned to sketch maps and forge escape documents and money to facilitate escapes. He told his daughter Susan: 'We made the money from the insides of the chocolate bar wrappers as that paper felt like real money. Then it was hand-inked with home-made inks. Many materials were used to make the coloured inks. The black ink was made from charcoal left after the fires.' The Germans had confiscated any traditional inks to prevent the forging of papers for escape.

Forgers worked on gate passes as well as travel documents. Often, and unbeknown to the forgers, a new German mark could be added to the back of the new gate passes to leave the camp for delousing, for instance, and Germans checked the new marks to watch for forgeries. The forgers, beyond applying their artistic talents, also experimented with clandestine photos to affix to travel documents, and they worked with map makers in the camp. A few of the best British forgers in the camp would have worked with Holmstrom, and several of those were later murdered after the Great Escape.

When his forging duties were completed, Carl found time to illustrate camp life. 'For drawing paper, I tore pages out of hymn books and sketched on the backs of music sheets,' Carl told a reporter after the war. 'Later, the YMCA sent over paper and paint. In the camps, it was really the Red Cross that saved us – so far as food and cigarettes went.'

In late January 1945, Russian guns were heard east of Stalag Luft III. Adolf Hitler ordered the prisoners to be evacuated immediately so that the Russians could not liberate the camp. In reality, the PoWs were preparing to leave days before they did, sewing blankets, mittens and packs. They knew it was likely that they would leave despite the frigid weather, and they would likely march at night. When the call for the march was given, Carl stuffed his clothes, along with his pictures, into his blanket rolls and backpack. The PoWs took only what they could carry, so many things were left behind. He took the pictures seen in this book instead of food or other necessities that would help him survive.

The PoWs had thirty minutes' notice to pack up their belongings and leave Stalag Luft III, whereupon they were forced to march for several days through the coldest winter in Germany in fifty years, sleeping in barns, factories and churches along the way. Carl was on the infamous 52-mile Forced March to Spremberg, Germany, where he then rode in an overcrowded and filthy 40&8 (forty men or eight horses) box car to Nuremberg, Germany, Stalag XIII-D. 'Why was I sent there? The Russians came,' recalled Carl after the war. The approach of the American Third Army caused another forced march. 'Two months later, I was marched to Moosburg, Germany, Stalag VII-A. Why? The Americans came.'

The American Third Army, led by General George Patton, liberated the prisoners in Moosburg on 29 April 1945. All around the camp, bullets were flying. 'We were out cooking breakfast on our "Kriegie burners" when the shots started,' Carl said. 'It didn't bother us. We just went inside to avoid the bullets and cooked breakfast there.'

At long last, the wait for freedom was over. Thousands of men from camps all over Europe were coming home after a great sacrifice to defeat a dictator and restore freedom to many countries. Former PoWs were reclassified as RAMPs: Returned Allied Military Personnel. Telegrams went out to their families stating that the men were being returned to military control.

After General Patton liberated Stalag VII-A, the American Army that liberated the camp, holding 120,000 Allied PoWs, tried to keep the men in the camp for their own protection as isolated SS troops were still fighting in the area. With German guards having fled or been taken away, routine operations of running such a huge camp stopped abruptly upon liberation. The prisoners were not fed, the latrines were not emptied and the men were still urged to stay in the camp. For the safety of the waiting men, the gates were locked and the newly-freed PoWs were no longer allowed outside. 'They had guards to prevent our escape, this time escape from the US Army,' Carl said.

After Stalag VII-A was liberated, Carl endured long lines and multiple delays which created frustration and impatience. As days dragged on, Carl and a friend from Chicago decided to make their own plans for departure and left the camp. Breaking through the wire, they commandeered any kind of transportation they could from German staff cars to bicycles to horses in order to make it to Paris or to friendly lines. They traded cigarettes and soap with civilians for food, especially eggs. They travelled through Germany from Munich to Frankfurt, and passed through many of the camps where they had been imprisoned before getting to Frankfurt, Germany. After reaching Frankfurt they flew to Paris.

Those who had waited in camp were flown out in two weeks after truck rides to recently-bombed local German airfields. Those men were flown to northern France, where they were processed home through Camp Lucky Strike. Names of cigarette companies, like Lucky Strike, were used for the transitional camps for security reasons. These camps were massive tent cities where men waiting in long lines transitioned back to pre-war life. PoWs were given several glasses of egg nog for days to prepare their stomachs for normal amounts and varieties of foods. Uniforms were issued, physicals were given, partial back pay was received, and souvenirs of war were registered.

Carl and his friend eventually ended up with the other PoWs at Camp Lucky Strike near Le Havre, France, on 7 May 1945, the day before V-E Day. There they got on a ship list and later arrived in New York. Those grateful men, Carl Holmstrom included, were finally going home.

Map of Prisoner of War Camps in Germany: Second World War

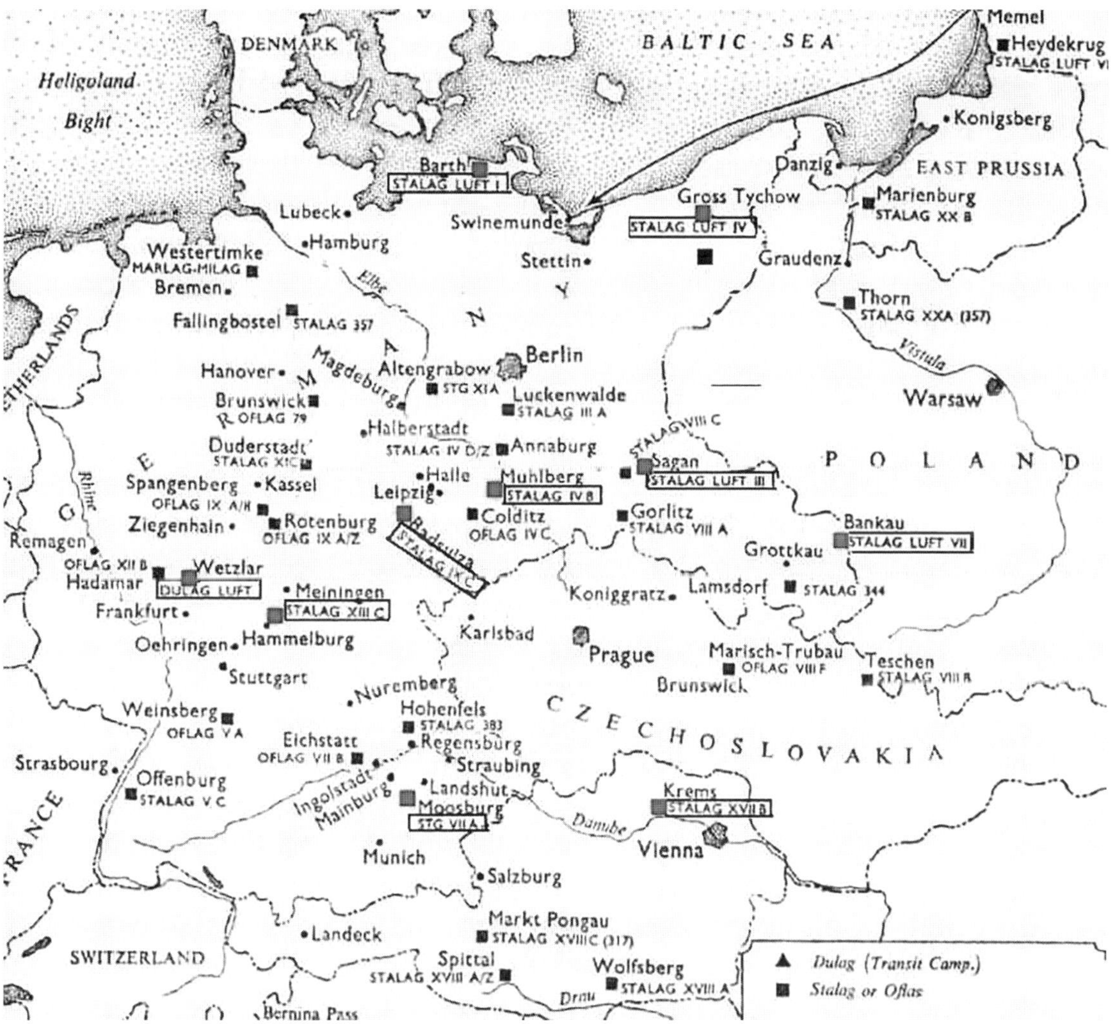

Dulag, a contraction of the word *Durchgangslager*, defines the camps that served as collection points for PoWs prior to reassignment to permanent camps. The designation stalag, a contraction of the word *Stammlager*, connotes a prison for the 'common stock' of the army or servicemen below officer ranks. Few NCO airmen and lower-ranking prisoners enjoyed the relative comfort of Stalag Luft III as they were typically sent to other Luftwaffe camps for enlisted men. Stalag Luft III should have been called oflag or officers' camp, but the Germans were consistent as all the Luftwaffe camps were labelled stalags. (*Courtesy of Pegasus Archive*: www.pegasusarchive.org)

Sketches of Oflag XXI-B

Buildings Identified in Oflag XXI-B

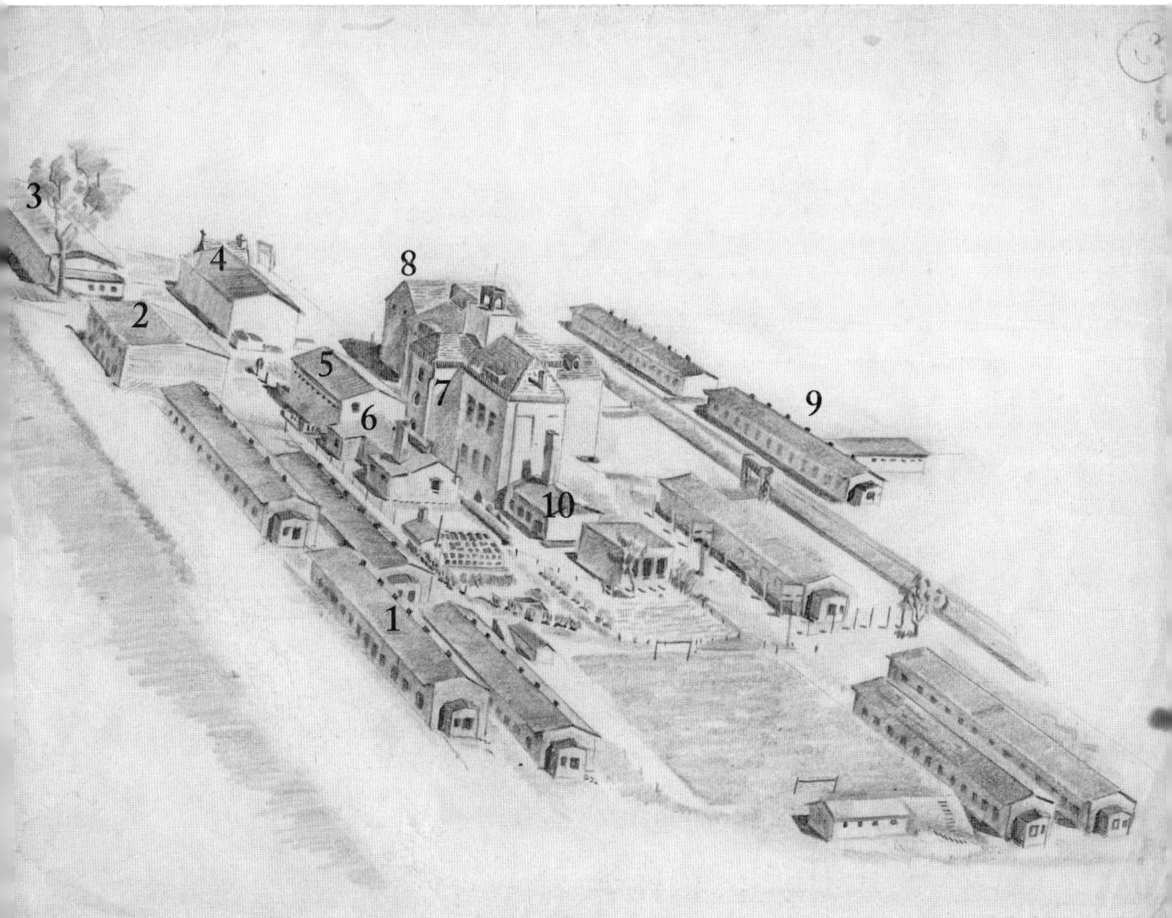

Please see page 79 for identification of camp buildings.

Hospital and Senior Officer's Building

The building with the three windows is the senior officer's building and the hospital is behind it.

The hospital staff at Oflag XXI-B were very competent and consisted of three English doctors, captains in the British Army and one English dentist. The hospital had a thirty-bed capacity but was not equipped to handle those seriously ill or injured.

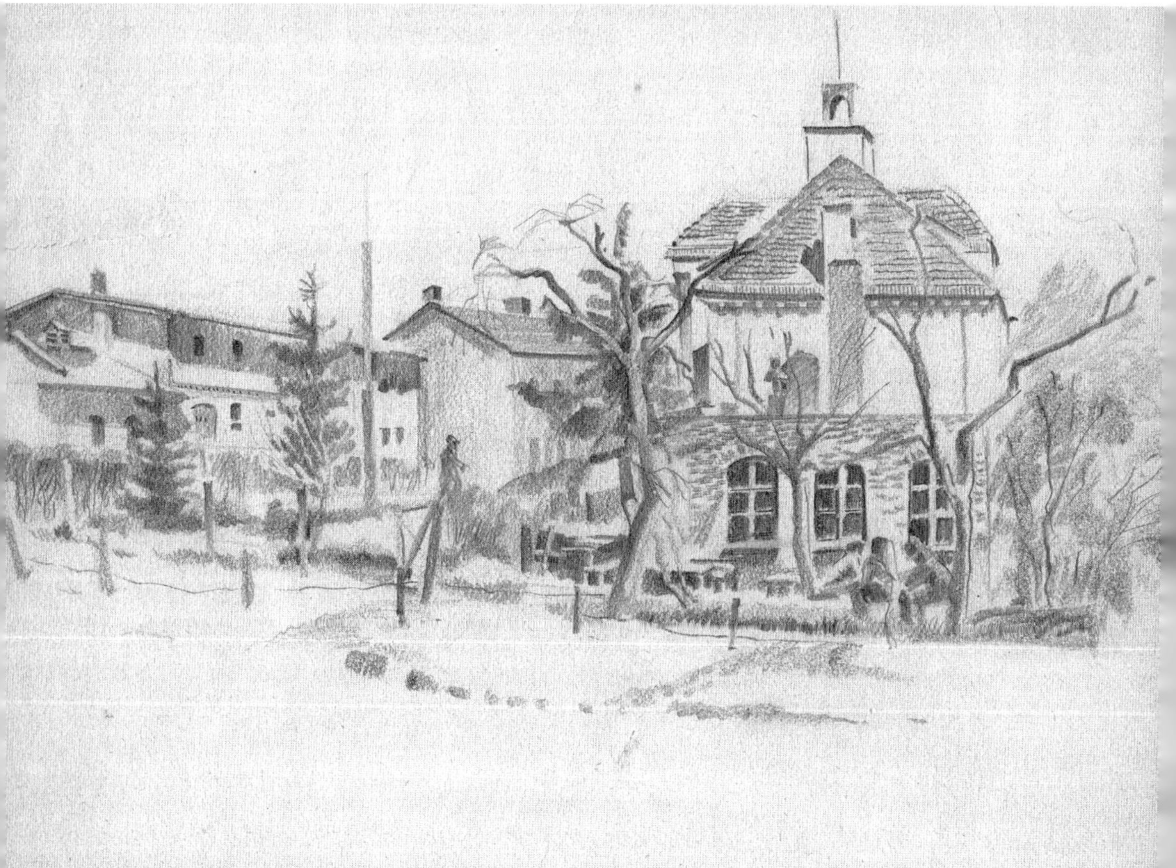

Hospital and the 'The White House'

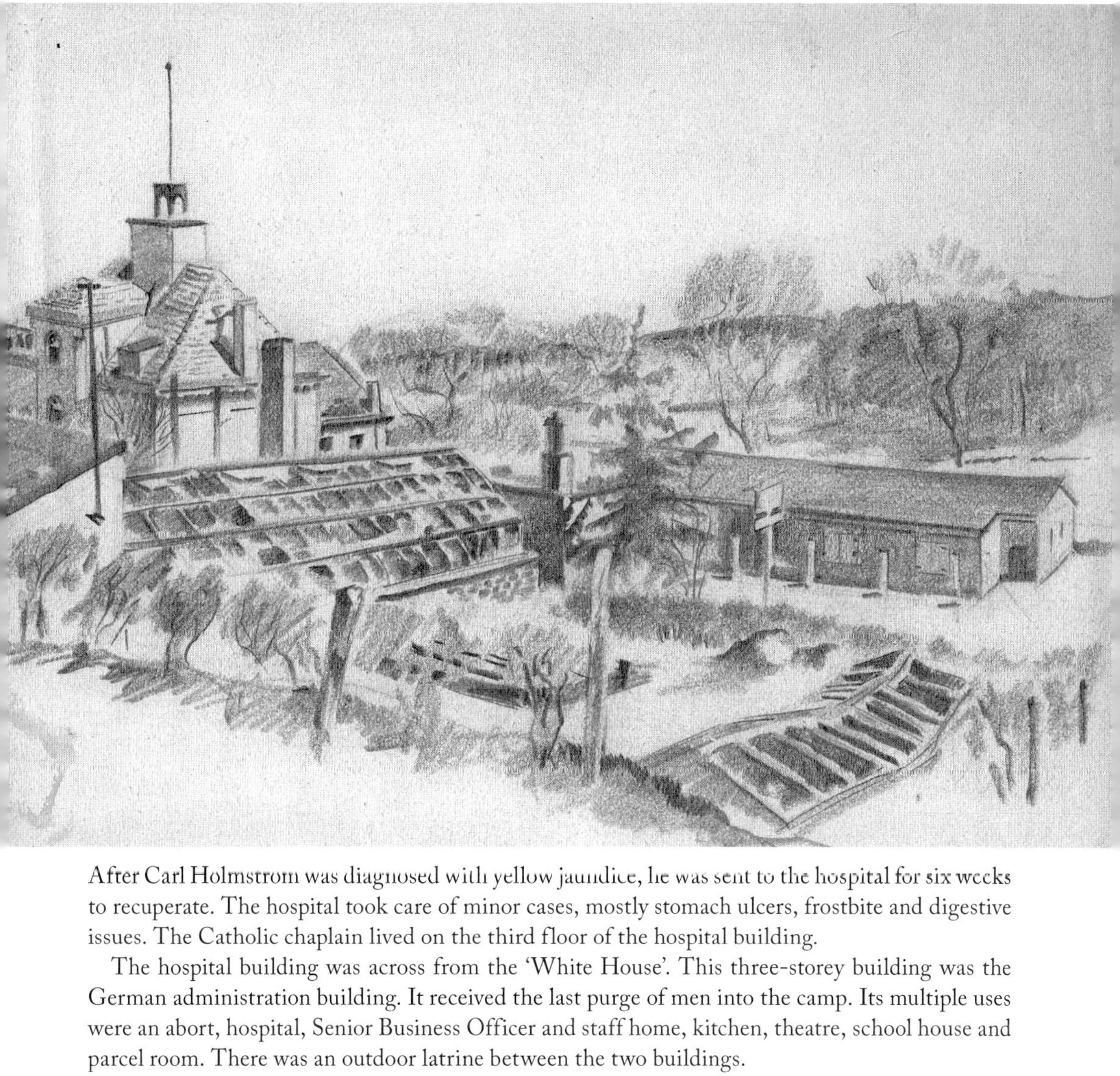

After Carl Holmstrom was diagnosed with yellow jaundice, he was sent to the hospital for six weeks to recuperate. The hospital took care of minor cases, mostly stomach ulcers, frostbite and digestive issues. The Catholic chaplain lived on the third floor of the hospital building.

The hospital building was across from the 'White House'. This three-storey building was the German administration building. It received the last purge of men into the camp. Its multiple uses were an abort, hospital, Senior Business Officer and staff home, kitchen, theatre, school house and parcel room. There was an outdoor latrine between the two buildings.

Cook House and British Red Cross Food Parcels

The PoWs were fed from British Red Cross parcels which supplemented German rations. They were treated to English food such as crackers, tea, oxtail soup and Yorkshire pudding.

Russian PoWs were held in the barracks, which were separated from the rest of the compound by barbed wire. The Russian PoWs were poorly treated by the Germans and were not allowed to share in the British Red Cross parcels. A voluntary contribution from each man's rations was made daily for a donation to the thirty-some Russian PoWs. The rations included cigarettes as well as food. Beer was much more attainable here than at Stalag Luft III.

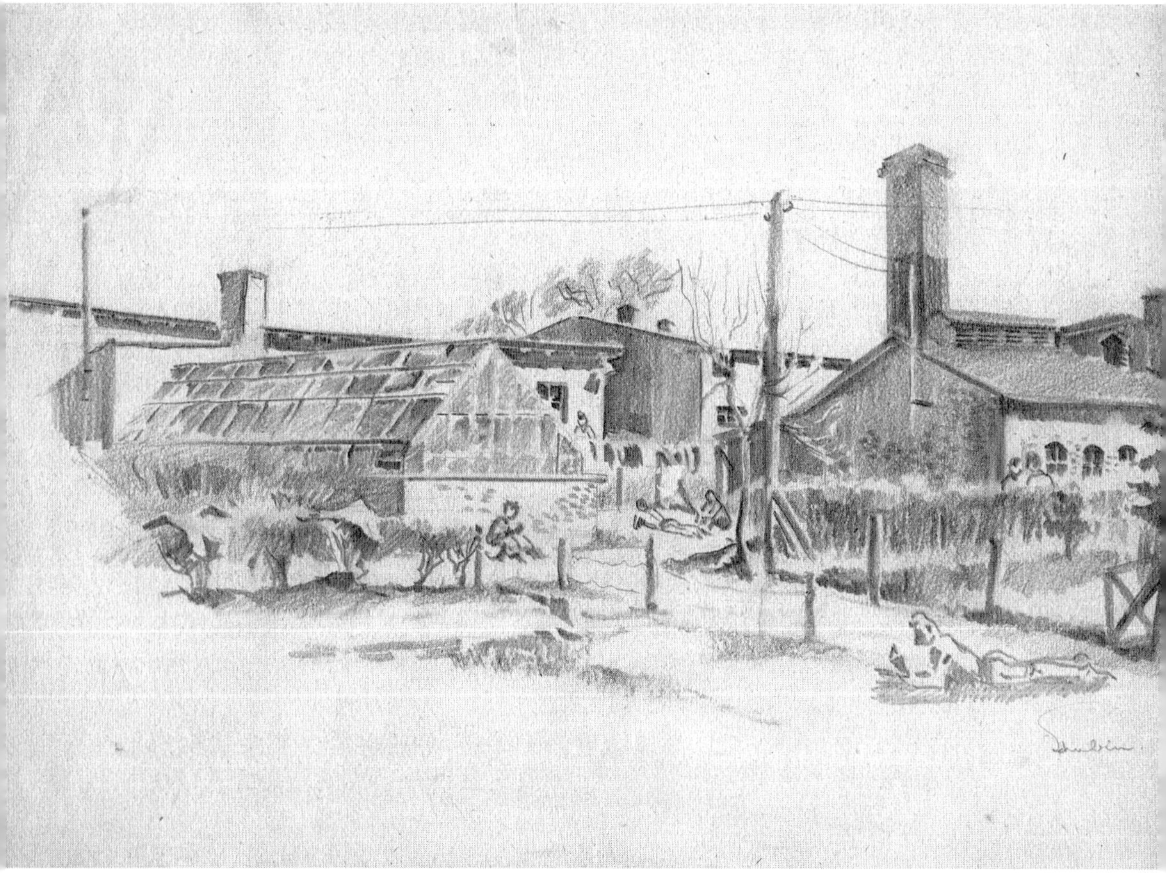

Small Kitchen

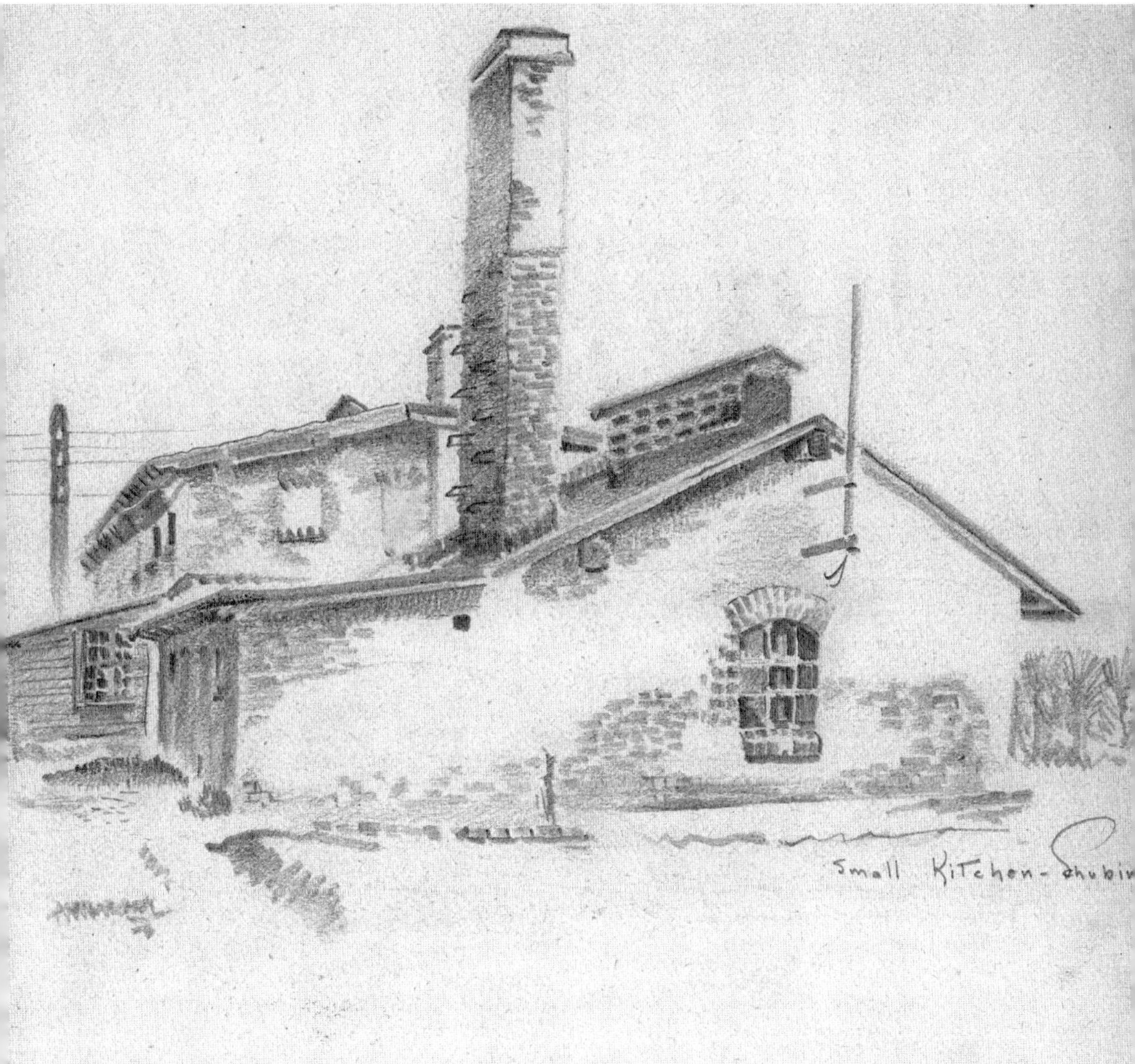

The cookhouse at Oflag XXI-B was located in a large room under the 'White House' in the western part of the building. The small kitchen is the building with the tall chimney.

Nourishment and entertainment revolved around food. Occasionally, potato-eating contests were arranged. One winner, an Englishman, consumed four-and-a-half bowls of mashed potatoes to win six chocolate bars. Some individuals with large appetites wagered that they could eat the contents of a British Red Cross parcel within a day, only to find their capacity was smaller than their imagination.

Barracks of Oflag XXI-B Showing Combines

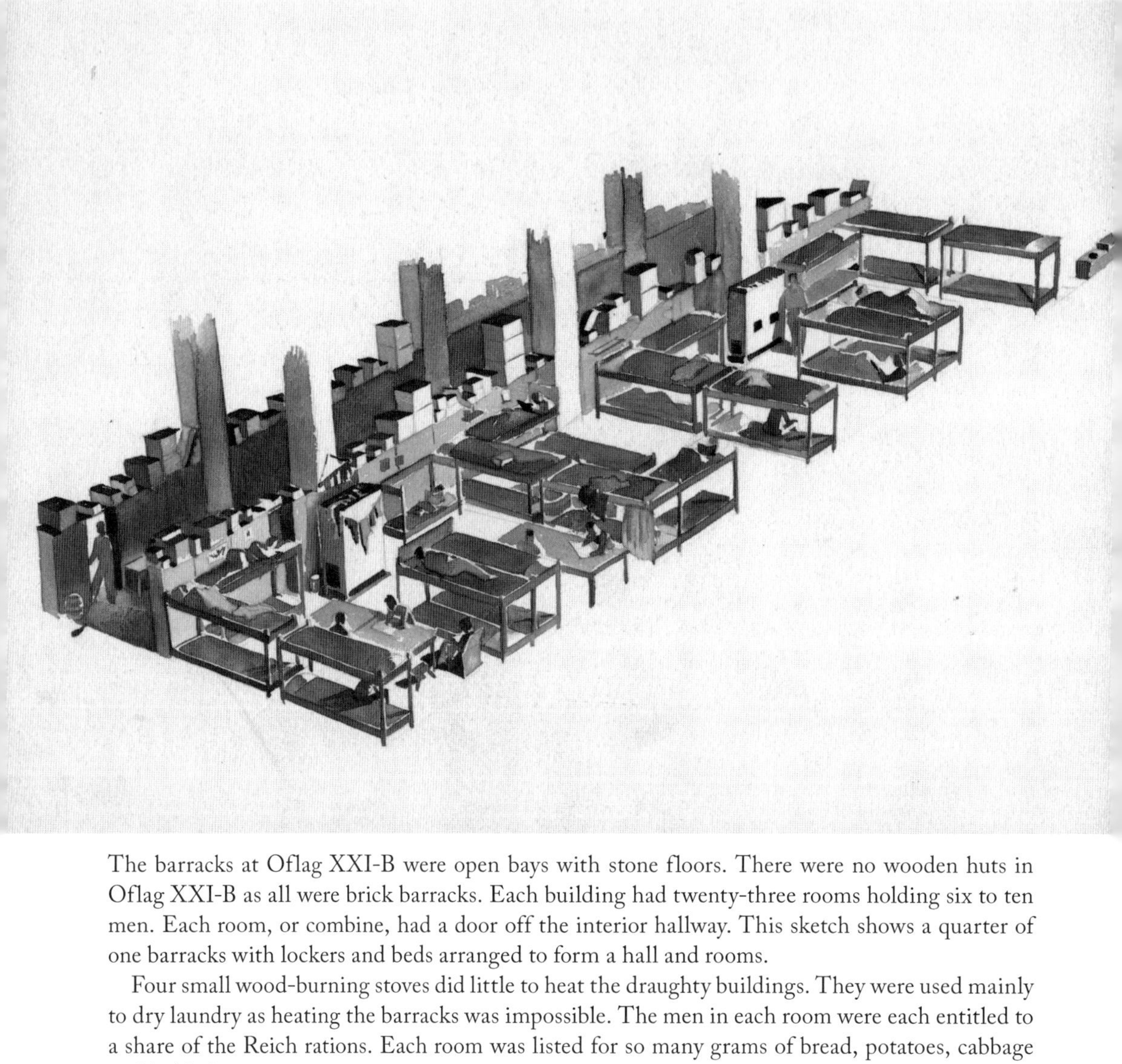

The barracks at Oflag XXI-B were open bays with stone floors. There were no wooden huts in Oflag XXI-B as all were brick barracks. Each building had twenty-three rooms holding six to ten men. Each room, or combine, had a door off the interior hallway. This sketch shows a quarter of one barracks with lockers and beds arranged to form a hall and rooms.

Four small wood-burning stoves did little to heat the draughty buildings. They were used mainly to dry laundry as heating the barracks was impossible. The men in each room were each entitled to a share of the Reich rations. Each room was listed for so many grams of bread, potatoes, cabbage and kohlrabi.

Washroom of Oflag XXI-B

Many days a week the water ran for only four hours. Hot washing water for clothes could be obtained twice weekly by individuals, but outside of the one washing vat per block, washing space was limited.

Soap was extremely scarce in Germany, but the PoWs received ample amounts from the Red Cross and from home.

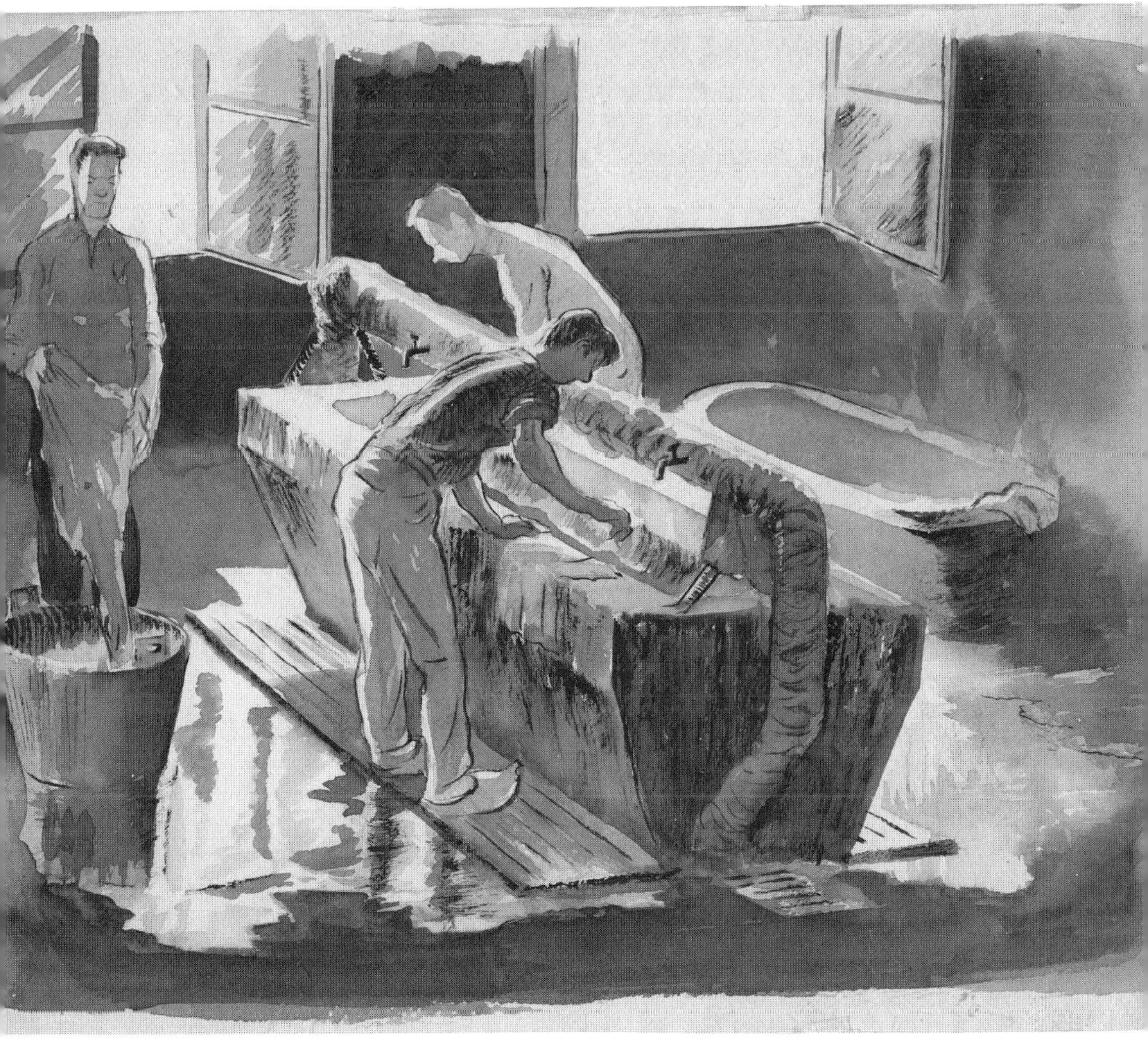

Sketches of the 'Great Escape Camp': Stalag Luft III

Stalag Luft III Background

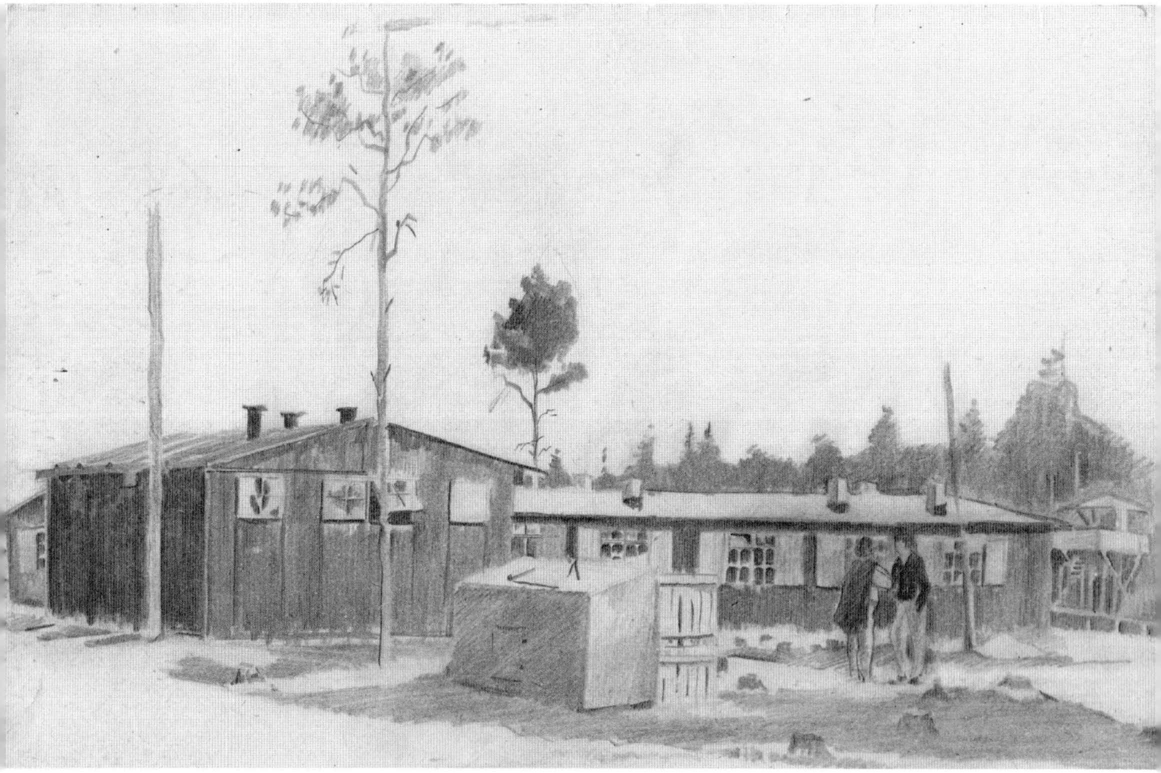

Stalag Luft III was constructed in a remote pine forest 100 miles south-east of Berlin. Prisoners were marched from the train station, a quarter of a mile away, down a rutted dirt road to enter through a very large gate at the camp. A crimson Nazi flag flew near the gate.

Barracks were made of pre-constructed sections of light pine wood painted a dull green. Weathering turned the colour to a dull grey. They were built on concrete stilts to thwart tunnelling and to allow ferrets to crawl underneath. Kriegies hid their contraband in the walls and the floors. Sometimes contraband was buried in the ground outside the barracks.

A tar paper roof covered each of the barracks. The thin walls contained cracks that allowed the winter cold inside. Due to the prevalence of high winds, dust circulated throughout the barracks continuously.

Prison Camp Surrounded by Barbed Wire

The perimeter fence consisted of two separate and parallel barriers about 7ft apart, each about 9ft high with an overhang at the top pointing inward. This consisted of barbed wire strands approximately 6in apart horizontally. Between these fences lay barbed wire tangles of concertina wire that were 2 to 4ft deep.

Inside the camp, about 30ft from the perimeter fence, a warning wire stretched about 2ft off the ground marking a no man's land. The Germans solemnly declared that anyone stepping over the wire in the direction of the perimeter fence would be shot without warning.

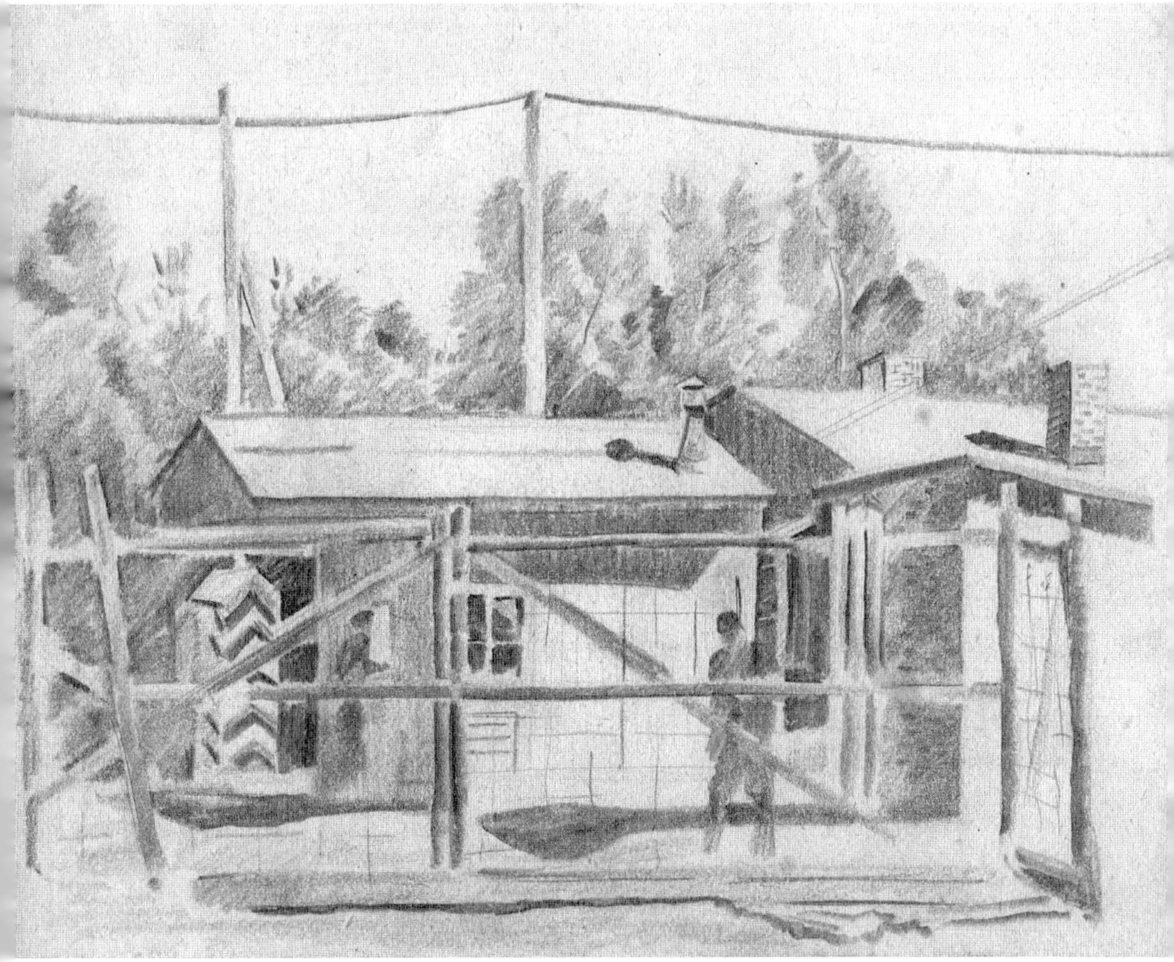

Barracks of Stalag Luft III

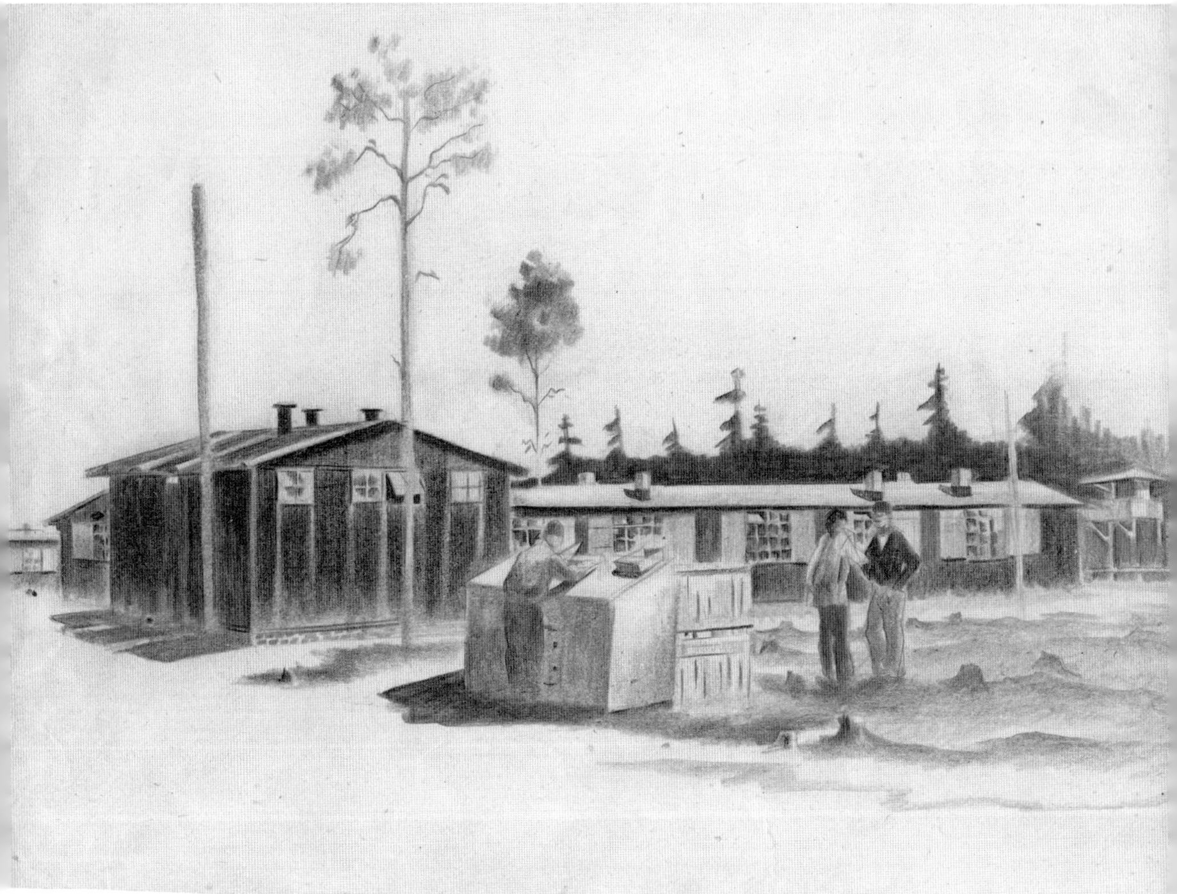

There were three barracks originally used in the camp and these were constructed of prefabricated materials made of wood, creating fourteen self-contained barracks per compound. Each building had sixteen rooms holding six to ten men with an indoor latrine with one urinal and two commodes, a washroom with six porcelain washbasins, and a kitchen with one cooking stove.

The barracks were 120ft long by 40ft wide, and subdivided into cubicles 7ft by 10ft. The camp was 300 yards by 200 yards and was surrounded by two barbed wire fences which did not necessarily prevent escape attempts.

Designed for Downed Airmen

Stalag Luft III was designated for downed airmen. *Reichsmarschall* Hermann Göring wielded tremendous influence with Hitler, and it is believed that he utilized his favoured position to secure good treatment for his respected fellow fliers. Göring had been impressed by the sense of chivalry that prevailed in the First World War and felt that there was a special bond among fliers of all nations.

The camp was designed by the Germans to be escape-proof. It held primarily American and Allied pilots, bombardiers and navigators. Although it was an officers' camp, early on some sergeants were held there as well.

Each compound had a large fire pool, which would have been pretty ineffective in case of fire. PoWs used the fire pools to sail model wooden boats and for the occasional *verboten* swim. Later in the war, theatres were built and small gardens were kept with poor results due to the sandy soil.

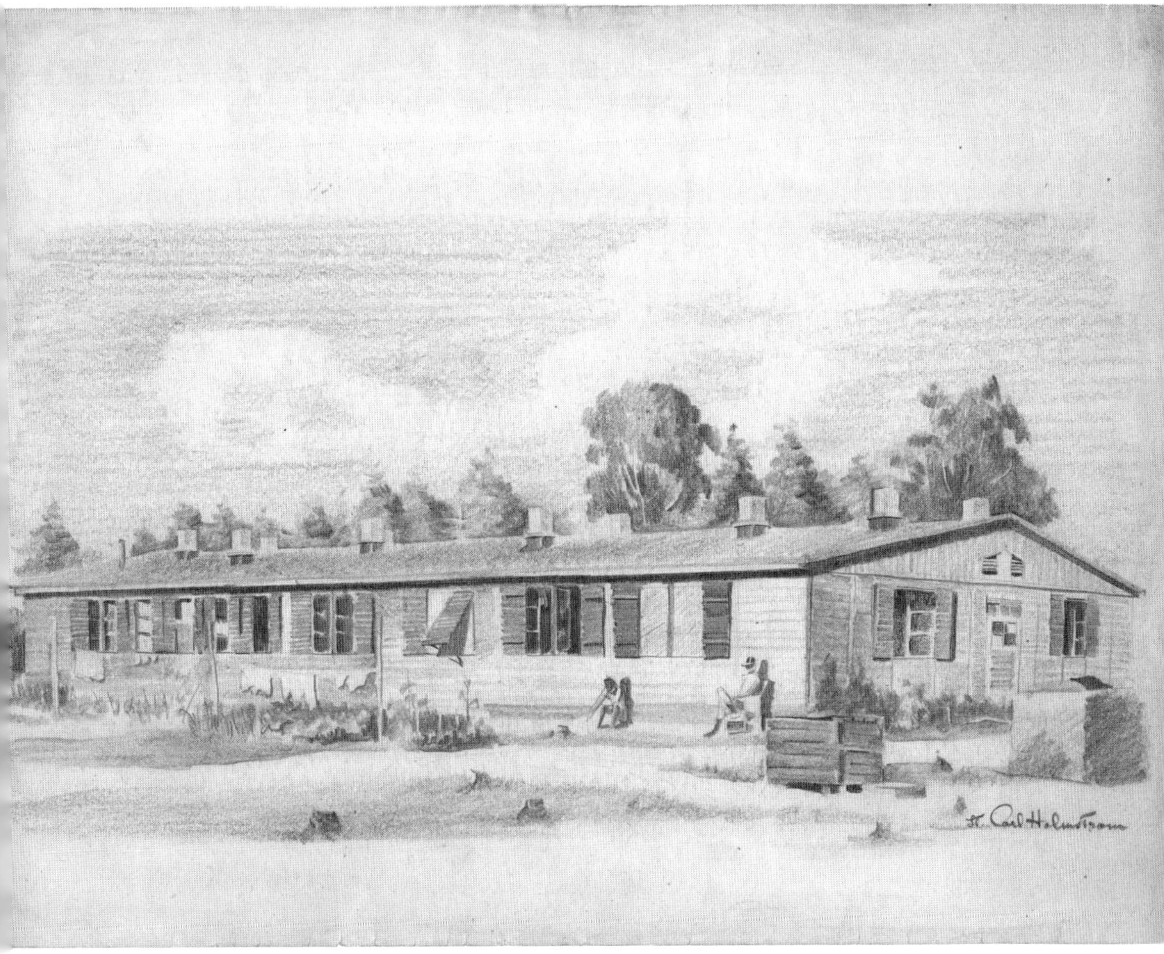

Later Escape Attempts

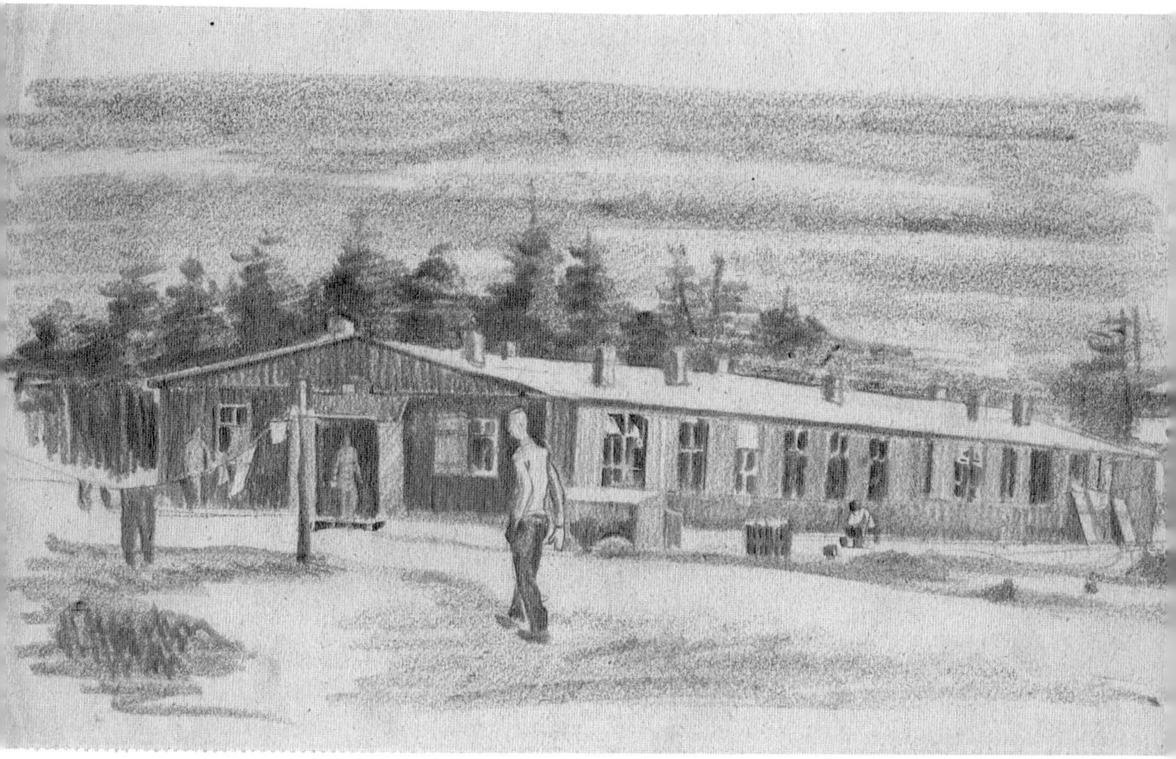

In late 1943, the escape committee started digging a tunnel that was to pass under the barbed wire fence, but after the news of the Great Escape in March at Stalag Luft III and the murder of fifty prisoners, the escape committee ordered a shutdown of the operation. Ferrets searched barracks and confiscated three Dobie sticks (see page 27) that they confused with escape aids.

Map of Stalag Luft III Buildings

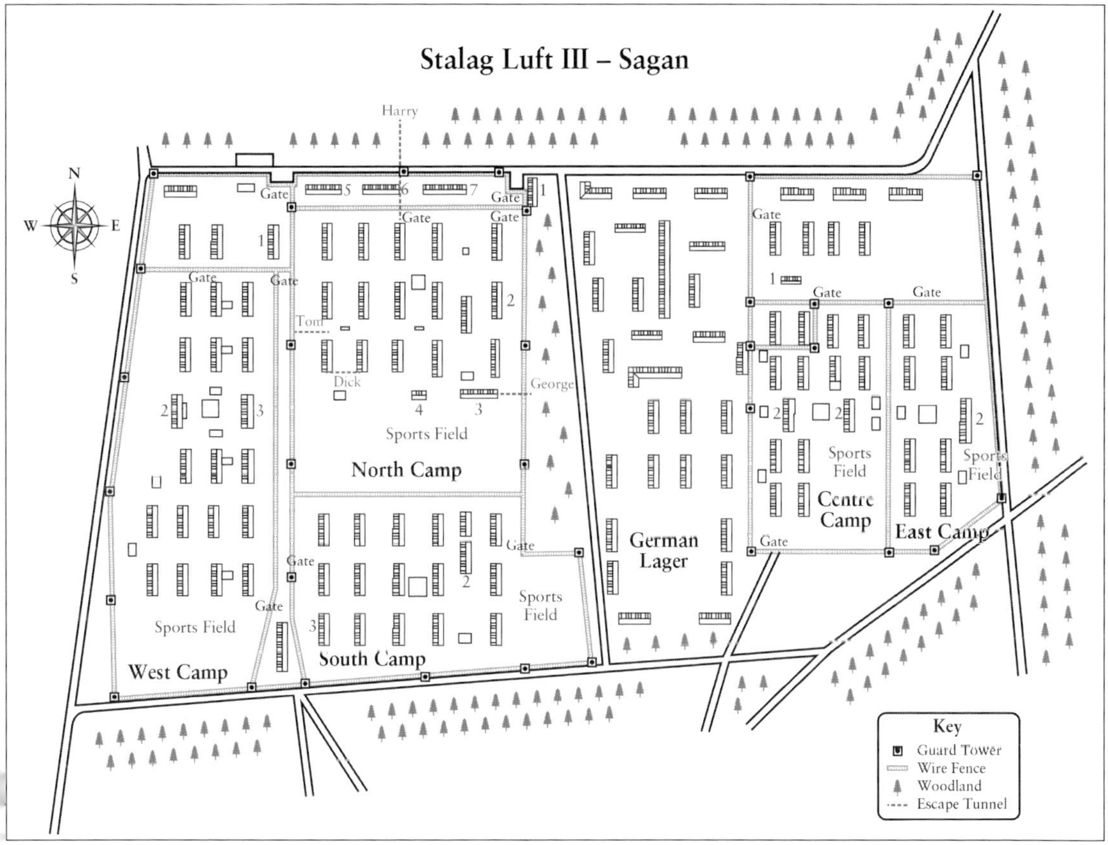

In 1942, the original camp itself when new contained four distinct areas. On the west side, a large area called the *Kommandantur* housed the Germans. In the north-east corner was the *Vorlager*, which contained facilities for the prisoners such as the cooler, sick quarters, bathhouse, coal shed and storage buildings, as well as several barracks for Russian prisoners who were used as camp labour. In the south-east corner was the officers' compound which was referred to as East Compound. In the lower centre of the complex was the NCOs' compound known as Centre Compound. It contained two cookhouses, twelve barracks (one was set aside as a theatre) and a large sports field.

South Compound was added in September 1943. All Americans from North Compound, which housed the British and some Americans from Centre Compound, were moved to South Compound. It had fourteen barracks. Each had an indoor latrine, a washroom with six porcelain washbasins, and a kitchen with one cooking stove. North Compound had been opened in March 1943 and was larger than East and Centre compounds. It had fifteen barracks, a cookhouse, a large theatre (built by prisoners) and a huge sports field. West Compound was the last compound constructed and was the largest, containing seventeen barracks, a cookhouse, a theatre, a shower building and a laundry hut. It opened in April 1944.

(*Courtesy of Pegasus Archive*: www.pegasusarchive.org)

Daily Life of Stalag Luft III

Introduction to Life as a PoW

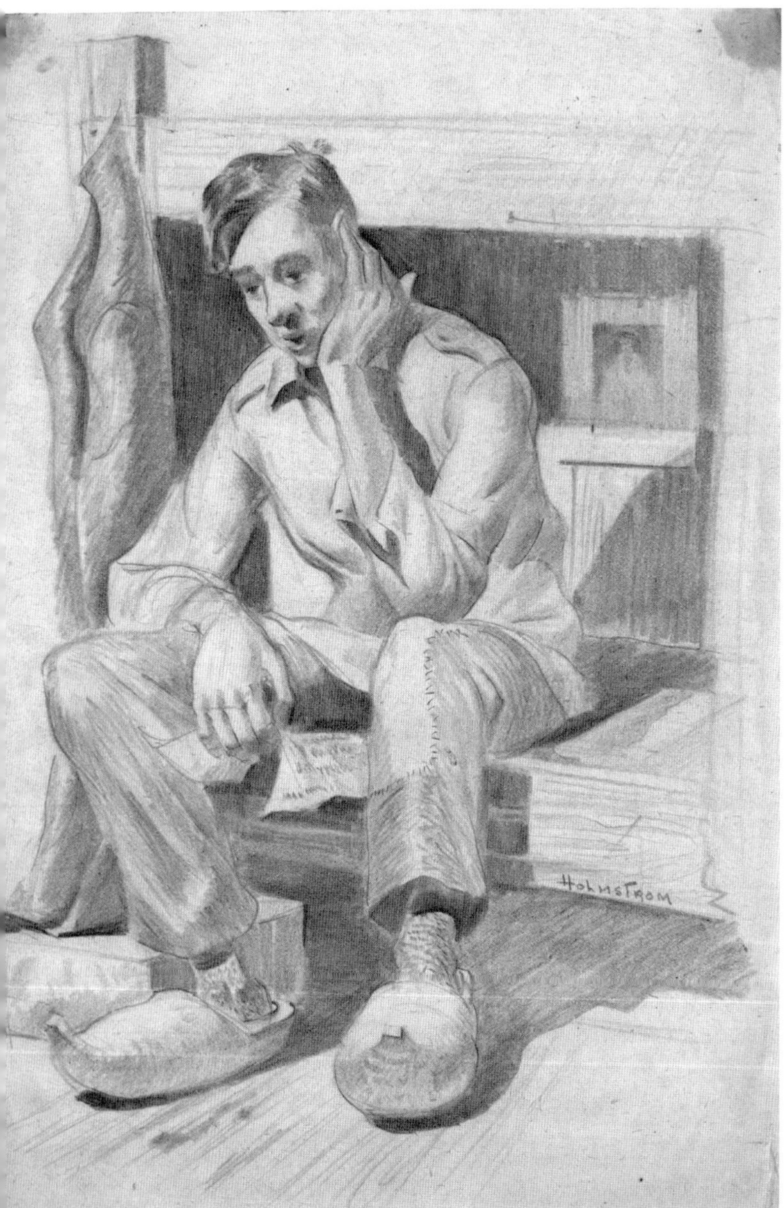

Upon entering the barbed wire enclosure at Stalag Luft III, the new Kriegie found a community with its own language, customs and code of ethics.

New arrivals from a purge, where hundreds of new men came into camp, were processed by a prisoners' interrogation unit anxious to learn the men's war experiences after being shot down and to have someone vouch for each man's identity. The new man had to be verified by a fellow Kriegie or successfully answer questions from the committee to ensure he was not a German plant. Men who could not verify their identity were subject to the 'silent treatment' with no one speaking to them until each man was deemed safe.

Breakfast with Ersatz Tea

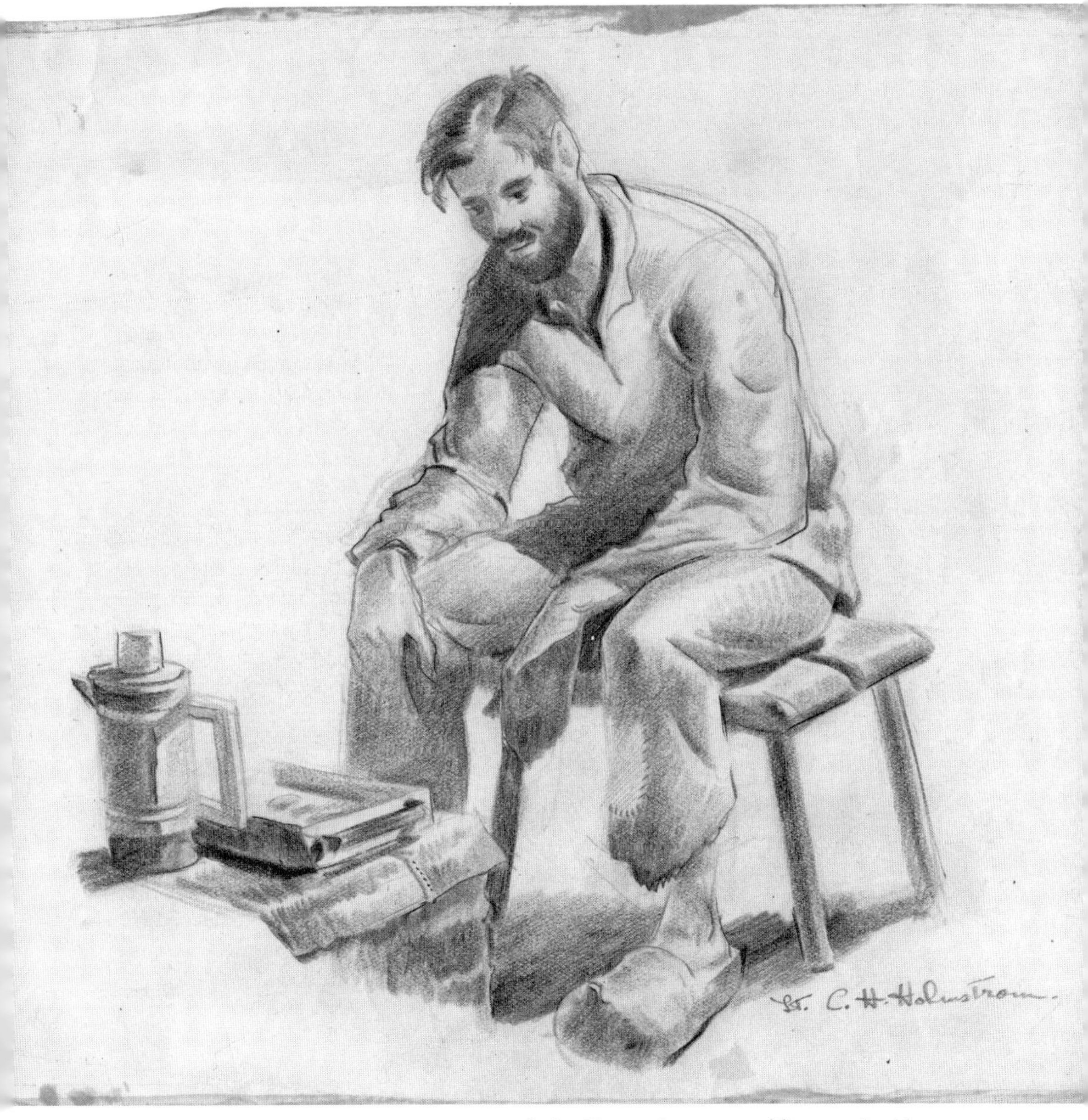

Coffee from a percolator or ersatz tea started the Kriegies' morning. The unpalatable tea was reminiscent of sassafras, but made of burned acorns and other unknown ingredients to replace tea or coffee.

Morning toast, German black bread held on a fork and toasted over an open flame, was made from wheat, rye, barley and potatoes. Heavy and sour, it included a large quantity of sawdust. The bread was smaller than standard US loaves and weighed 4.5lb!

Black Bread Recipe

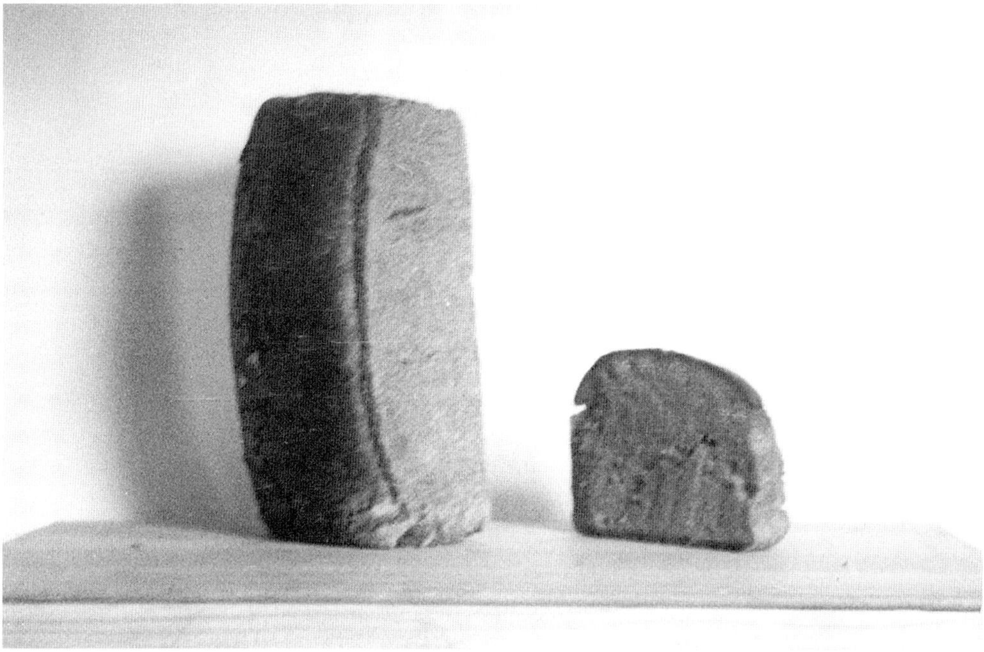

This is the actual recipe for the black bread provided to the Allied prisoners of war by the Germans. The black bread was the most common and readily available food to prisoners; many times this was all they had to live on for extended periods. The recipe comes from the Food Providing Ministry published in Berlin:

BLACK BREAD RECIPE

50% Bruised Rye Grain
20% Sliced Sugar Beets
20% Tree Flour (sawdust, likely pine)
10% Minced Leaves and Straw

Typically, a loaf per man would be provided each week depending on the supply and availability. Delivered piled high on a wagon, it was very common for the bread to be either rock-hard or under-baked and soggy when distributed. German boots often stepped on the loaves as they were being unloaded. Normally, the bread was sliced as thin as possible; not only to ration it for long periods of time if necessary but to check for pieces of debris.

(*Courtesy of US Air Force Academy McDermott Library SMS 329*)

Cooking Duty

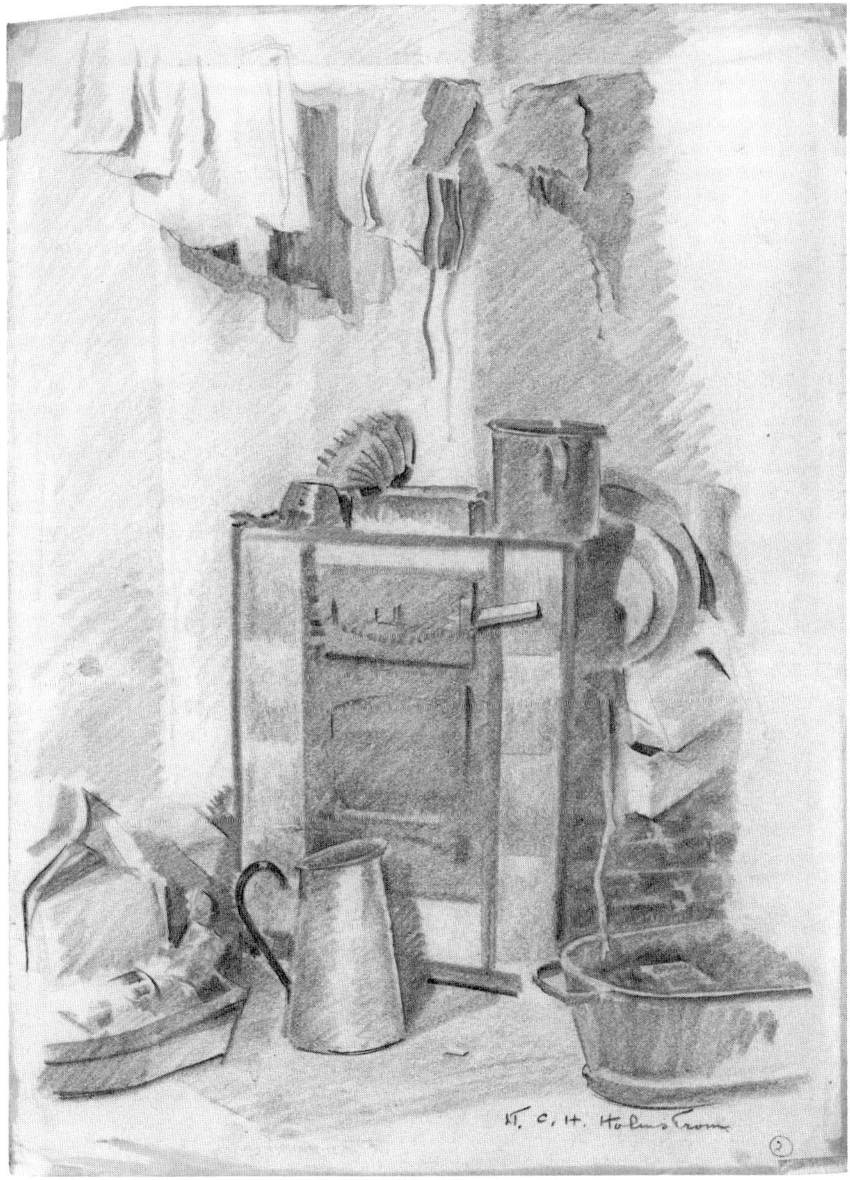

Within the blocks, the cook for the day had to prepare an entire meal for twelve to sixteen men in about half an hour. Cooking duty was usually decided by rotation unless someone was a bad cook, which usually resulted in the bad cook trading this chore for something else for his turn.

Once food was prepared, it often took an hour to divide it evenly. All roommates watched the process for fairness so no one was short-changed. The man cutting and dividing was always the last to choose his portion. Like all communities, it was customary to make weekly social visits. Close friends were asked to come down to the room for a brew.

Percolators were left on stoves all day with a hot drink filling in for lack of food. The camp's food supply came from five sources: German rations, Red Cross food parcels, private parcels, occasional canteen purchases and gardens, with the latter yielding very little.

Cooking Challenge

Cooking became a challenge to ingenuity since the German rations offered only the monotonous diet of potatoes, barley, kohlrabi, black bread and Green Death Soup, with a variance of fish-cheese, blood sausage or turnip jam. The Red Cross parcels provided supplementary foods that added the necessary vitamins and minerals.

With such meagre rations, hungry Kriegies dreamed of food and spent hours interviewing other Kriegies from other states to record in their wartime logs the best restaurants in each man's respective home states. Kriegies described their favourite meals to each other that they would eat when they returned home.

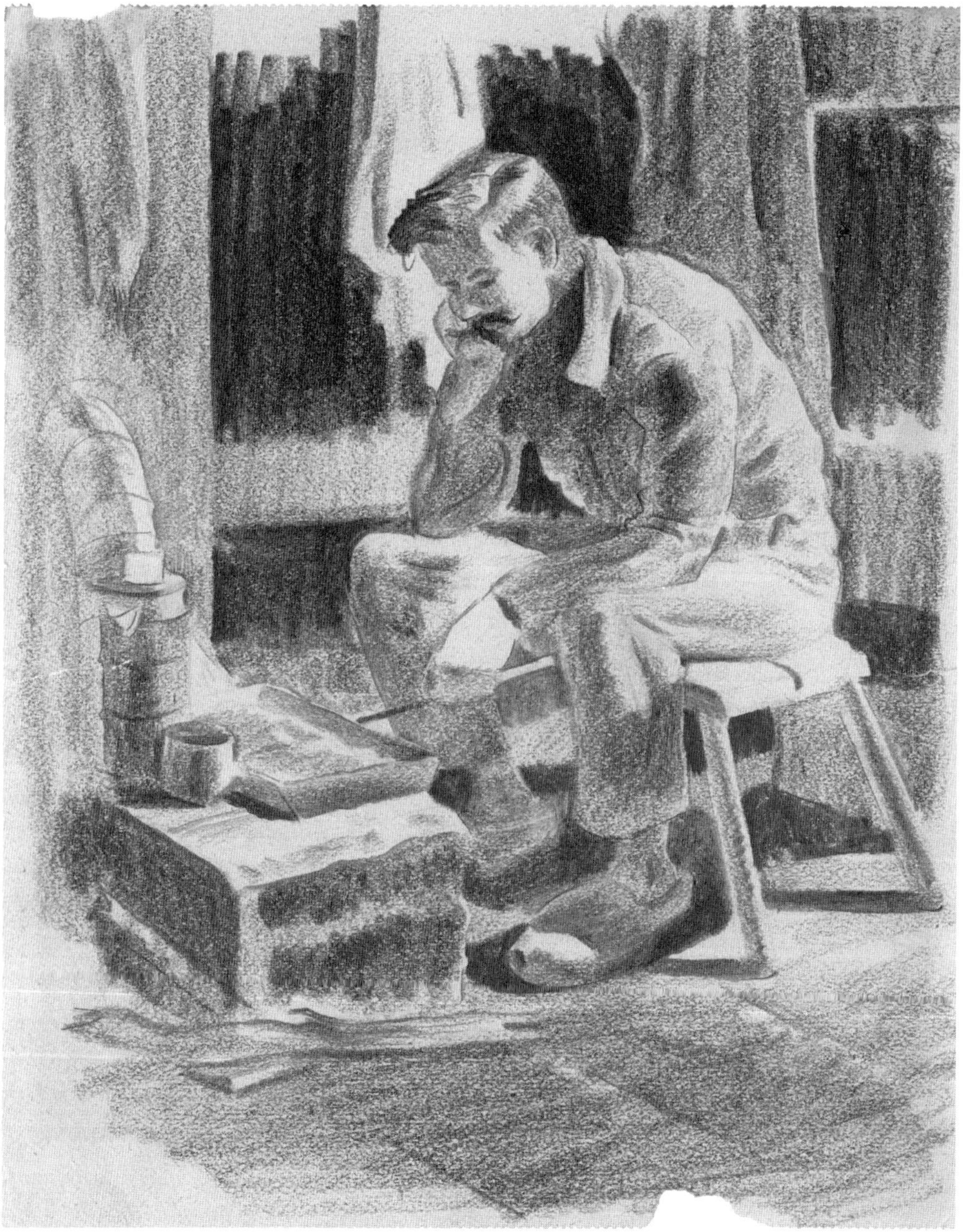

Bashes

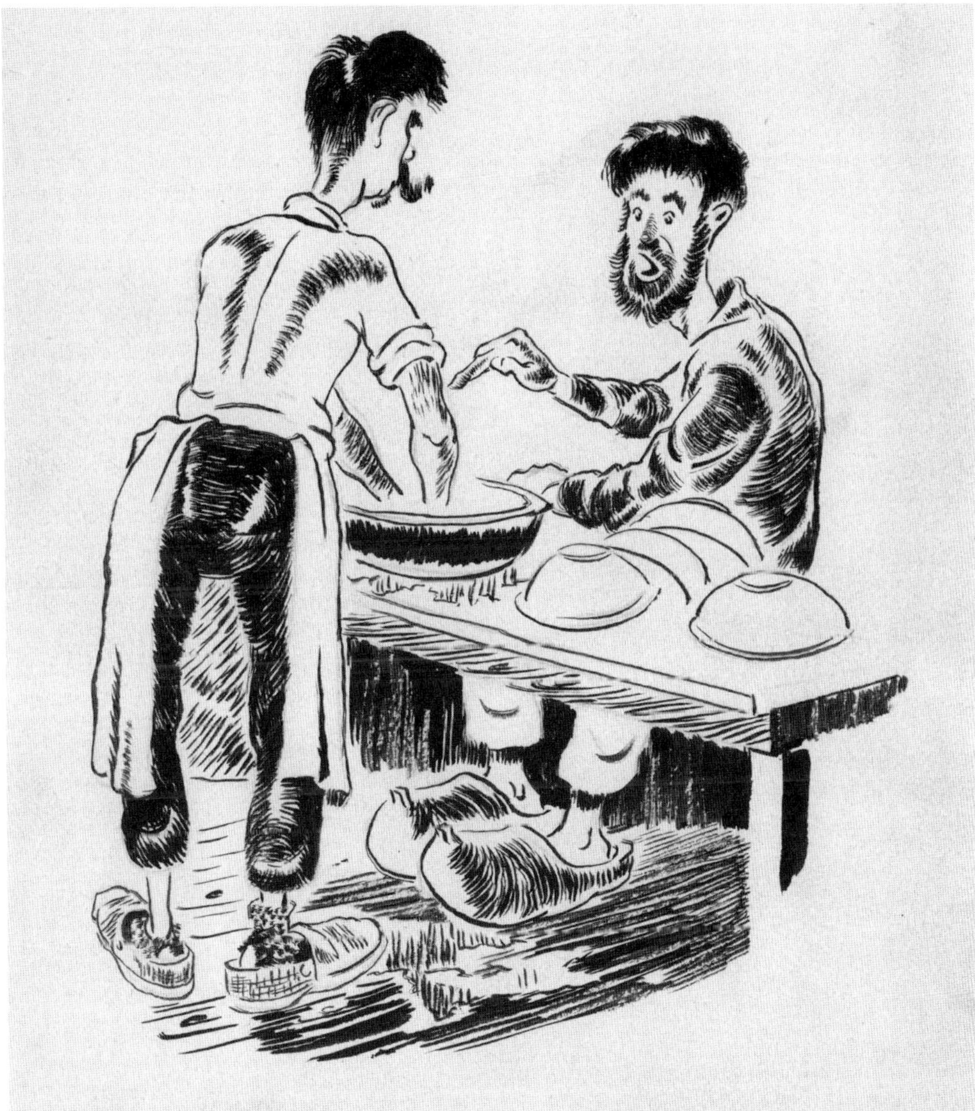

Mundane tasks in the kitchen were known to all Kriegies, but special holidays and planned activities that involved their food broke the monotony. Every Kriegie remembers the raisin brew when he stored up his sugar and raisins for months to properly celebrate Christmas, New Year's Day and the 4th of July. After the raisins had fermented for thirty days, an old trombone attached to a jam bucket was used as a still.

Great trouble was taken in food preparation, with special occasions such as a birthday or Christmas requiring months of hoarding. Holidays also meant 'bashes' and concoctions made up of everything in the cupboard. The occasional celebrations were overlooked by the German authorities until they noticed that their ferrets were partaking. Confiscating containers used in the fermentation process did not help, so the Germans demanded that all dried fruit be cooked in the kitchen before issue. This put a strain on the limited kitchen facilities, so senior officers promised that the fruit would no longer be used for alcoholic purposes, thus ending the compounds' breweries.

Second World War Red Cross Package Contents

Published by the American National Red Cross for the relatives of American Prisoners of War and Civilian Internment, August 1943:

One full Red Cross parcel was a box about 3in deep and 12in square. It contained the minimum amount of food required to sustain a man for one week at approximately 1,700 calories per day.

In an American box, were small portions of SPAM, corned beef, powdered eggs, jelly or jam, powdered milk (KLIM), soda crackers, dried raisins or prunes, powdered coffee, cigarettes, sugar, a chocolate 'D' bar and salt and pepper.

The rule in most of the camps was that both 'individual' (for a named person, sent and paid for by relatives and containing a mixture of goods) and 'bulk' parcels (for general distribution, sent and paid for by the International Red Cross) were pooled. This ensured that replacement clothing, shaving and washing kit, coffee, tea, tinned meat, jam, sugar and essentials were distributed equally.

Ever since the early years of the war, the Germans had punctured the tins of the Red Cross when they were handed out to the prisoners so they could not be used as escape rations, but the prisoners found that they could keep the meat for several days before it went bad.

(Courtesy of US Air Force Academy McDermott Library SMS 329)

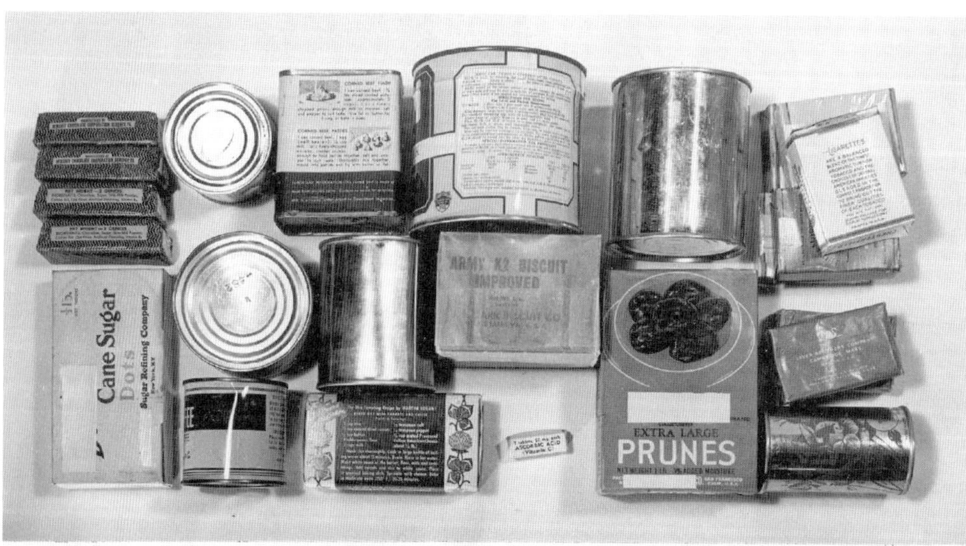

AN AMERICAN RED CROSS STANDARD FOOD PARCEL

FEBRUARY - 1944

1 6-oz. carton of Type K-2 biscuit
1 8-oz. carton of processed American cheese
4 2-oz. bars of chocolate
1 2-oz. tin of soluble coffee
1 12-oz. tin of corned beef
1 16-oz. carton of dried prunes
1 6-oz. tin of liver paste
1 16-oz. tin of whole powdered milk
1 16-oz. tin of Vitamin A fortified oleomargarine
1 6-oz. tin of Jam
1 12-oz. tin of pork luncheon meat
1 7-3/4-oz. tin of salmon
1 8-oz. carton of white lump sugar
5 pkgs. containing 100 cigarettes
2 2-oz. bars of odorless soap
1 pkg. ascorbic acid tablets (Vitamin C)

German Food Rations List with Calories

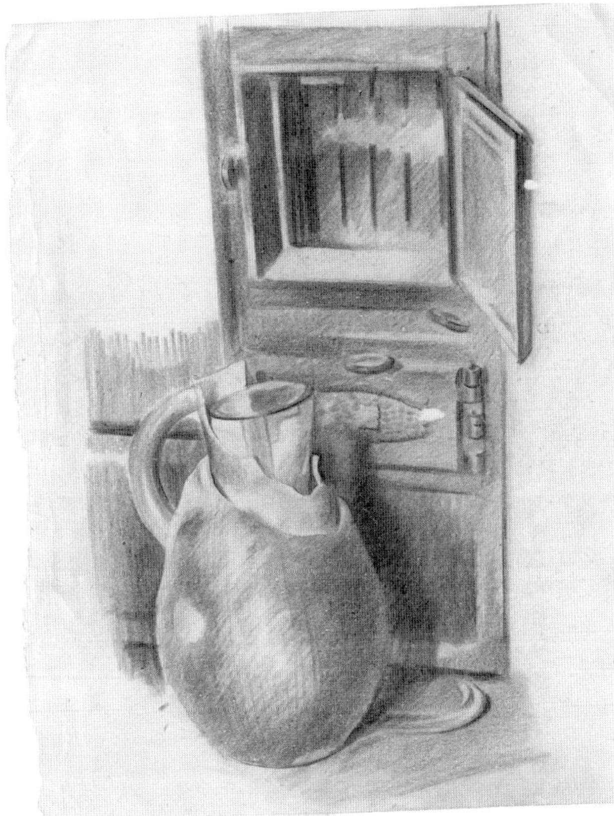

German rations at Stalag Luft III, instead of being the equivalent of those furnished to depot troops, compared with those received by non-working civilians, the lowest category in Germany. While insufficient, these foods provided the bulk of staples, mainly through bread and potatoes. A PoW's average daily issue of foods, with caloric content included, was as follows:

TYPE OF FOOD	GRAMS	CALORIES
Potatoes	390	331
Bread	350	910
Meat	11	20
Barley, oats, etc.	21	78
Kohlrabi	247	87
Dried vegetables	14	38
Margarine	31	268
Cheese	10	27
Jam	25	69
Sugar	25	100
TOTALS	1,124	1,928

A conservative estimate of the caloric requirement of a person sleeping eight hours a day and getting very little exercise is 2,050 calories. German rations therefore fell below the minimum requirement for healthy nutrition.

Cooking Equipment

Cooking within the blocks at Stalag Luft III was done on a kitchen stove with a heating surface of 3 sq ft and an oven that could hold two flat pans at a time. Two rooms shared the stove at one time in order to allow everyone time on the stove, so some rooms had to eat their dinner as early as 2.30 pm, while others ate at 8.00 pm. During the winter months, a small amount of cooking was done on the heating stoves in the rooms, which helped to relieve the overcrowded camp kitchen.

The kitchen equipment consisted of ten boilers, two ovens, three cooking pots, fourteen milk cans and pails, four ladles and five wooden pails for washing potatoes, completely inadequate for use by so many prisoners. The men had to rely on hand-made cooking and eating utensils.

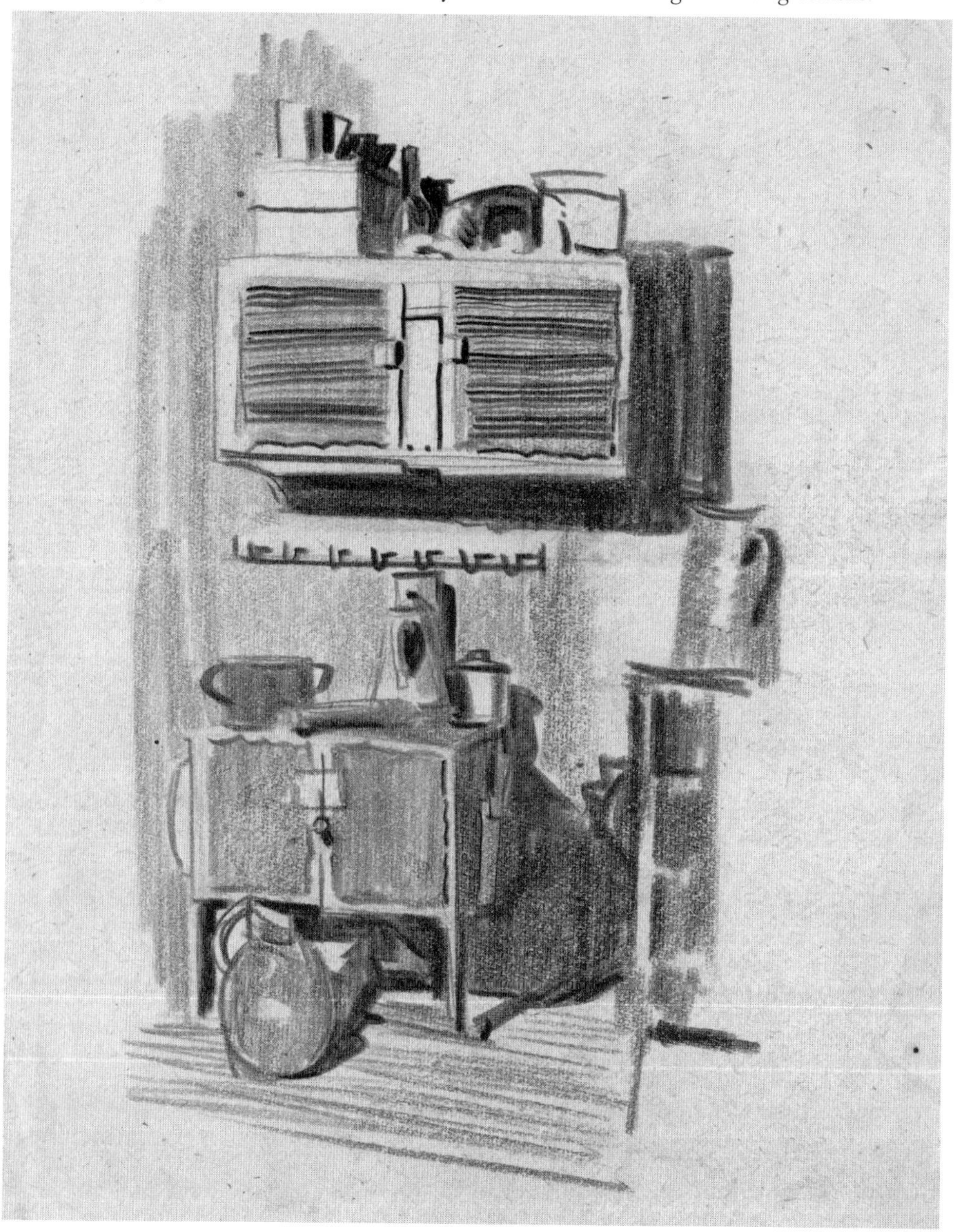

Cooking Utensils Made of Barbed Wire and Tin Cans

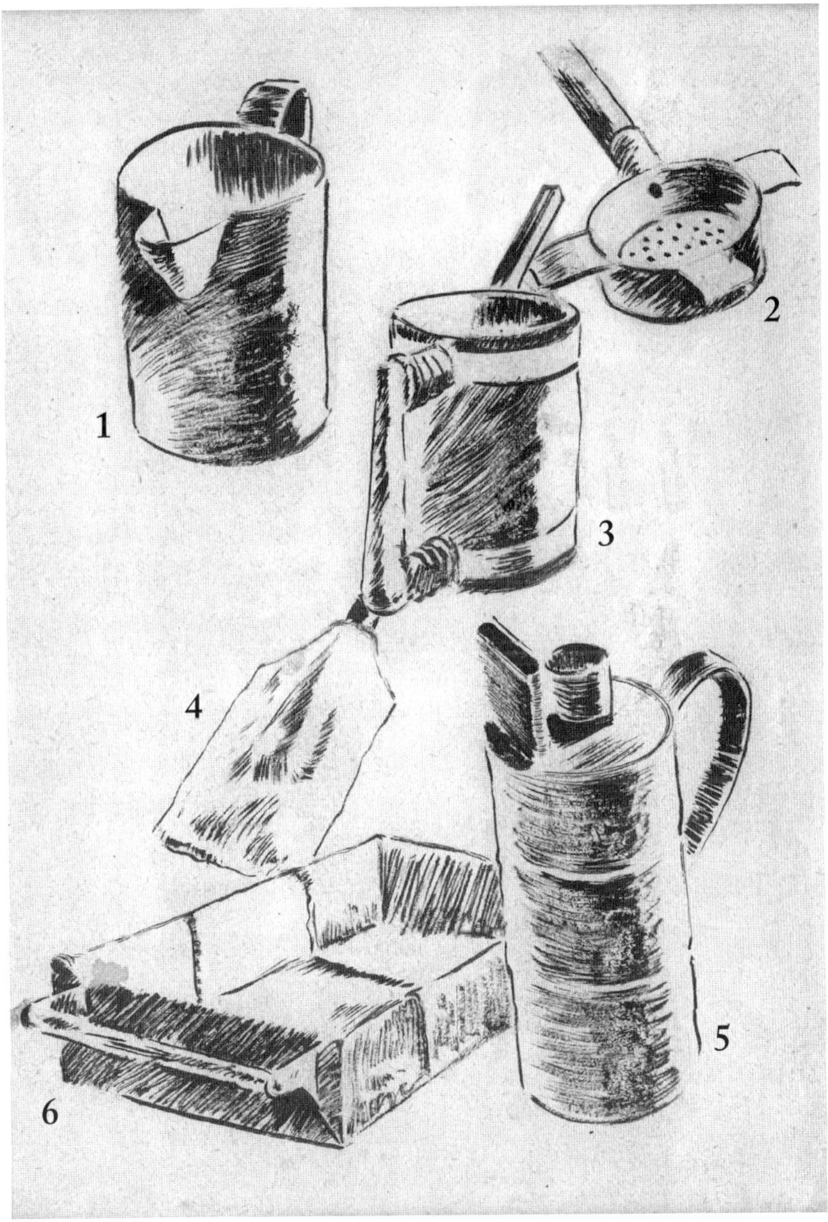

Kriegie cooking utensils were made from bits of wire, moulded clay and tin cans: (1) pitcher, (2) tea strainer, (3) cup, (4) pancake-turner, (5) coffee pot, (6) all-purpose cooking pan.

Pots and pans were scarce, leading to 'Who's got the communal pot?' being often heard. Custom-made pans fashioned from KLIM cans and cocoa tin cans supplemented by barbed wire prevailed to the end. PoWs removed the bottoms from the KLIM tins and hooked them together to form airtight pipes to provide air while digging escape tunnels.

Percolators were made with tin cans and solder laboriously gathered from a few types of cans, tin foil and toothpaste tubes. Every compound had its own tinsmiths as the Germans claimed that the prisoners destroyed what was issued them and refused to replace lost or broken items.

Pancake Turner and Pitcher

Typical kitchen implements could be used by the cooks to create imaginative delicacies. More accomplished cooks in camp could create cakes and pies using crackers for crust and cans of tooth powder for leavening, items both found in their Red Cross parcels. Pulverized crackers were the primary source of 'flour' for pie crusts, cakes and cookies.

To exist, the prisoner had to develop talents and latent skills to provide the necessities of life. Material from Red Cross parcels were converted into tools such as hacksaws made from the steel bands around the cardboard cartons.

Canadian packing crates of plywood yielded cupboards and other room furniture. Another source of supply was the heavy wooden boxes in which the YMCA shipped art materials. Paints, inks, and pencils were used by camp artists in every compound and their fellow Kriegies who wrote in YMCA logbooks and drew pictures. The supplies could also be used for forging documents. Wooden Red Cross crates used for food parcels were used to build seats for the camp theatres.

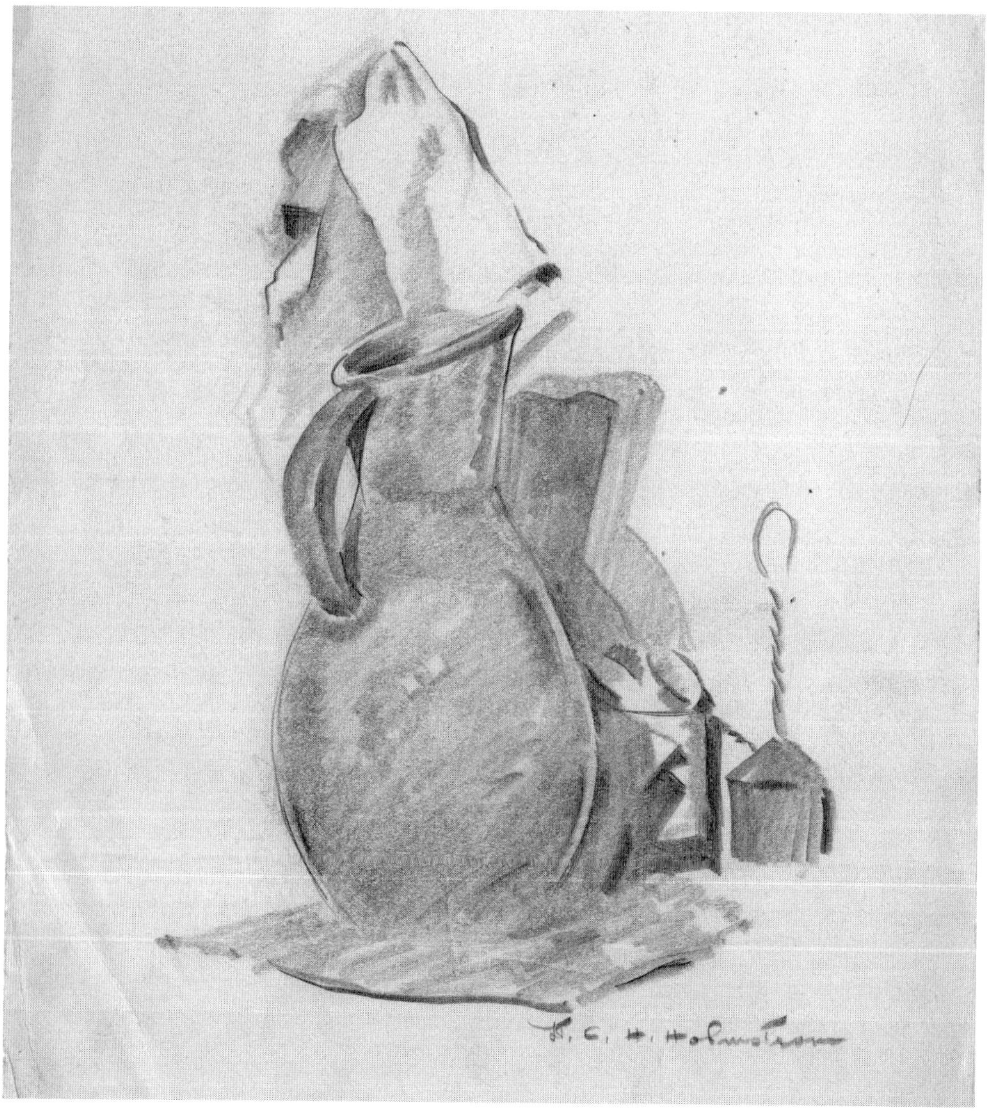

Cleaning Clothing and Barracks

Daily Duty Roster

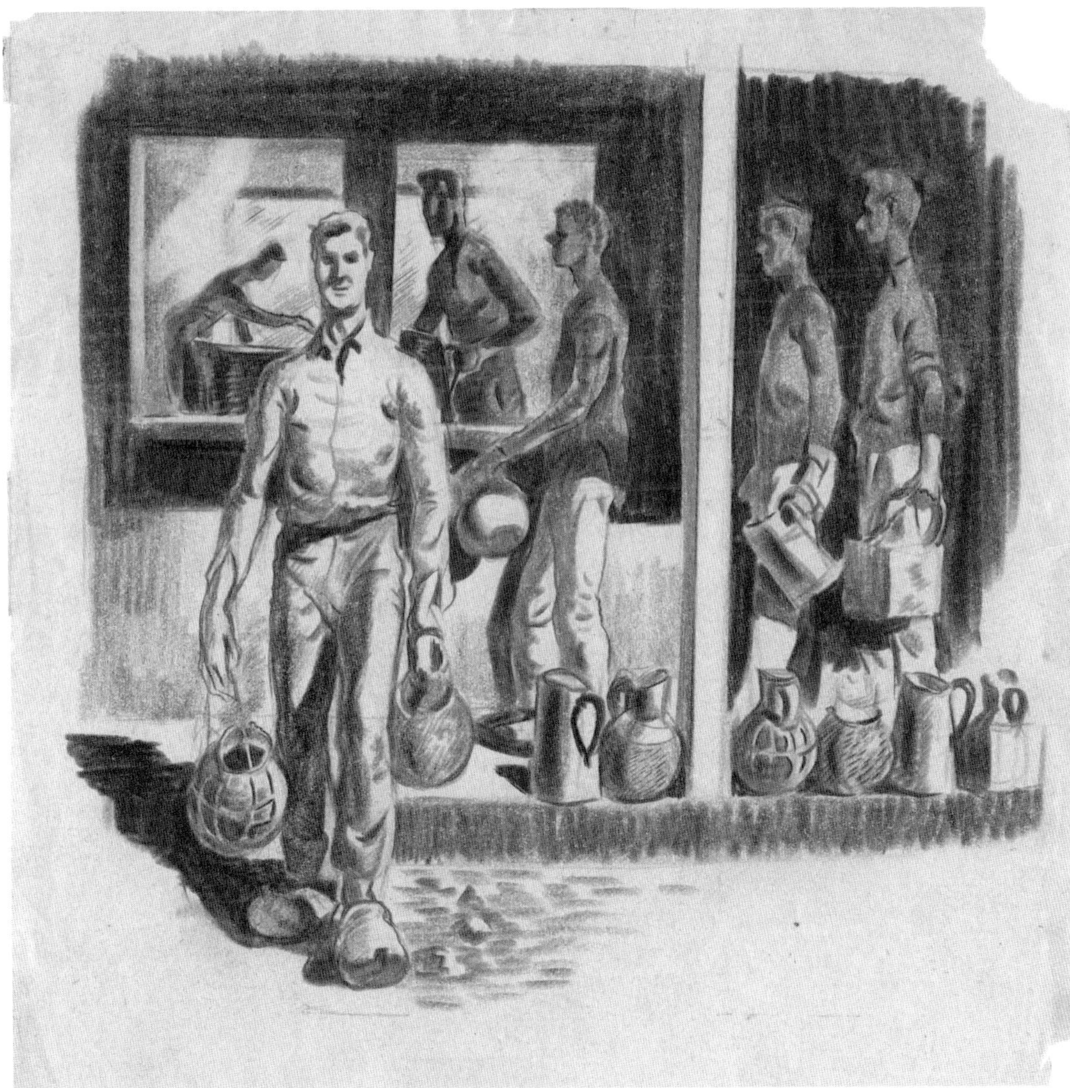

All work at Stalag Luft III was carried out according to a rotating roster drawn up by the room members. A daily stooge performed the duties of sweeping the room, peeling potatoes, preparing vegetables and fetching water.

Fetching Water with a Lead *Keintrinkwasser*

At Stalag Luft III every morning, a designated man from each room went to the cookhouse to fetch hot water. He had two pitchers, one for drinking water and the other, made of lead and marked *Kein Trinkwasser* (not drinking water), for washing up. Huge vats in the cookhouse supplied the camp with hot water. Normally, the men waited in long lines.

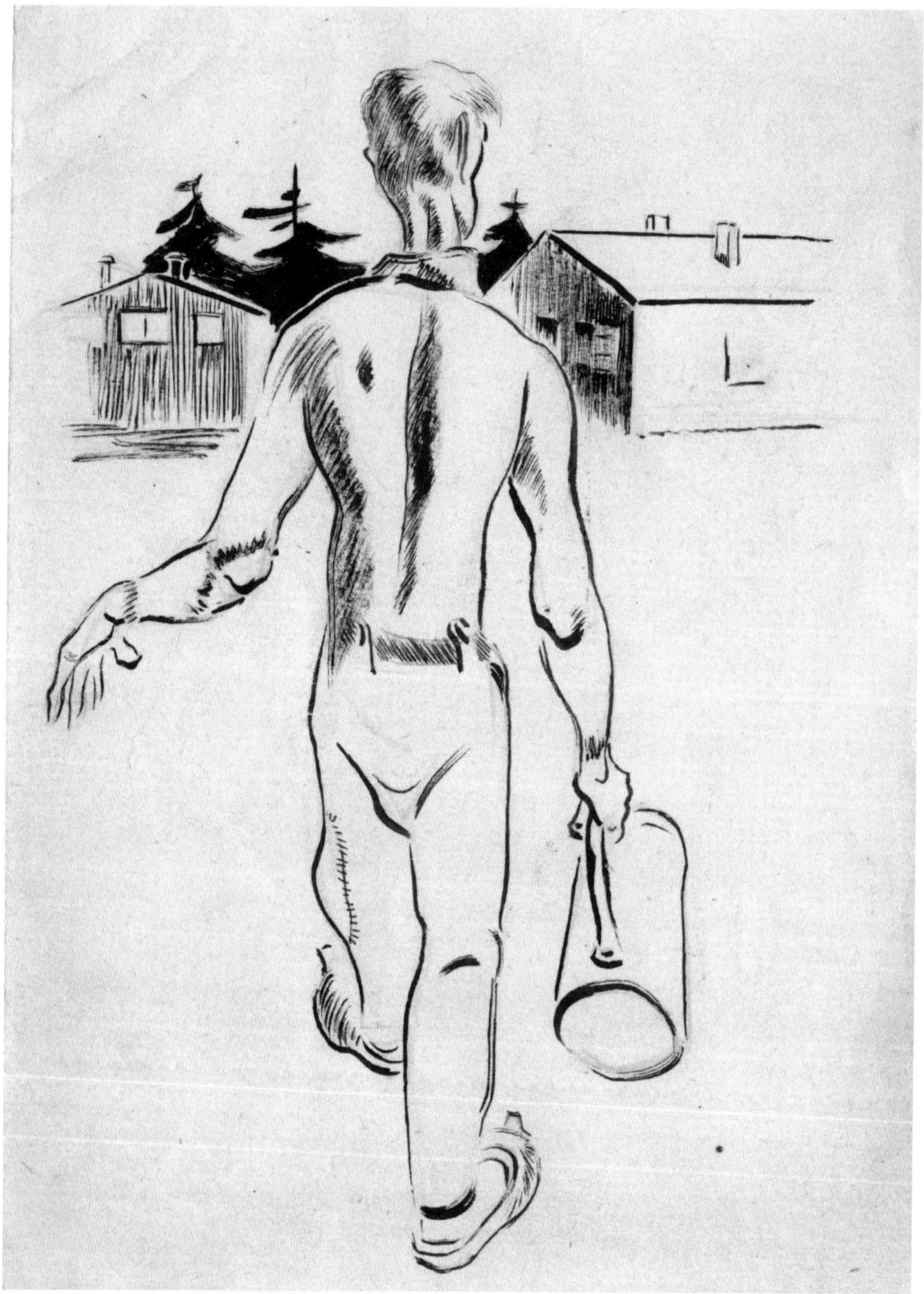

The Dobie Stick

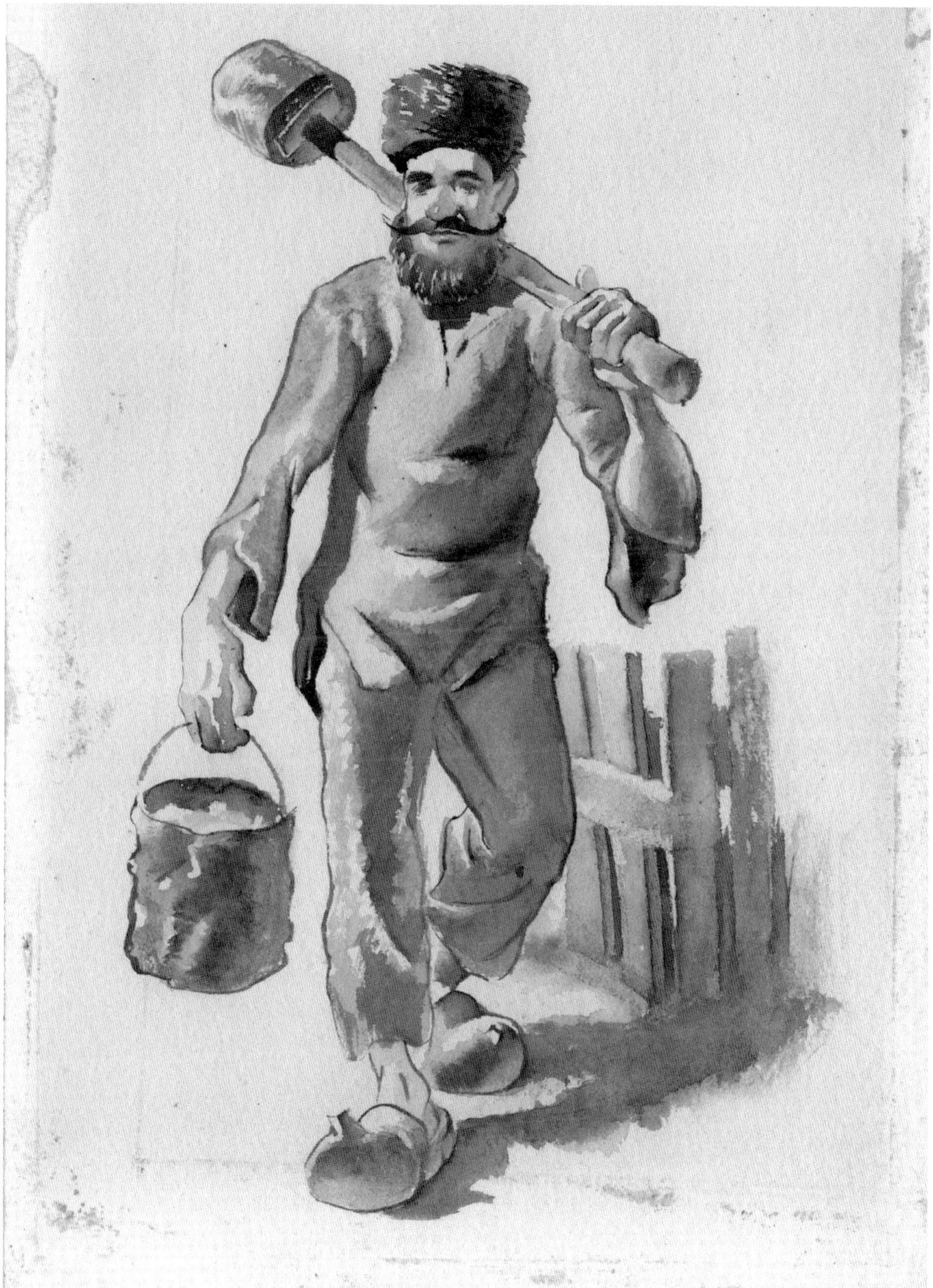

Washing clothes was difficult as cold water removed little grease and dirt. A Dobie stick used with a jam bucket became the washing machine. It consisted of a small tin can inserted into a larger one with both nailed to any available stick. Washing clothes with a buddy provided time for conversation. An average of 200 men used the cement basins and troughs every day.

Limited Clothing

The camp goal was to provide everyone with at least an overcoat, a blouse or jacket, three pairs of socks, a pair of wool trousers, three shirts, three pairs of winter underwear, one sweater, one pair of high shoes, a scarf, a pair of gloves, one belt or suspenders, a cap, four handkerchiefs and one blanket.

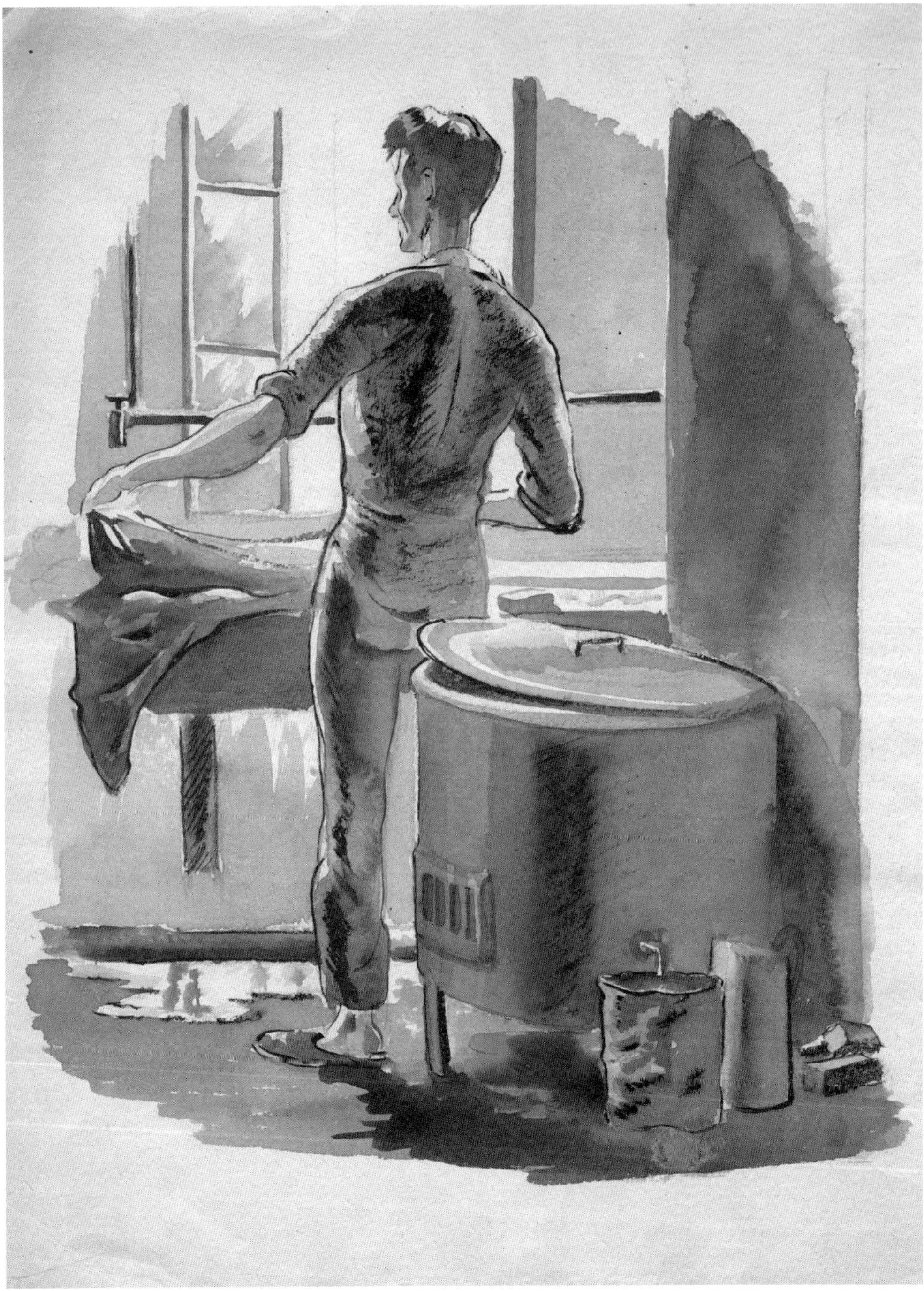

Washing Clothes

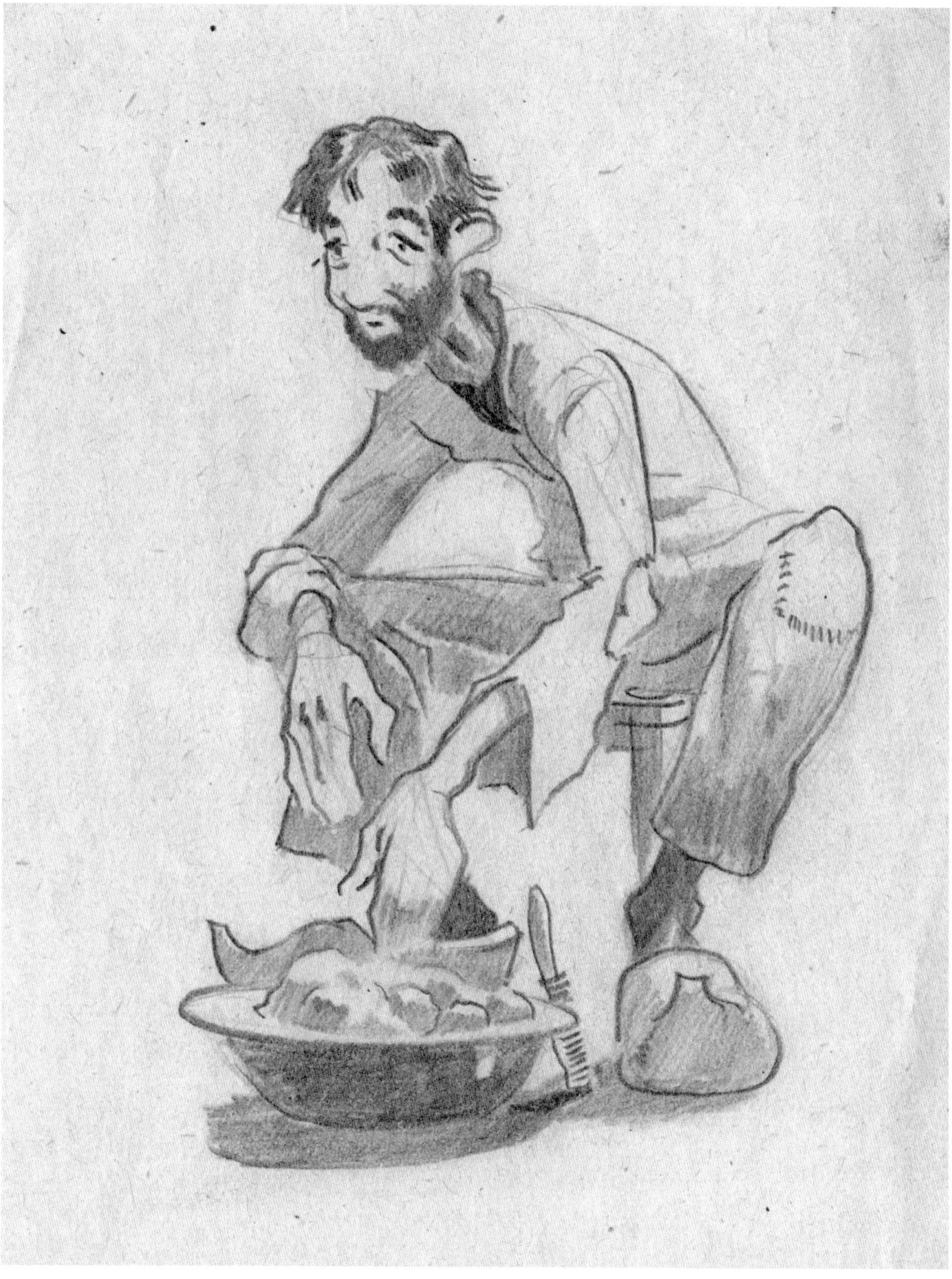

Life in camp was never without its humorous moments, even during the blackest days. Some Kriegies, after boiling white laundry, found a blue sock had been overlooked that had dyed everything a tropical pattern.

The military clothing received through the Red Cross was regular enlisted army issue and quite durable, as it needed to be, since a pair of trousers that was worn every day was expected to last one year.

Washing Clothes with a Buddy

Washing clothes was a necessary chore for all the PoWs and a very important one. Clothing never assumed more importance than it did in a PoW camp. There was always a critical shortage. Items of civilian nature were strictly forbidden and military uniforms were often put together from whatever was available, regardless of branch of service.

Bulk parcels for general distribution and Red Cross Parcels were pooled. Thus, replacement clothing, shaving and washing kit, coffee, tea, tinned meat, jam, sugar, and essentials were distributed equally. When a Kriegie received items of clothing in parcels from home, he was expected to return the Red Cross items they replaced.

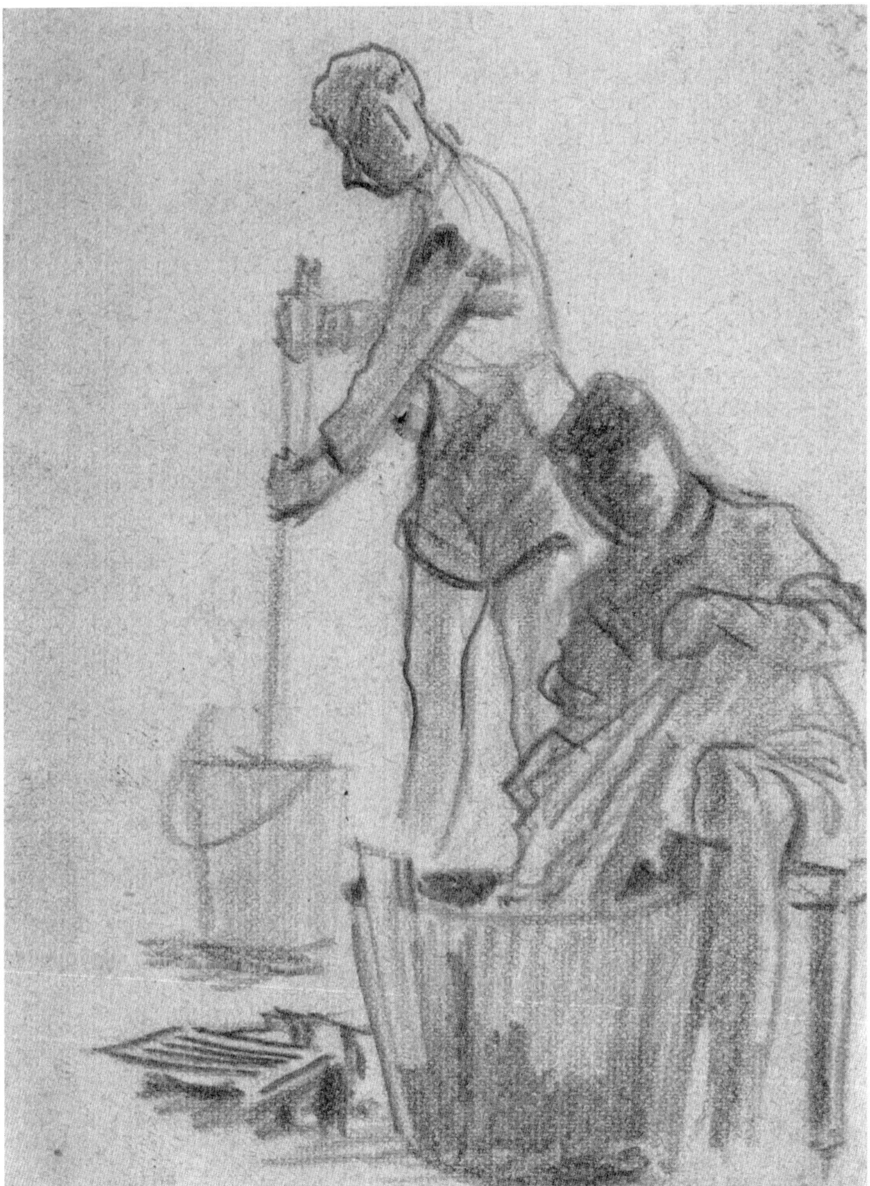

Clothing Repair

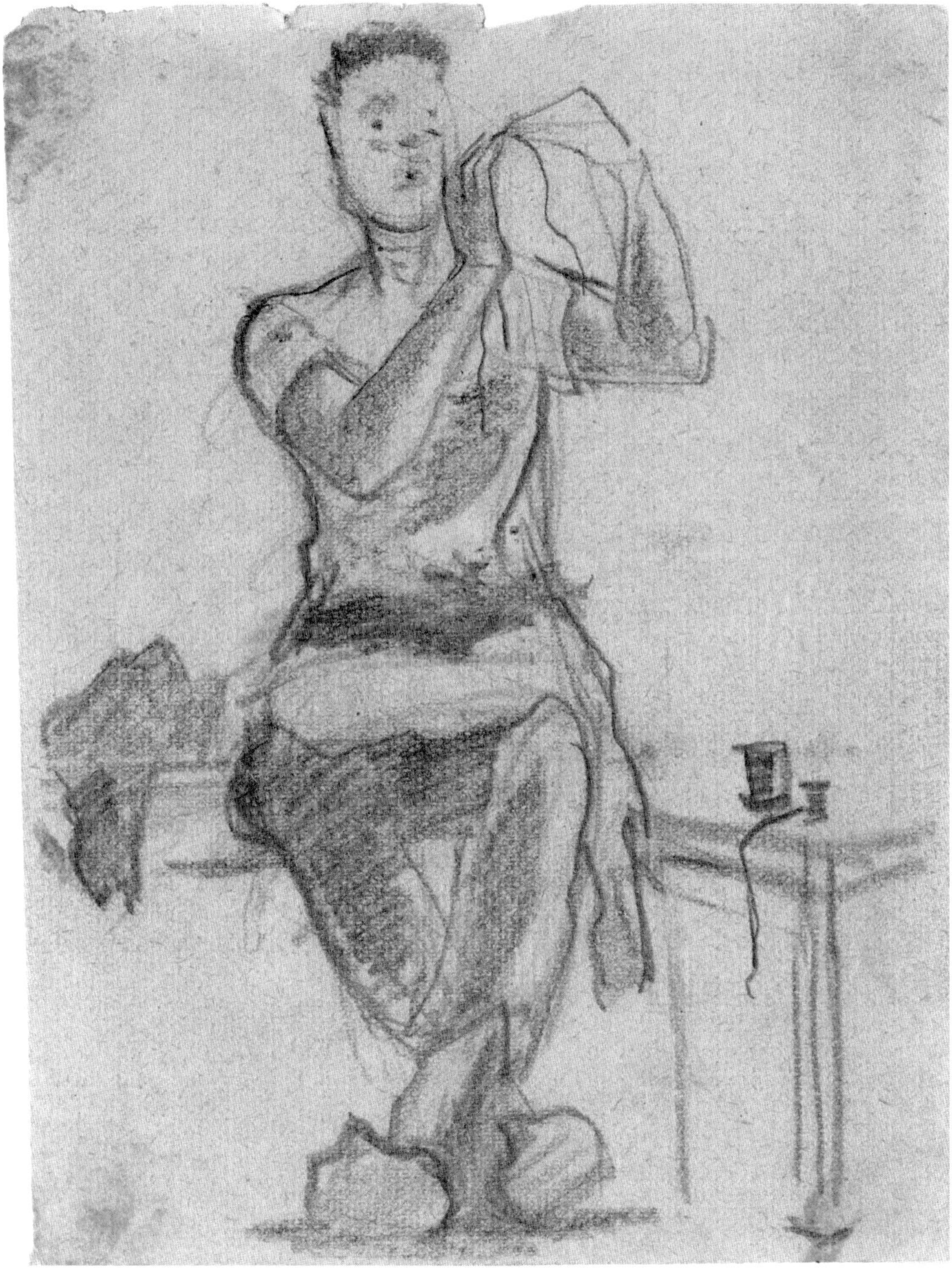

Kriegies, who had never sewn, learned to knit socks and scarves, crochet and repair all their clothing to make it last.

The PoW had to convince his block clothing officer that his threadbare pants had room for no more patches, his shoes soaked up water like a sponge and that he surely wouldn't live through the winter in that lightweight, robin's egg blue French overcoat issued last year. This list would be added to the 'master list' as clothing was in short supply.

Laundry Drying Outside

Washed clothes drying outdoors were a frequent sight. For security reasons, the Germans had most trees in camp cut down, allowing warm sun into the former pine forest.

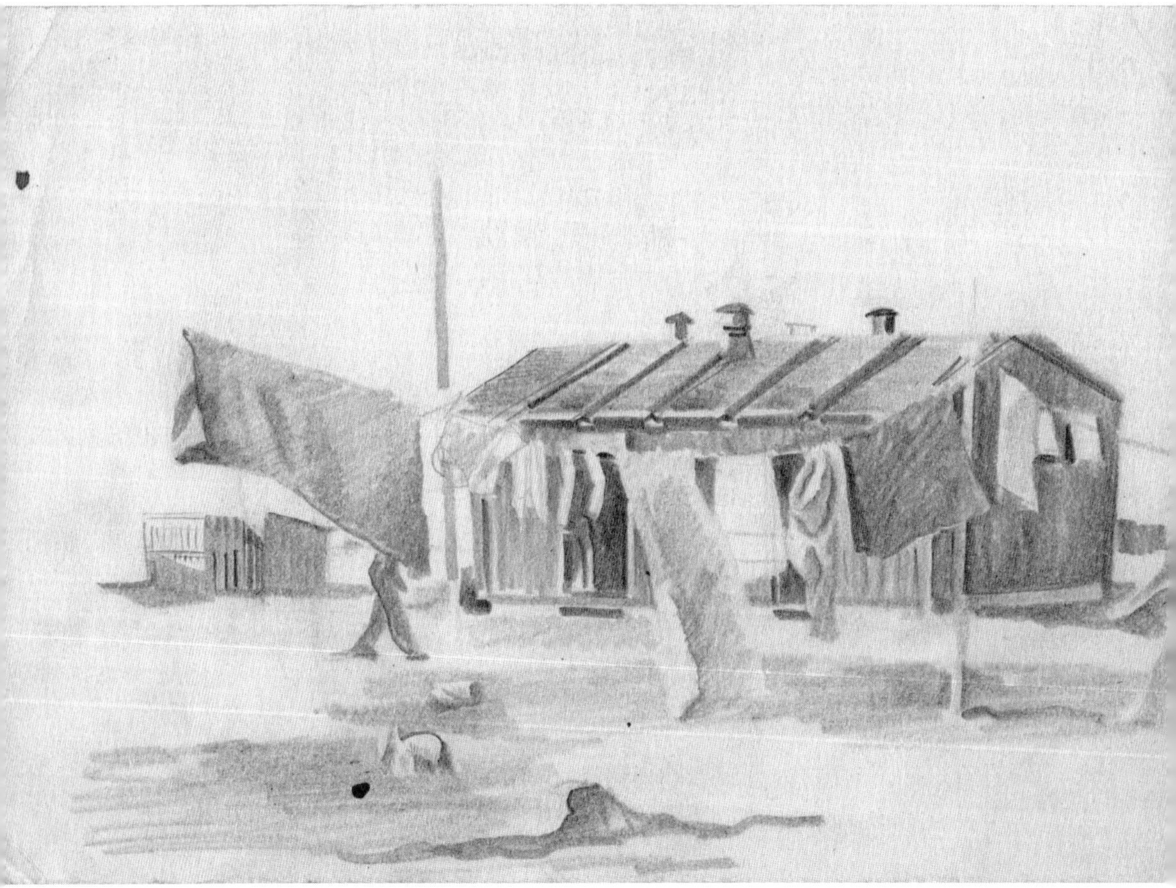

Issued by the Third Reich

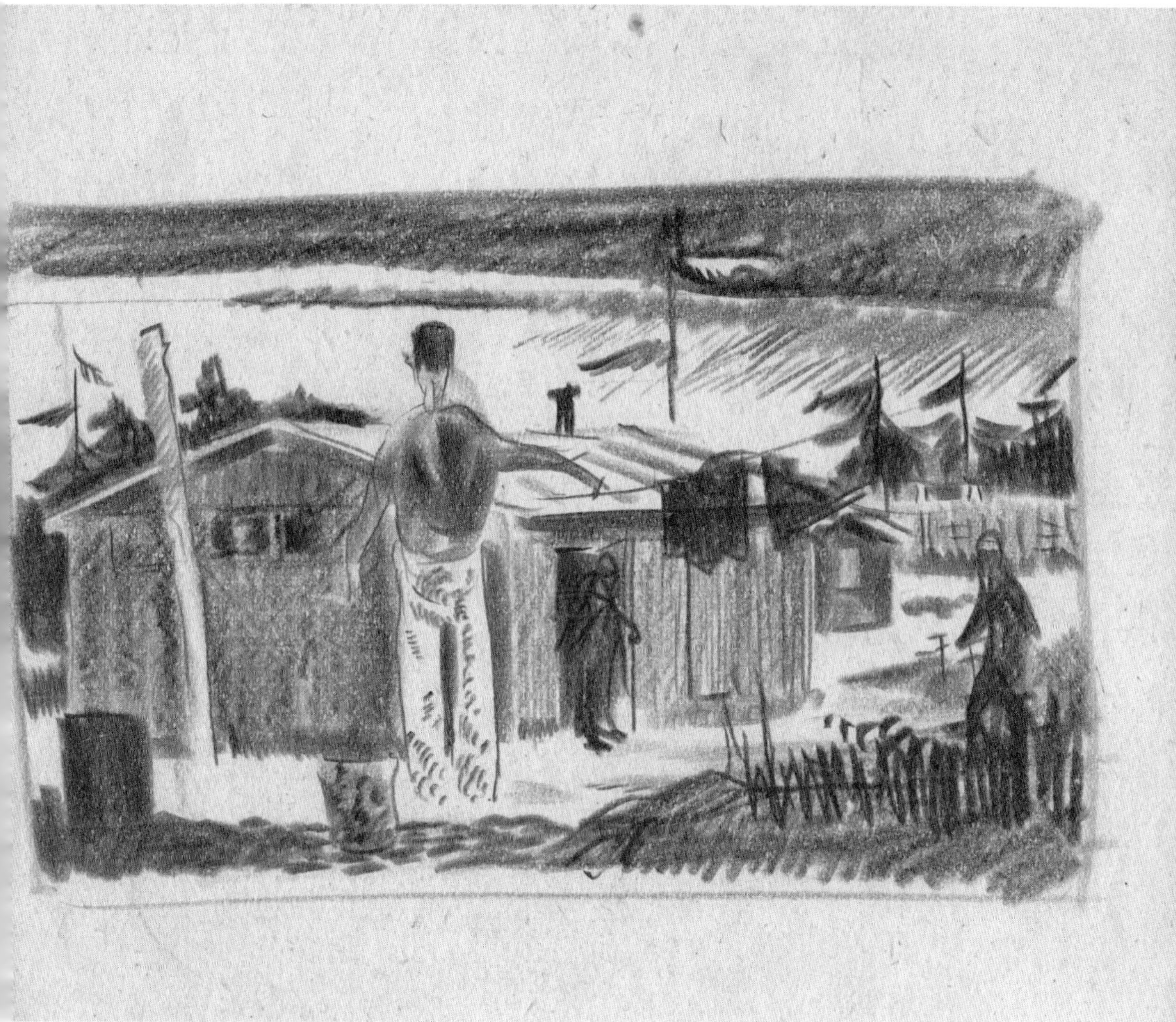

Each PoW received two thin blankets, one sheet, one palliasse (straw mattress), one pillowcase, one pillow filled with straw and one small face towel. Linen for the camp – mattress covers, pillow cases and sheets – was provided by the Third Reich. Clean linens were provided every three to four weeks.

For kitchen implements, each PoW was given one two-quart mixing bowl, one cup, knife, fork, and spoon. If any item was lost or stolen, it would not be replaced.

Poor Quality Brooms and Brushes

Brooms and brushes were of poor quality and wore out quickly. The usual monthly issue of brooms and broom handles at Stalag Luft III did not suffice for cleaning rooms, kitchens, halls, latrines and washrooms.

Cleaning materials were difficult to obtain, but regular cleaning had to be done in order to keep the bedbugs and lice under control. A typical monthly issue of cleaning supplies for the entire camp was eighteen brooms, twenty deck scrubbers, fifteen hand scrubbers and 25 kilos of chlorine-based cleaner per month.

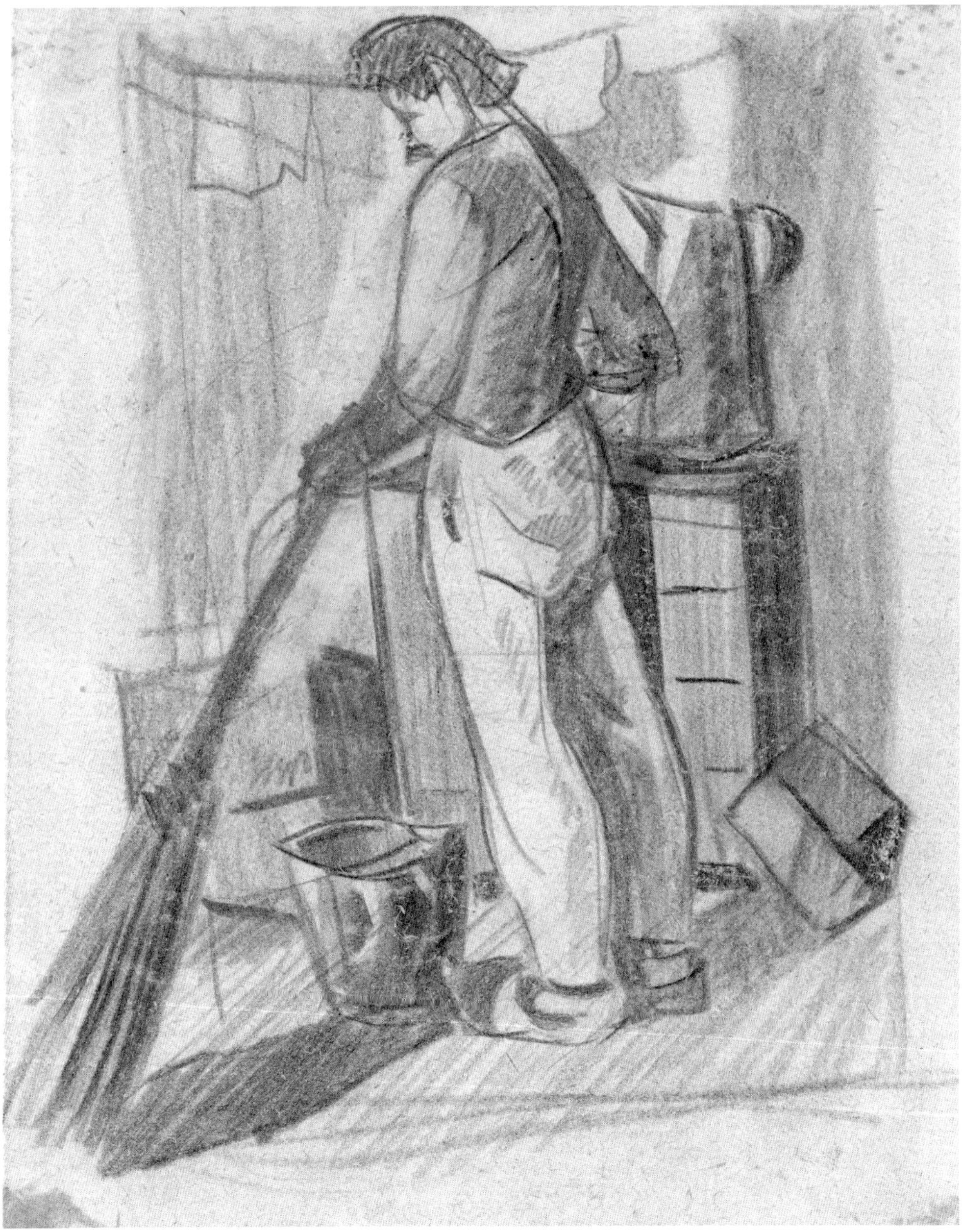

Cleaning Was a Team Effort

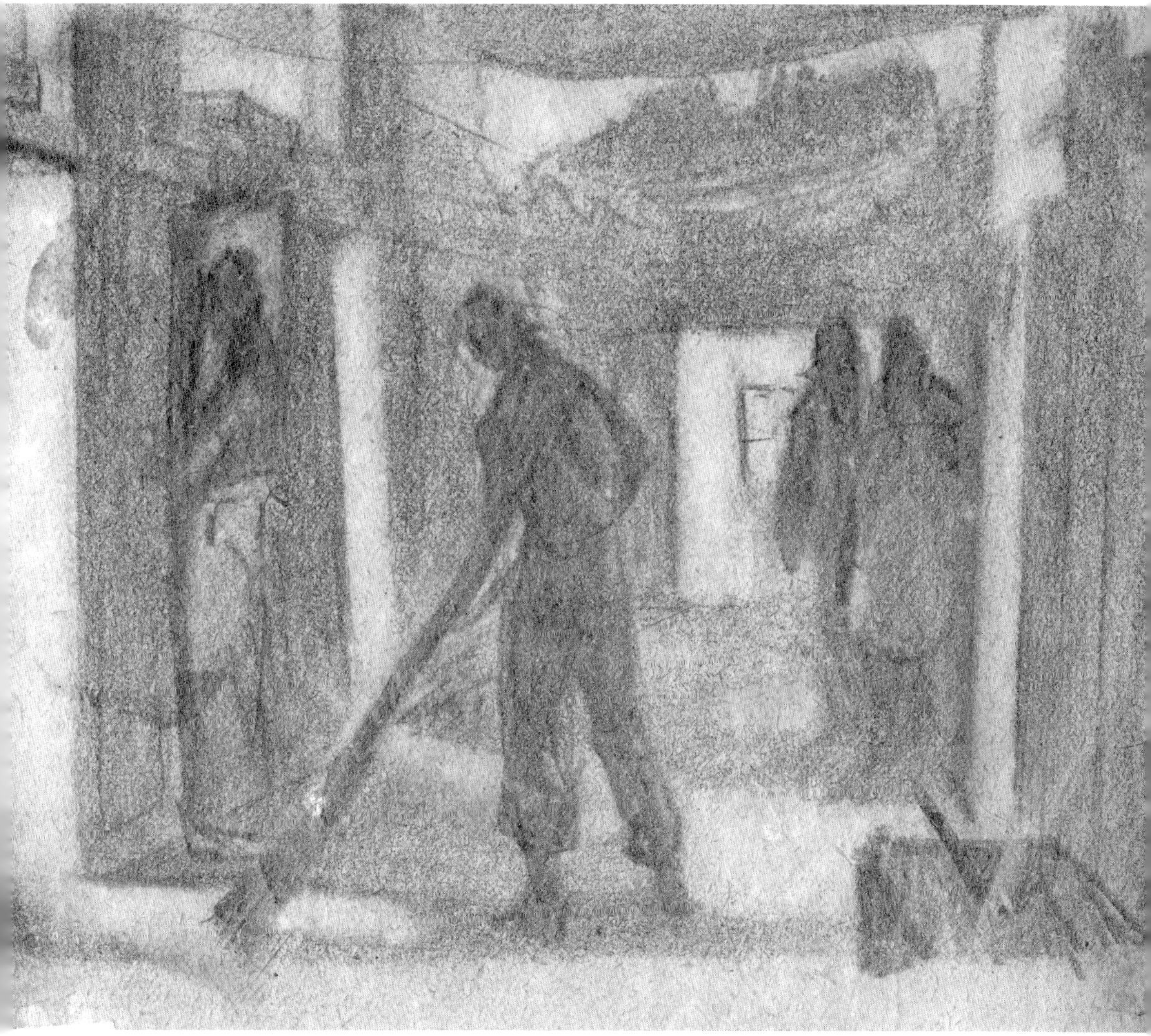

Room members helped with the monthly floor-washing task, but bunks were made up and cleaned by each of their occupants.

In May 1944, Lieutenant Colonel R.M. Stillman and Lieutenant Colonel A.P. Clark initiated a 'spring Buck-up' in sanitary standard of their blocks. The rate of dysentery and skin disease would go up when the flies arrived unless these new sanitary standards were followed. Block COs would be required to inspect all rooms in their blocks at 11 am each Saturday morning. Lieutenant Colonels Stillman and Clark would accompany Block COs on their inspections from time to time.

Kriegie Carries His Essential Belongings

The Kriegie learned quickly in his new life that food and wearing apparel were the prime essentials for existence. A few months of cold, wet weather proved the importance of shoes and clothing. When moving from camp to camp, these items received preference as all belongings were limited to the amount a man could carry.

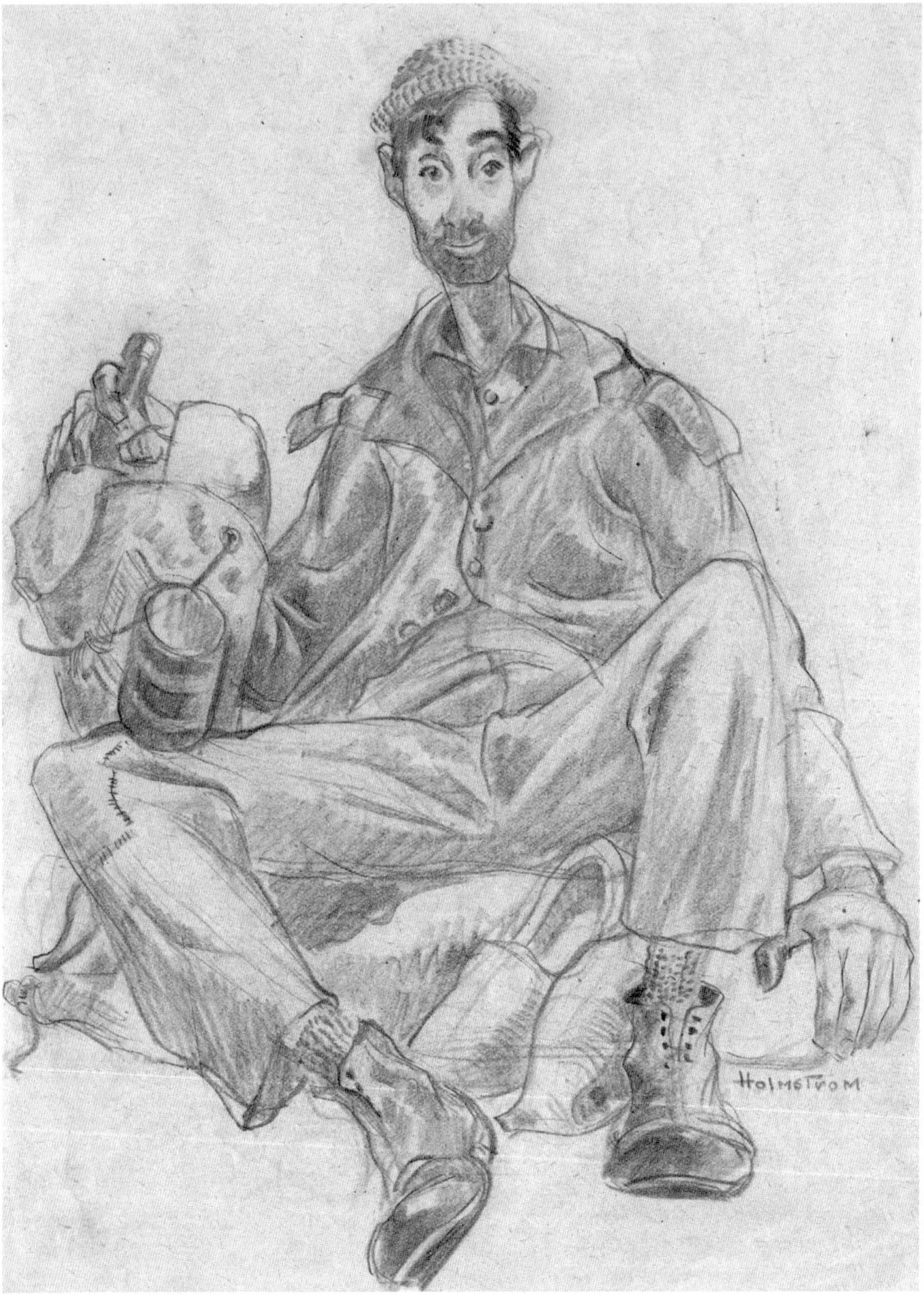

Wooden Clogs

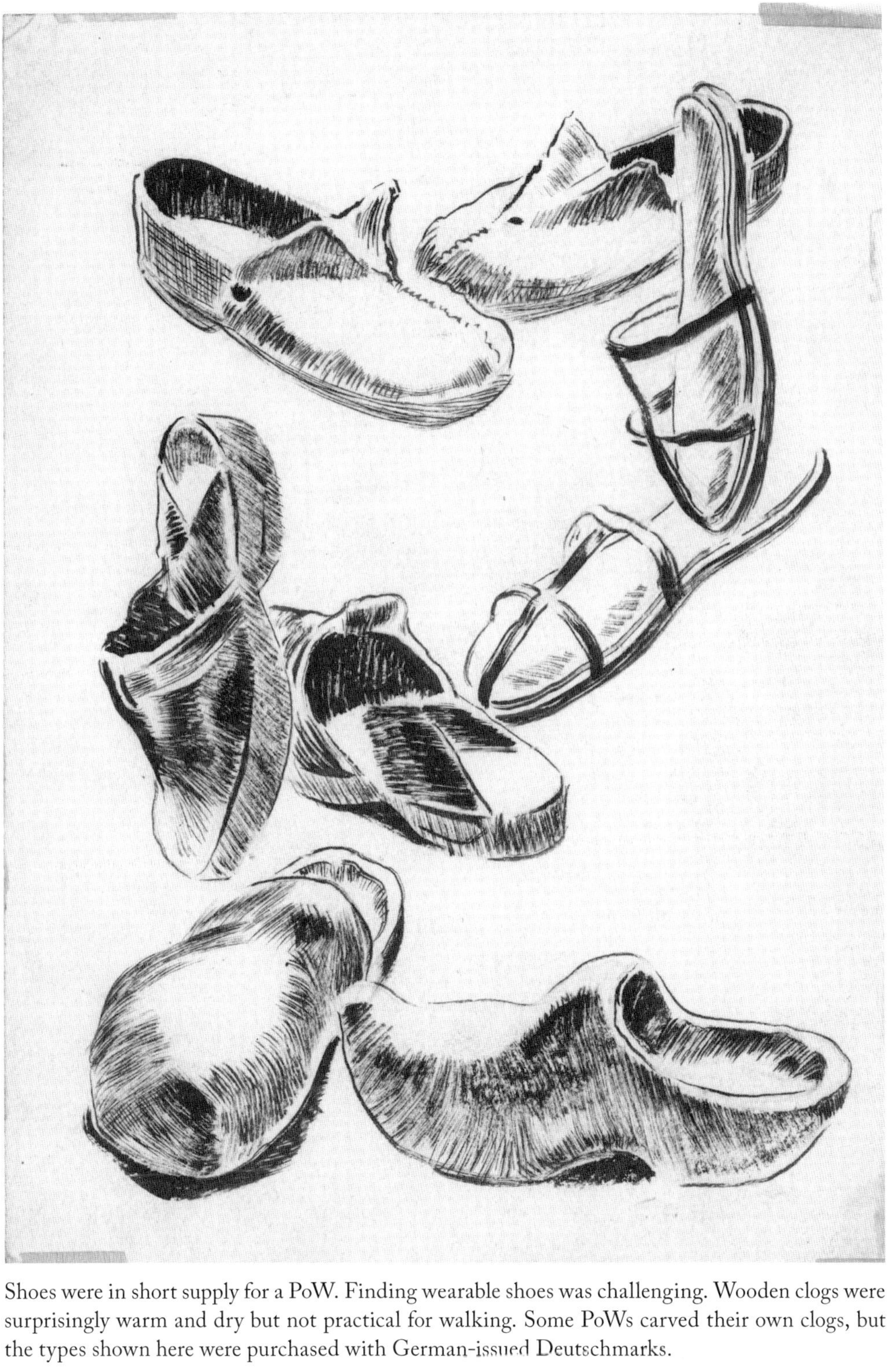

Shoes were in short supply for a PoW. Finding wearable shoes was challenging. Wooden clogs were surprisingly warm and dry but not practical for walking. Some PoWs carved their own clogs, but the types shown here were purchased with German-issued Deutschmarks.

A Kriegie's Private Time

A Bunk of Warmth

In the entire Stalag Luft III camp, the only place of privacy was the Kriegie's own bunk as nobody sat there without his permission. It consisted of a palliasse, two ersatz blankets and a pillow filled with straw with a pillowcase. The mattress was supported by eight bed boards. Nightly bed checks by the Germans required that PoW numbers be printed on the side of the bed.

During the winter, lack of heating facilities, in addition to food deficiencies, compelled many prisoners to stay in their bunks in order to keep warm and try to forget their hunger. Others remained there simply logging sack time to become "sack artists".

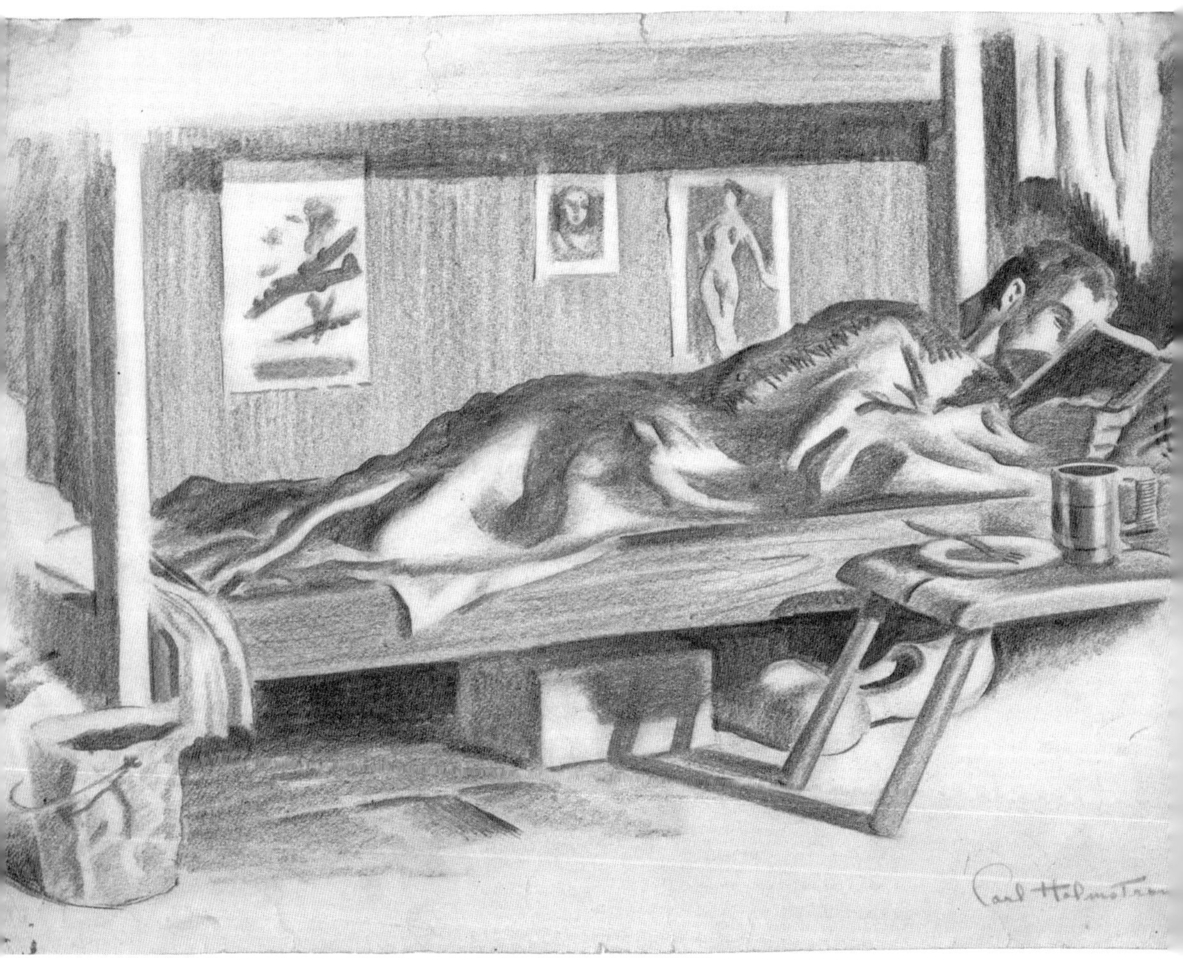

Not All Were Sack Artists

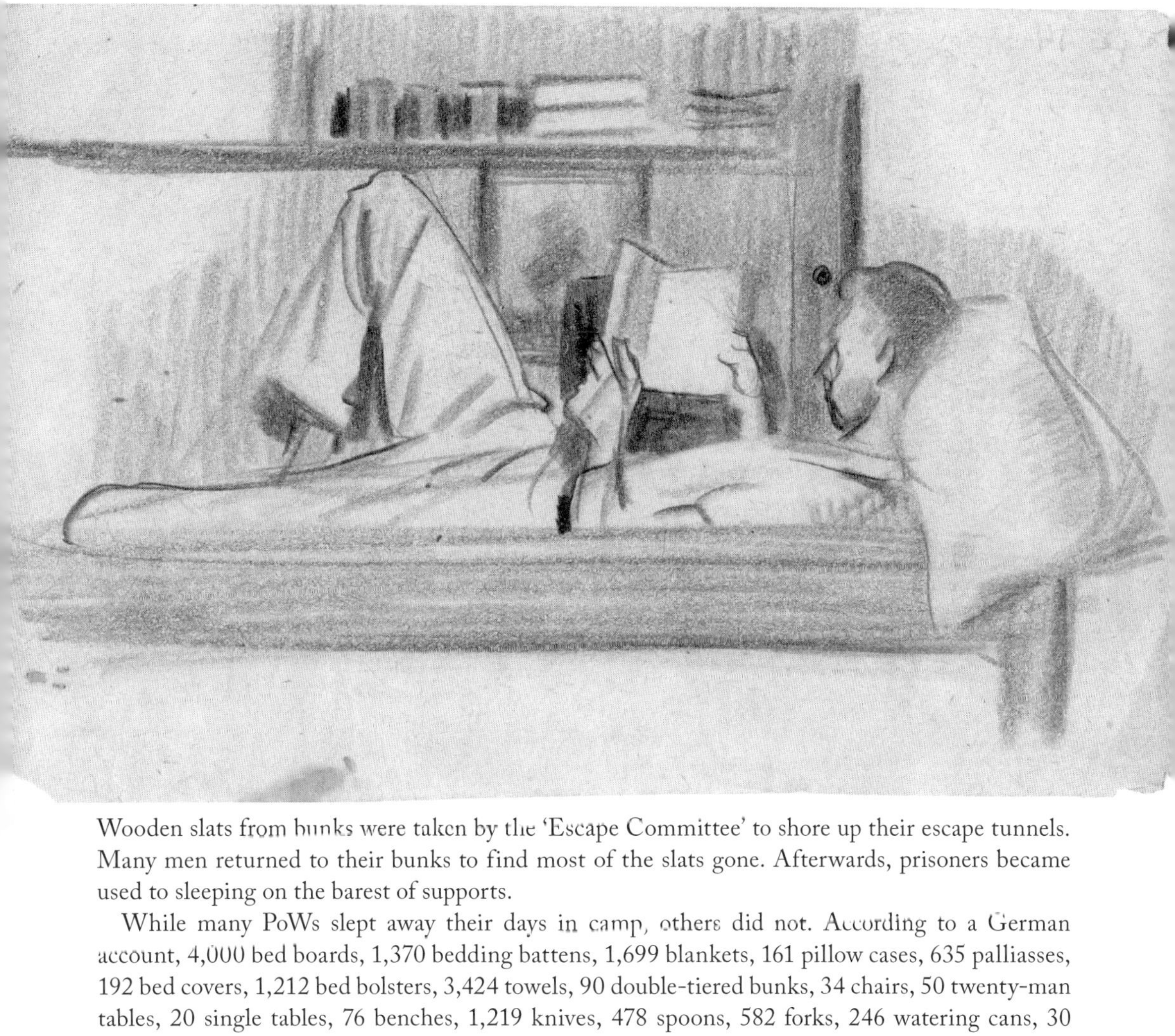

Wooden slats from bunks were taken by the 'Escape Committee' to shore up their escape tunnels. Many men returned to their bunks to find most of the slats gone. Afterwards, prisoners became used to sleeping on the barest of supports.

While many PoWs slept away their days in camp, others did not. According to a German account, 4,000 bed boards, 1,370 bedding battens, 1,699 blankets, 161 pillow cases, 635 palliasses, 192 bed covers, 1,212 bed bolsters, 3,424 towels, 90 double-tiered bunks, 34 chairs, 50 twenty-man tables, 20 single tables, 76 benches, 1,219 knives, 478 spoons, 582 forks, 246 watering cans, 30 shovels, 1,000ft of electric wire, 600 feet of rope and 69 lamps went missing after being issued to the prisoners. This list does not include the materials used for false papers or fake civilian clothing.

A Kriegie's Own Bunk

Retreating to one's own bunk created a time of self-reflection and relative solitude. Each man adorned the walls around his bunk with pictures from home, letters and poems. It was the only place in camp where he could be somewhat alone.

> The Kriegie's life was an empty, monotonous routine. Bewildered as to his future, and hungry from morning till night, he passed his days dreaming of home. Moods of depression came in cycles developing from lack of mail, self-pity and cramped living conditions. Excessive brooding caused some men to 'go around the bend', which made everyone in the room suffer. Such men were sometimes removed from the camp to local mental hospitals, changed to another barracks or repatriated if severe. Everything had to be done to prevent this so PoWs were encouraged to occupy their minds with reading, studying, drawing, crafts and taking classes to keep mentally fit. Sports were also encouraged to stay physically fit.
>
> Second Lieutenant Carl H. Holmstrom, POW #221

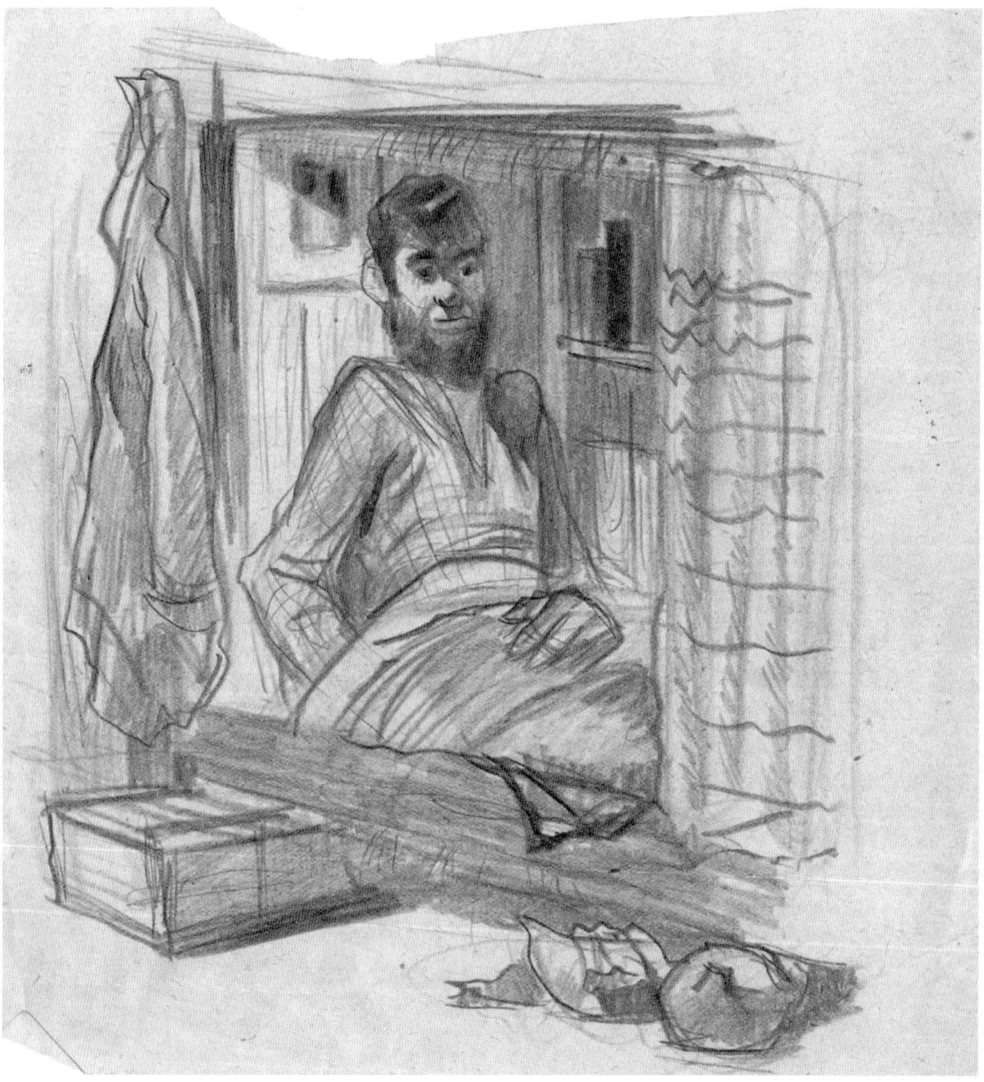

Reading and Libraries

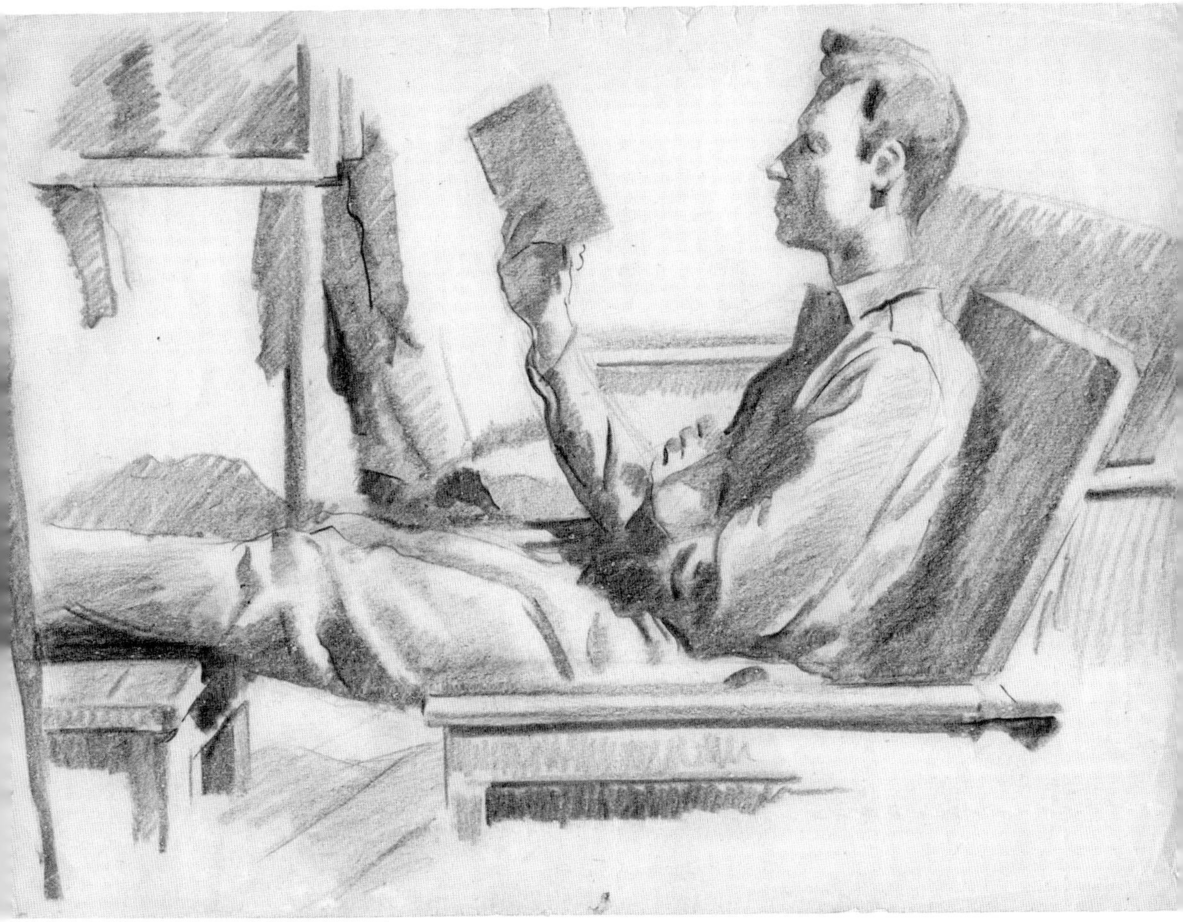

Each compound at Stalag Luft III had at least two libraries, one that served as a general lending library with fiction and non-fiction books, and one for reference materials in which sports equipment, phonograph records, art materials and books that would occupy the prisoners making life a little easier at the camp. In South Compound, the library held 400 books for 600 officers but gained many more as the war continued. The YMCA provided many of the books and others were sent from home.

Libraries provided one of the few places where prisoners could study and keep warm in the winter. PoWs taking courses had to share textbooks for their course work. Books were often read aloud for the benefit of other Kriegies. The library could seat only sixty-five men, so the rest found other places to read.

Wartime Logs

With much time on their hands, Kriegies depended on reading to occupy their time. Books sent from home were shared with other Kriegies and were read and re-read many times.

Many Kriegies read hundreds of books while confined and kept a list of books read in their wartime logs which were diary-style books issued by the YMCA to each prisoner. Nothing negative was allowed to be written in them about the Germans or the camp, and a daily diary of activities in them was *verboten*.

As a result, most men wrote recipes, had others sign their books, drew pictures, copied poems and recorded menus. The covers became works of art, some inlaid with names and initials in vari-coloured wood. Ingenious means of binding the books and adding new pages took hours of time.

A common theme in the wartime logs was the recording of Kriegie jargon. As Kriegie slang developed in the camp, and men quickly learned it, the most common expressions heard repeatedly were recorded on the book's pages.

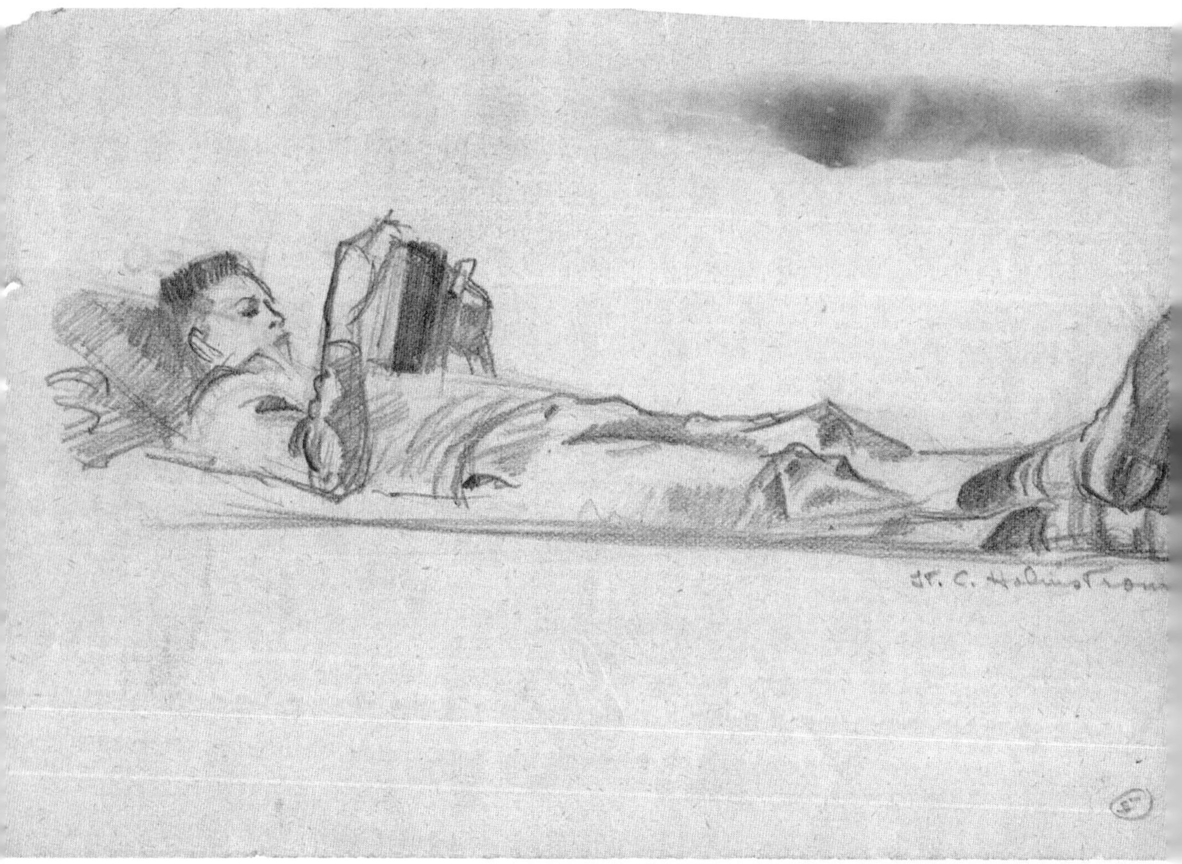

From Double to Triple Bunk Beds

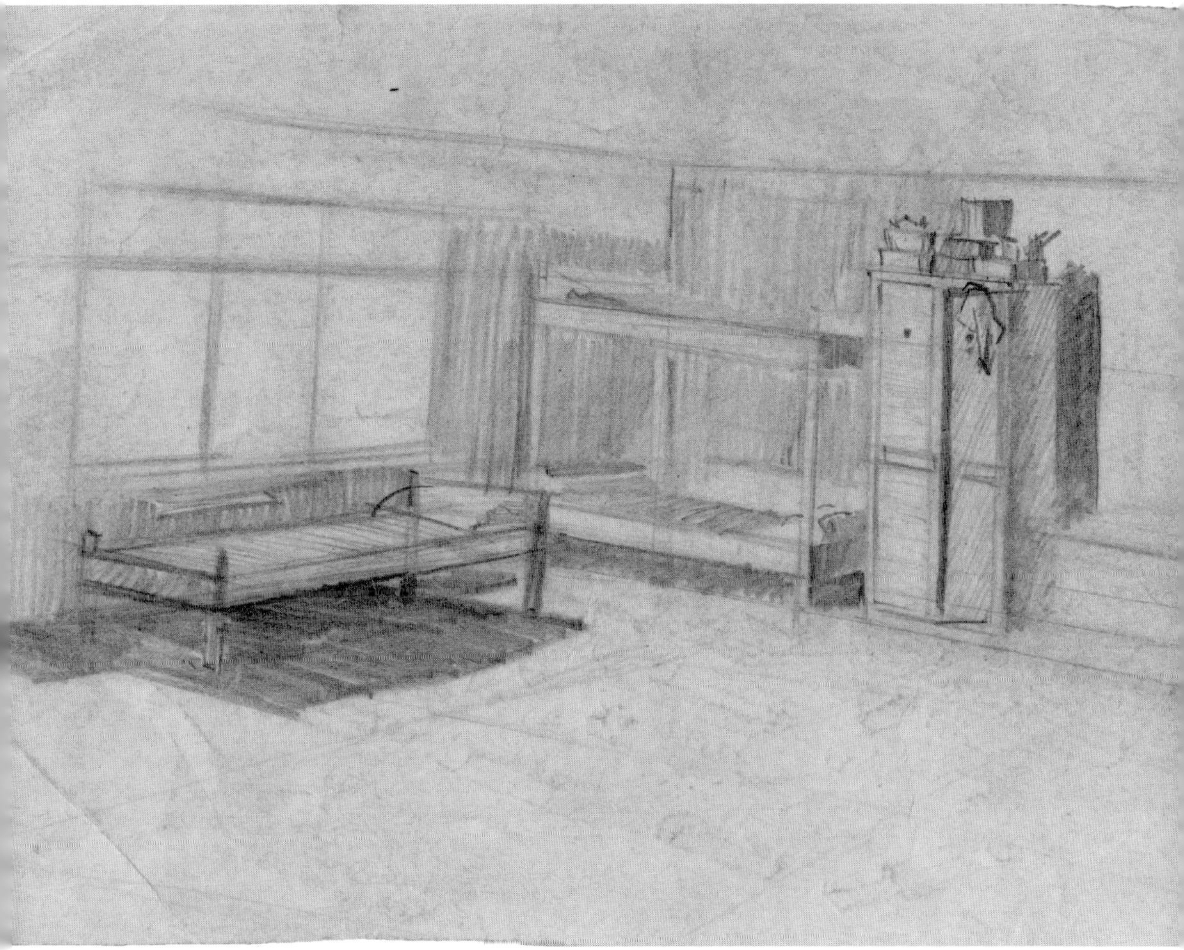

USAAF prisoners began arriving at the camp in significant numbers after 1943, filling rooms beyond maximum capacity. Earlier in the war, double bunks were adequate but as the war dragged on and more men were brought into Stalag Luft III, it was necessary to use triple bunks. The room or combine that was made for eight men now held as many as ten or more.

To arrange fifteen beds in a room three-high, PoW John O'Neill and his staff of carpenters came in. While some PoWs were allowed to borrow German tools for approved projects with restrictions strictly enforced, O'Neill and his staff were the only PoWs in the compound permitted to regularly handle tools. However, when the waiting lists for help were too long, men got their 'prangers' and knife saws from their hiding places and fixed the bunks themselves.

New arrivals discovered that of the eight bed slats many had already been donated to the escape committee. PoWs would lose more slats as the war went on. Soon they were carefully getting into their bunks as many had two slats left. Many PoWs began replacing loose boards with nets of rope in order to sleep in comfort and safety.

Eventually, the camp grew to approximately 60 acres in size and housed about 2,500 Royal Air Force officers, about 7,500 US Army Air Forces and about 900 officers from other Allied Air Forces. This was a total of about 10,900 inmates, including some support officers.

Parcel Day

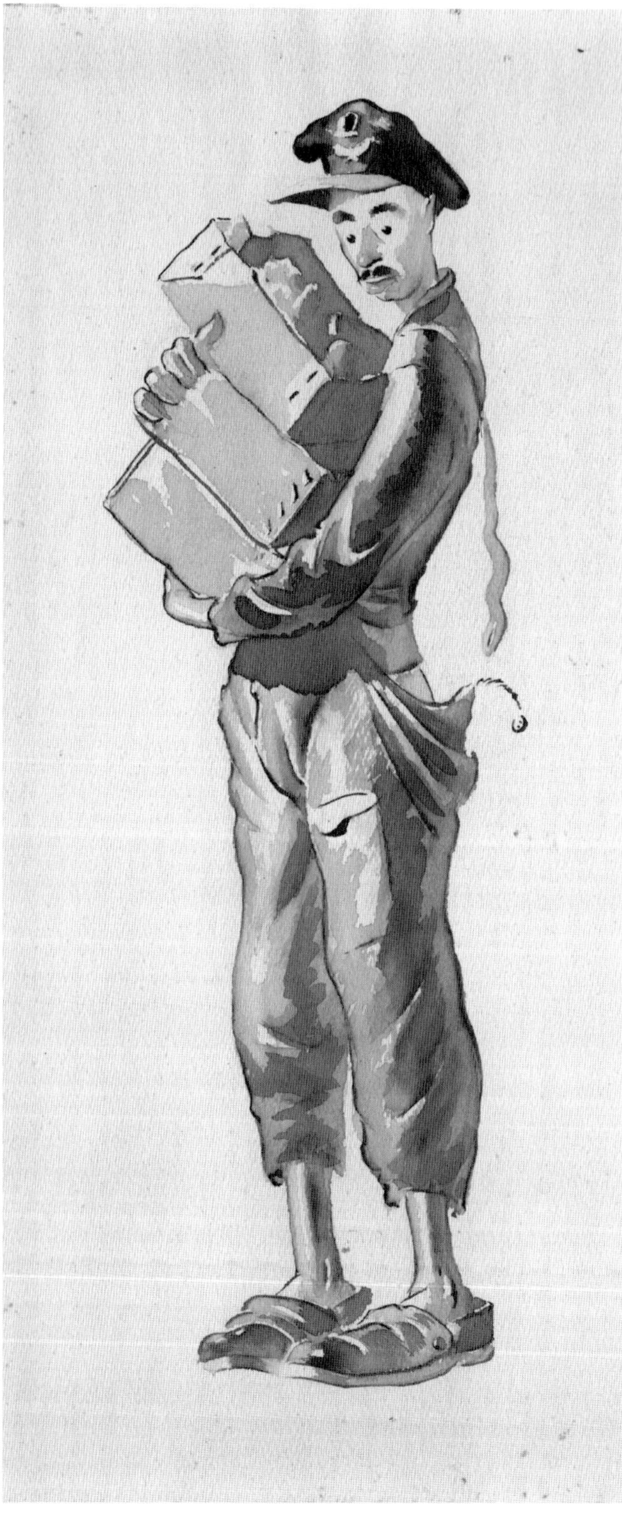

Parcel day was the Kriegies' dream of heaven. Red Cross parcels brought supplementary food that prisoners depended on. It meant a chocolate bar or sweet condendo, and extra special items that allowed for a 'bash'. Cans of KLIM contributed to the creation of special recipes. Parcels were brought into camp and checked by PoW parcel officers as well as German officers.

Months or years could go by without a letter from anyone. Allied bombing of railways often delayed the delivery of mail as it did for the Red Cross food parcels. It could take months for a letter to go through both American and German censors and finally be delivered, so news was often four months old or more. A picture from home brought great joy. Letters with good news were read and re-read and shared with buddies who received nothing.

As the tunnels advanced in 1943, the boxes were coded, usually in the return address. They contained escape materials that looked like everyday items. The boxes came from both military intelligence entities – MI9 in Britain and MISX in the US. Monopoly games with real German money, brushes that came apart to reveal contraband, including inks for forging documents, sports equipment that hid the same, and compasses hidden in uniform buttons.

Censors and Letters

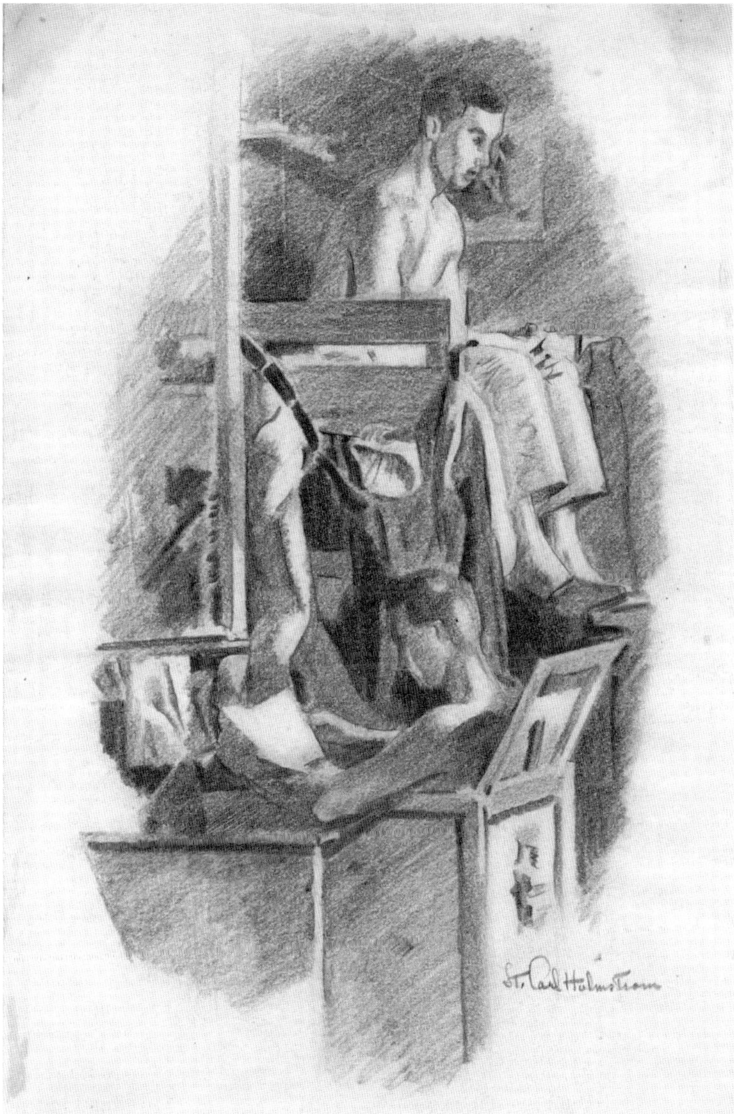

Every man looked forward to mail delivery. Every other day mail was delivered. PoWs were not restricted in how much mail they could receive, but were only allowed to send three letters and four postcards every month. Letters averaged three weeks to arrive from Canada, four from England, and five from the United States. For security purposes, outgoing mail was censored by block commanders before delivery to Germans for further German censorship before leaving the camp. Young German women fluent in English and some German men were hired as mail censors. The women lived in the camp but were never permitted access to the PoWs. Practically all letters had words deleted by the censors. Some men received no mail for the entire time they were incarcerated.

Mail was never lacking in surprises. Often men heard from wives or girlfriends, tired of the long separation, who chose to leave them. These letters were called 'Dear Lieutenant letters'. The bulletin boards were used to display humorous mail as well as 'Dear Lieutenant letters' which informed all Kriegies how the 'girls they left behind' were being entertained by the boys at home.

Bull Sessions

Bull sessions covered every possible subject as no prisoner hesitated to give his opinion on anything. Incidents of one's life were of interest, but personal problems or complaints usually brought the remark: 'See the chaplain and have your ticket punched!'

'There I Was' stories, detailing all the aspects of a man's shoot-down story, were told and re-told whenever an audience was available. The stories became more embellished and exaggerated with each re-telling. Many compounds imposed the rule that a prisoner could tell the story when he got to camp, and he could not tell it again afterwards other than on his birthday.

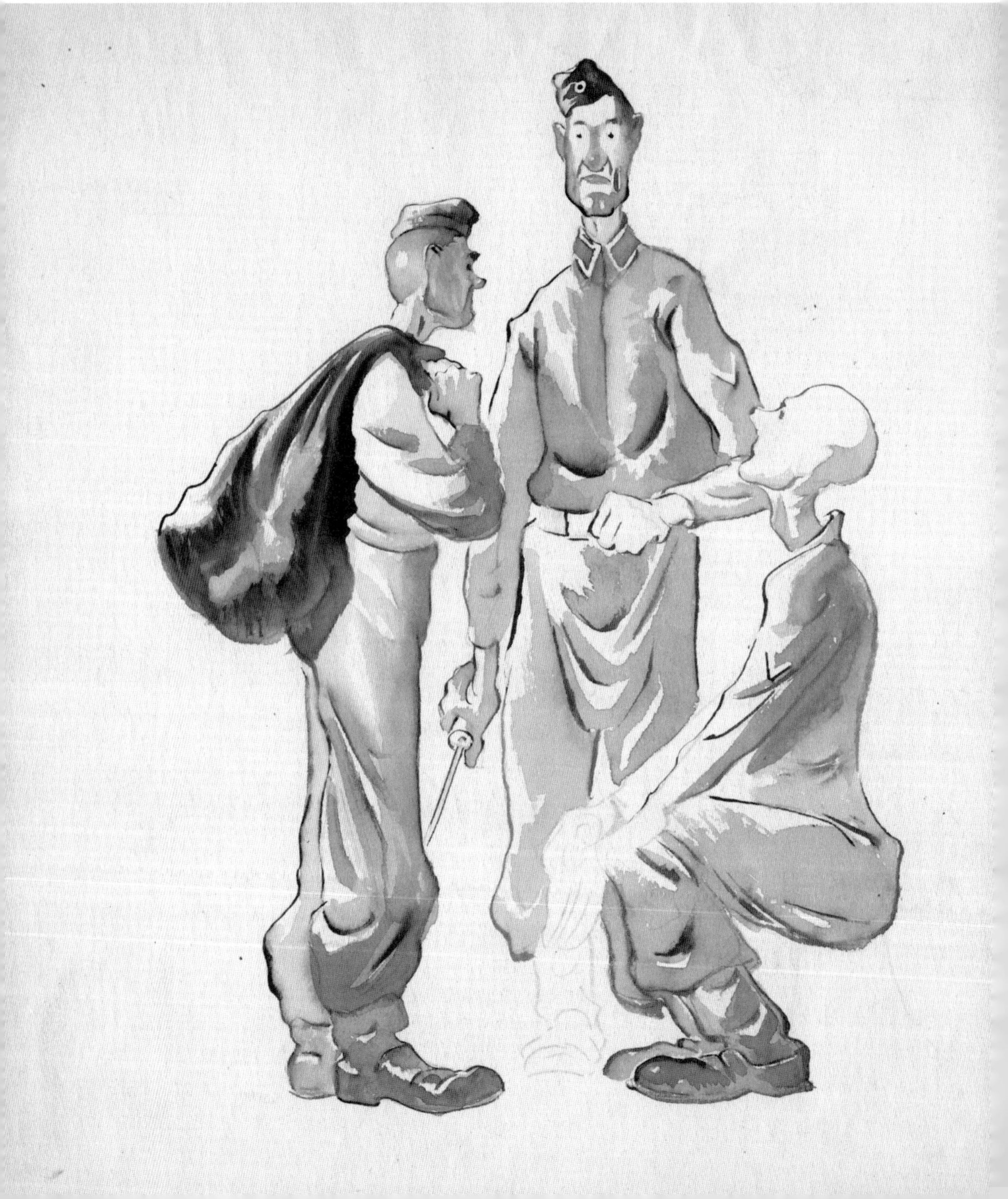

Kriegies Perform in Theatres

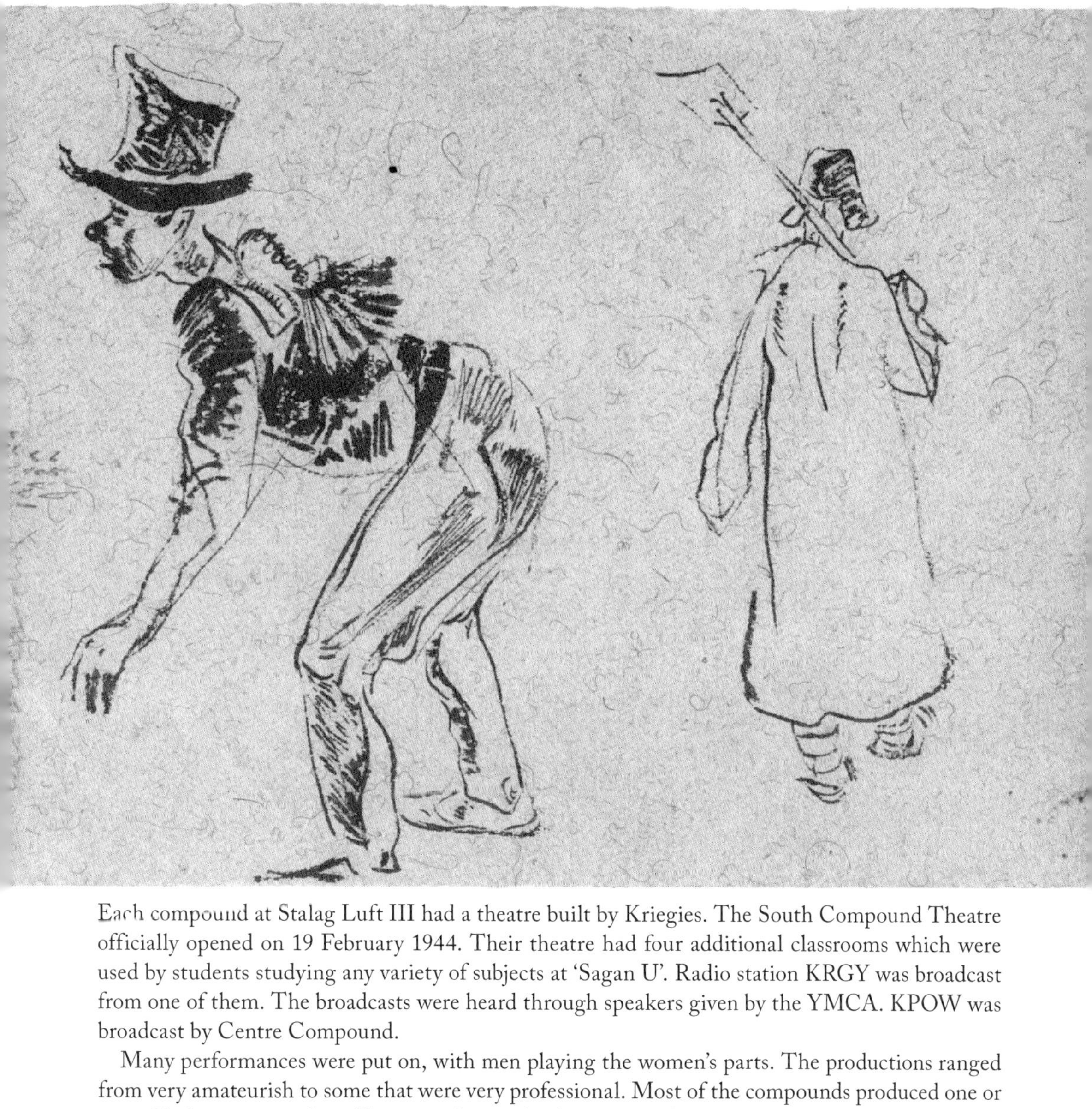

Each compound at Stalag Luft III had a theatre built by Kriegies. The South Compound Theatre officially opened on 19 February 1944. Their theatre had four additional classrooms which were used by students studying any variety of subjects at 'Sagan U'. Radio station KRGY was broadcast from one of them. The broadcasts were heard through speakers given by the YMCA. KPOW was broadcast by Centre Compound.

Many performances were put on, with men playing the women's parts. The productions ranged from very amateurish to some that were very professional. Most of the compounds produced one or more Shakespearean plays. Variety and comedy shows were the most popular with the prisoners. Men's choirs performed regularly. During winter, the audience had to bundle up and sit together listening to the choirs and Christmas productions as there was no heat.

Red Cross parcel boxes were made into seats. The YMCA provided artificial cosmetics, and in one compound they donated a red silk curtain. Many professionals and well-known actors, playwrights, musicians and screenwriters after the war had gotten their starts in the theatres of Stalag Luft III. Once when an American marching band played *God Save the Queen* outside North Compound for the British PoWs, the Germans forbade the bands from performing for many months as a punishment.

Tunnel Sand Disposal and the Theatre

Digging tunnels was dangerous – both below ground and above it. The sand was treacherous and would come crashing down with little warning. No one was killed but several diggers were forced to take days off after almost being suffocated. A cave-in left a large space above the tunnel to be repaired. The damaged roof was shored up and the sand packed back above it. The diggers found out that sand dug out, while making the repair, occupied 30 per cent more space as it would normally, placing extra burdens on the disposal teams.

Sand disposal from the tunnels was a problem. Originally sand dispersal was done by 'penguins'. PoWs filled long, thin bags which were slipped inside their trousers, suspended by a cord around their necks. The 'penguins' then walked around the compound, releasing the sand from the bottom of the bags after pulling a pin to drop it from each bag. The tunnel sand was yellow so it had to be carefully kicked into the dirt where men walked, PoW gardens in particular.

Later, a huge closed-off area under the theatre was utilized. Seat 13 was hinged and camouflaged so the vast triangular space beneath could be used for sand disposal. The sand's pungent but not unpleasant odour was distinctive and easily detected during the theatre disposal operations. Pipe smokers were engaged to sit near the hinged seat, and puff away to camouflage the smell of the sand.

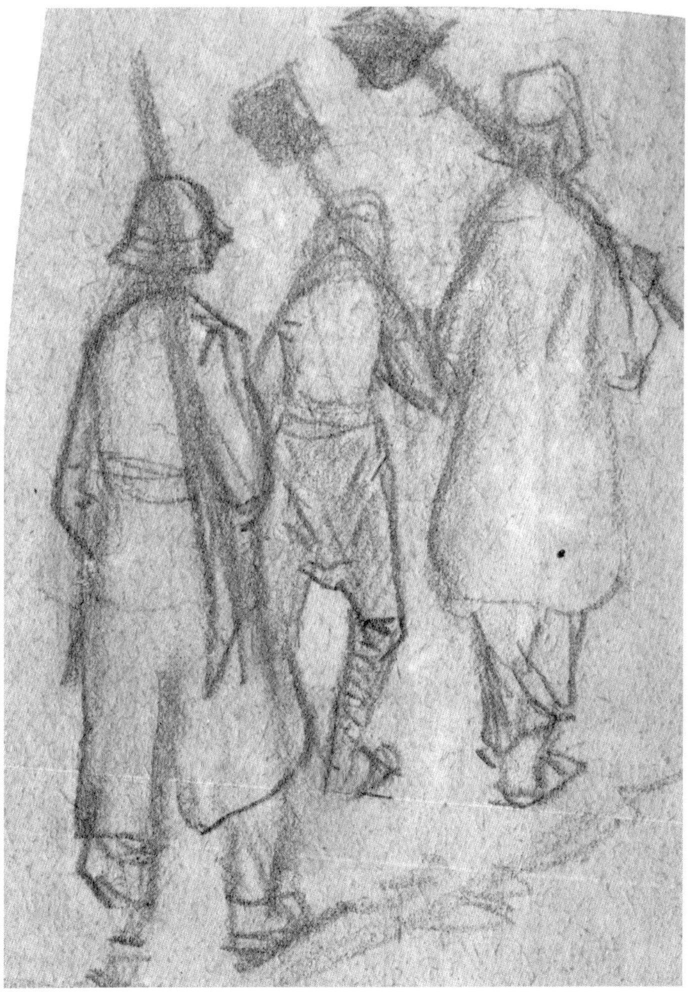

American Pride at Stalag Luft III

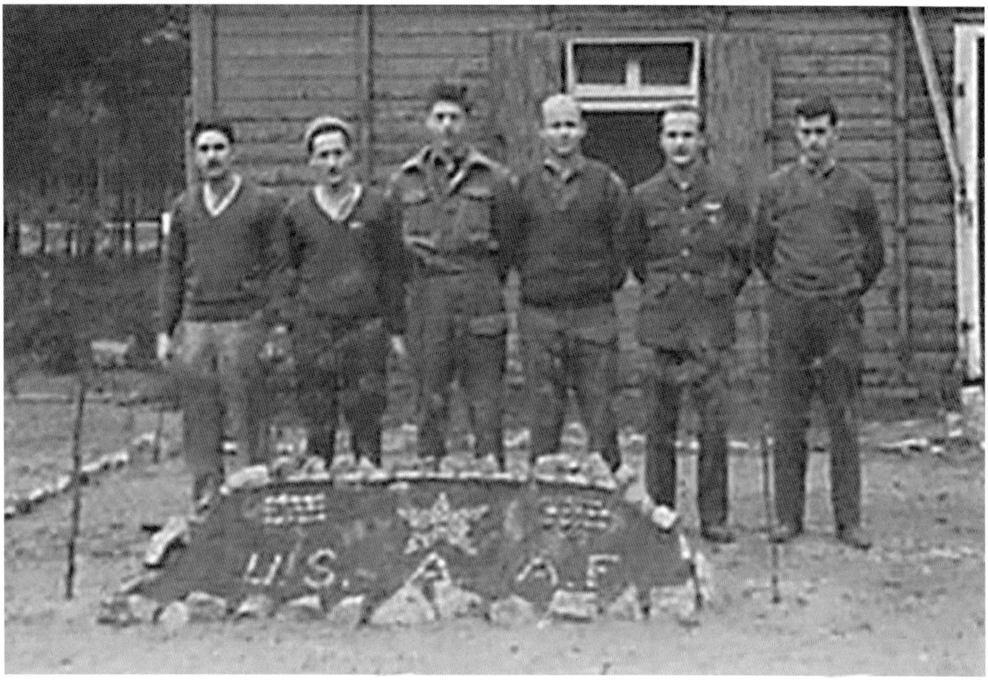

Many roommates had their pictures taken standing behind this 'memorial' that sat in front of barracks 108, made by American PoWs in North Compound. Carl Holmstrom is third from the right with the noticeable bald head. The mound hid sand removed from a tunnel that was under construction. Barracks 108 was initially known as 'the American barracks', holding only Americans who were shot down early in the war and lived with the British in North Compound.

Barracks 108 held only American prisoners shot down early in the war who initially lived with the British. As more men were shot down later in the war, the Americans were moved to South Compound where Carl lived in barracks 135, room 14. Some Americans helped to dig Tunnel Harry and served in the massive security operation to maintain its secrecy. Some were even on the list to escape through it, but their move to South Compound denied them that opportunity.

Forged Documents Produced at Stalag Luft III for the 'Great Escape'

Carl was one of the fifty men in the forgery department who turned out money, phony passports and identity cards. Those chosen as forgers had to be able to hand-stencil to make a finished product look like a typewritten script, and also draw the background of a master document's watermark with pen, ink brush and watercolour so it looked authentic. Carl's art training with his speciality in calligraphy came in handy.

The forgery group was called 'Dean & Dawson' after the English travel agency. Some of the guards could be bribed with a gift of coffee or chocolate. Afterwards, they couldn't refuse more because the PoWs could report the transgression to the commandant, who could have them sent to the Eastern Front. In this way, the forgers got coloured inks, pens, brushes, special types of paper, magnets with which to make compasses and radio parts to build the illegal receiver on which they got daily news bulletins. In addition, they got a camera and equipment to make photos for fake passports and also maps.

The faking of documents was an incredibly tedious job. Whole sheets of simulated typesetting were drawn by hand, complete with strike-overs, imperfect letters and bad shifts. Forgers ripped fine paper from bibles and linen covers from books to make identification books. One document needed in crossing frontiers was so complicated that it would take a skilled forger five hours a day for a month to make one. One mistake and the forger had to start all over again. German eagles and swastika stamps were cut from rubber boot heels. Altogether 'Dean & Dawson' provided the escapers with more than 400 forged documents.

(*Courtesy of Pegasus Archive*: www.pegasusarchive.org)

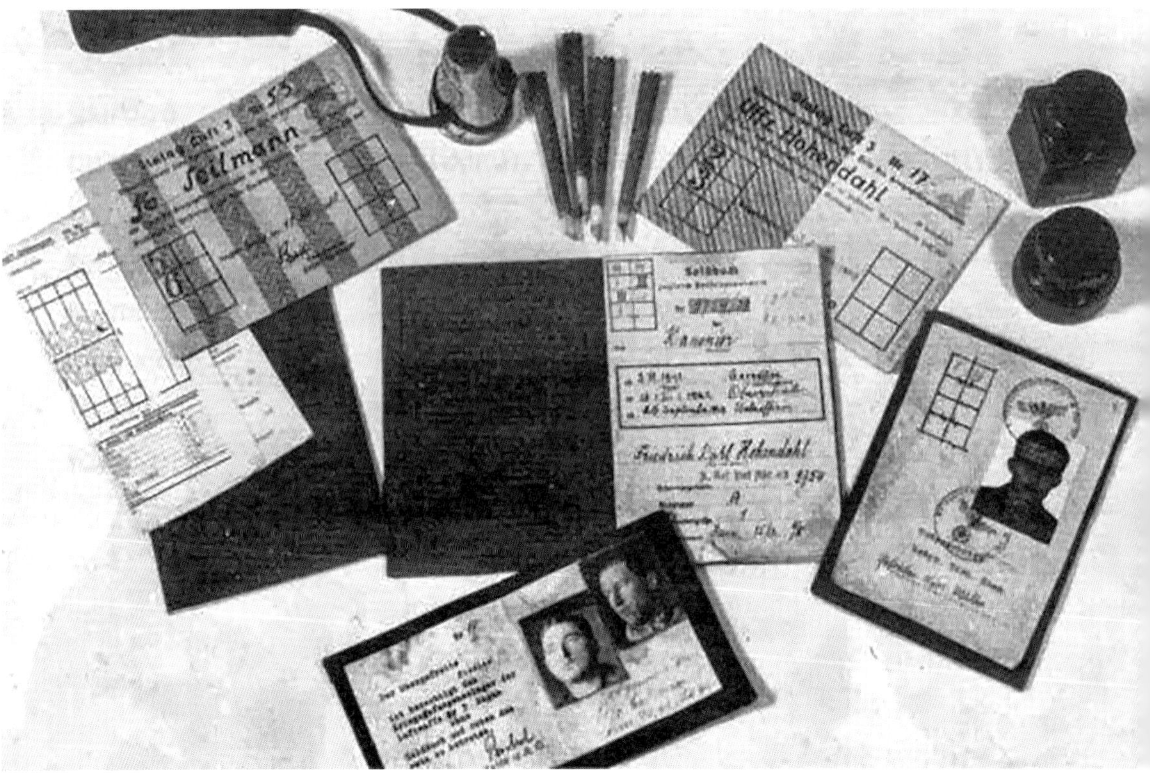

Sketches of Workers and Guards at Stalag Luft III

Honey Wagon Man and Gardens

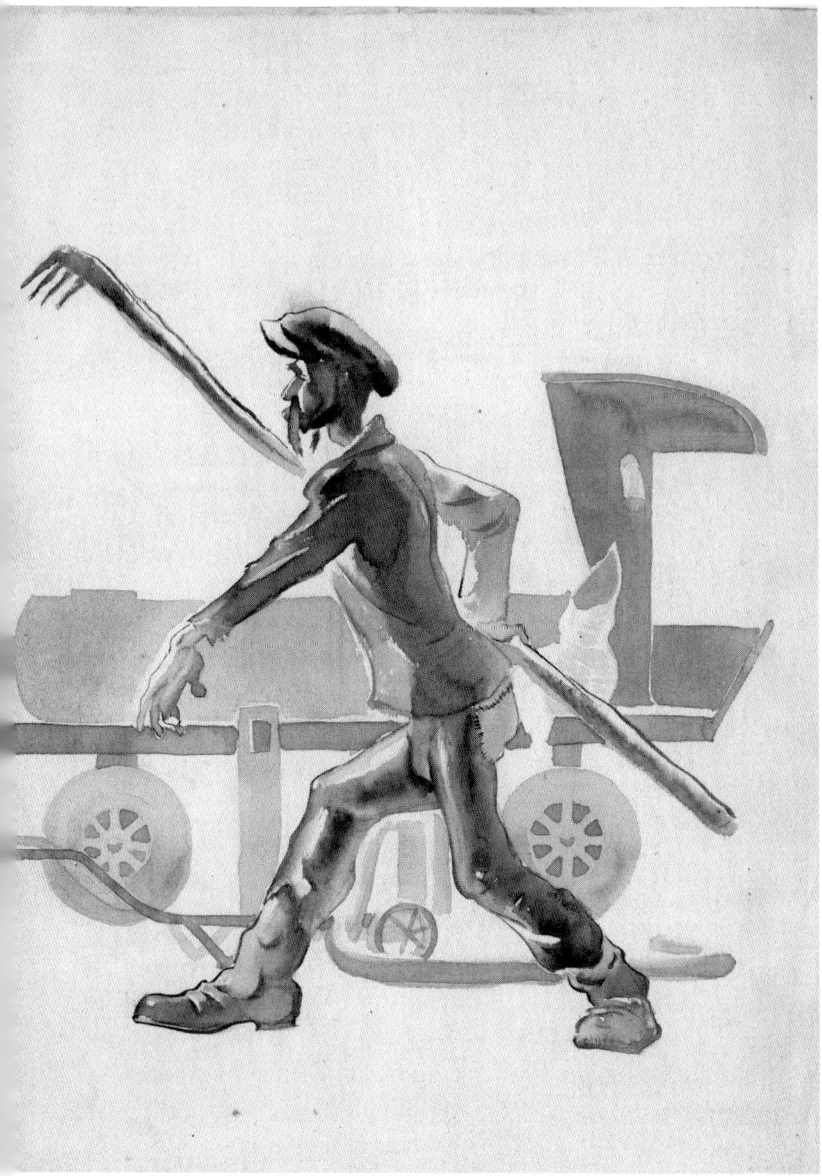

The Honey Wagon Man was Polish, Juliusz Koziol, and Holmstrom sketched his portrait. Koziol was assigned the task of pumping out the aborts. His battered pipe, ragged clothes and sandwich in the back pocket of his trousers identified him. The prisoners marvelled at the fact that a man with such a job could eat a sandwich at the same time he was working. His fellow Polish workers ate their lunches also without ever leaving the pump.

As of 1944, camp-wide gardening was under way with each room cultivating a small plot outside its windows using seeds supplied by the Red Cross. The sandy soil required lots of water and fertilization. As the Honey Wagon Man's wagon passed into a compound, some PoWs ran behind the horses that pulled it to collect the 'road apples' dropped by the horses to use as fertilizer in their gardens. Crops were usually tomatoes, radishes, lettuce and onions, making up for the lack of green vegetables in the camp.

Improvements to Latrines by PoWs

Continual visits by the Honey Wagon Man kept disease at bay in the camp. When American Lieutenant Colonel Albert P. Clark arrived in August 1942, he was disturbed by the unsanitary conditions. He knew what a pit latrine should look like and how it should be maintained. He volunteered to improve sanitary conditions.

The Germans provided tools with the provision they not be used for escape, and Clark gave them his word. With a group of volunteers, the pits were sealed to the flies, the latrines were screened with mosquito nets or burlap, and a stack was installed so that circulating air would take out the foul odours. After the improvements, the flies disappeared, and the illnesses cleared up. The Germans were so pleased with the results that they adapted these measures whenever possible in other compounds and camps in Germany.

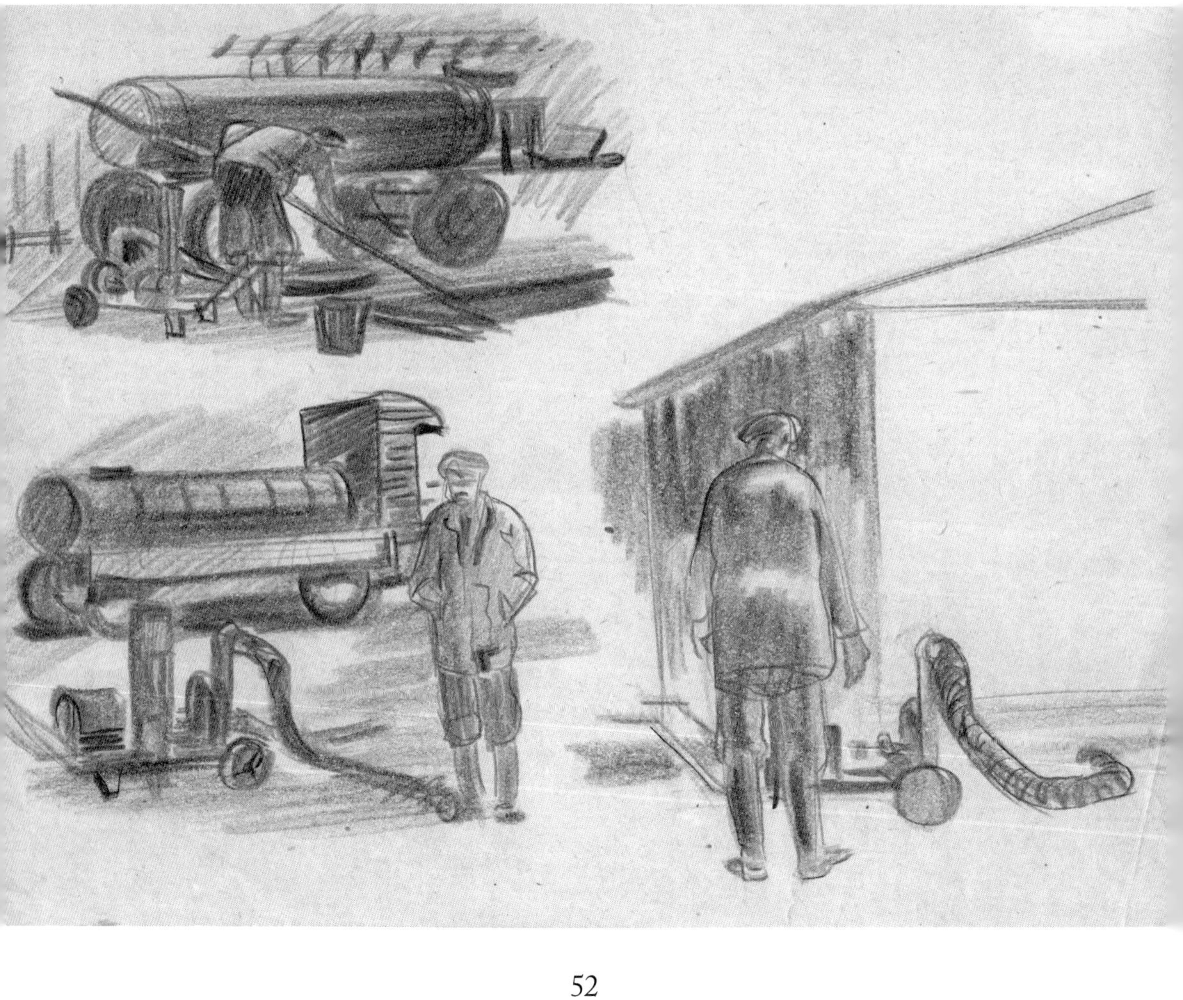

Goon Boxes

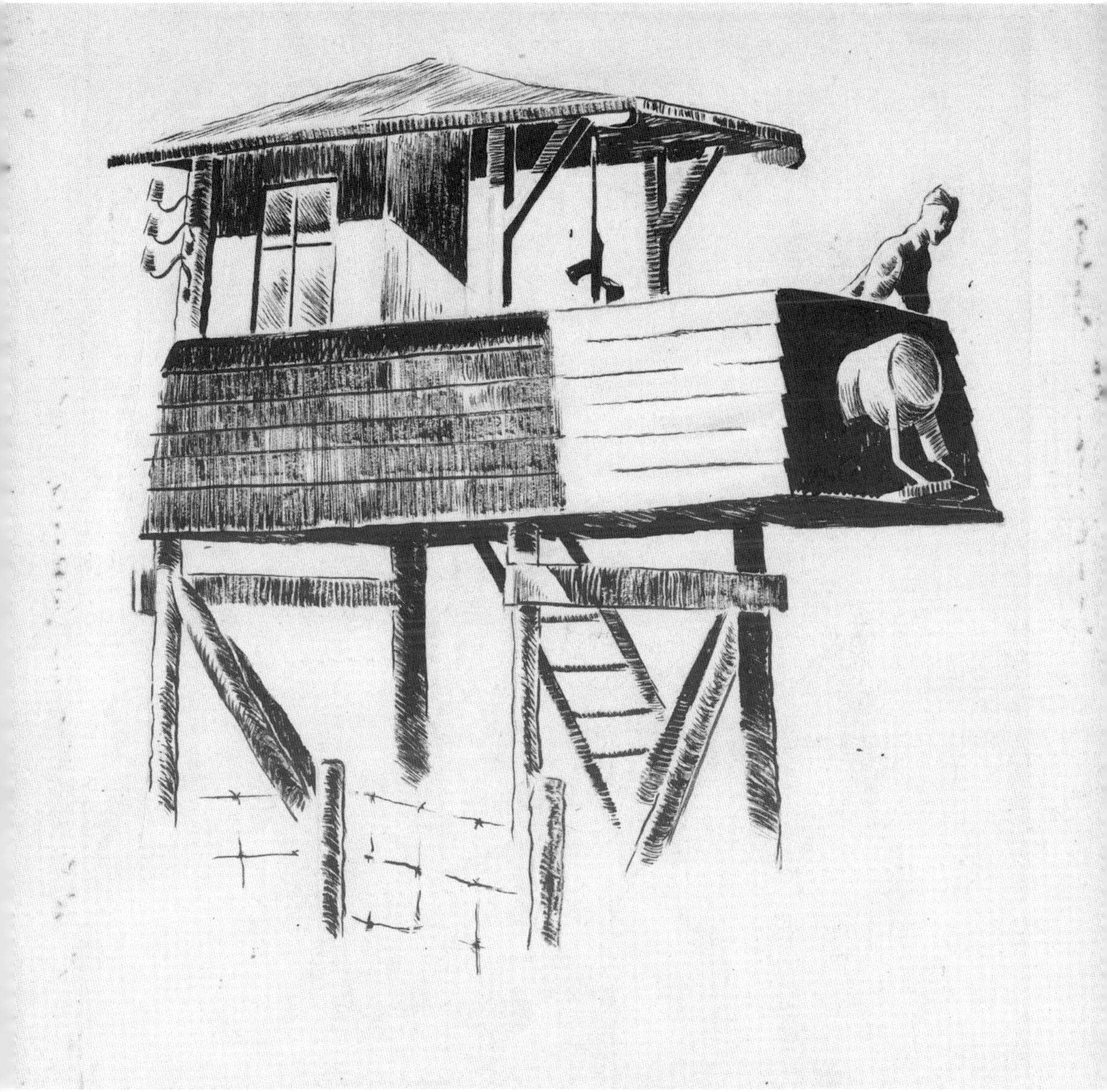

Goon boxes, or guard towers, at Stalag Luft III stood at the perimeter of the camp and contained every possible device to prevent escape, such as searchlights, machine guns, telephones, field glasses and a seismograph to detect tunnelling.

Kriegies told the German officers or soldiers that 'Goon' stood for a 'German Officer or Non-Com', but it was a derisive term shortened from 'Gooney' and was named after a popular cartoon character 'Alice the Goon' in the series *Thimble Theatre* by E.C. Segar.

The name gained wide popularity due to a comic strip in the UK *Daily Mirror* that depicted goons as low-browed, primitive ape men of great strength and stupidity. The Germans never knew where the word came from.

Baiting the Goons

The act of provoking the enemy was 'Goon baiting', the often organized annoying and harassing of the guards. Baiting the Goons was always enjoyed and provided relief from boredom. The PoWs generally knew their limits and not to go too far.

The Kriegies lost many things of value as guards tore rooms apart in their searches, breaking prized items, so searches, even in the middle of the night, could go far beyond the finding of contraband. While employed at the camp, many guards lost their entire families and homes in Allied bombing raids as they guarded the men who killed their families. Yet the guards had to continue their duties.

On one occasion the Germans, in an attempt to destroy a tunnel, blew the roof off a barrack and destroyed a German building by using too much dynamite. The PoWs thought it hilarious. It always amazed the Germans that Kriegies could work, endure, play and laugh all at the same time.

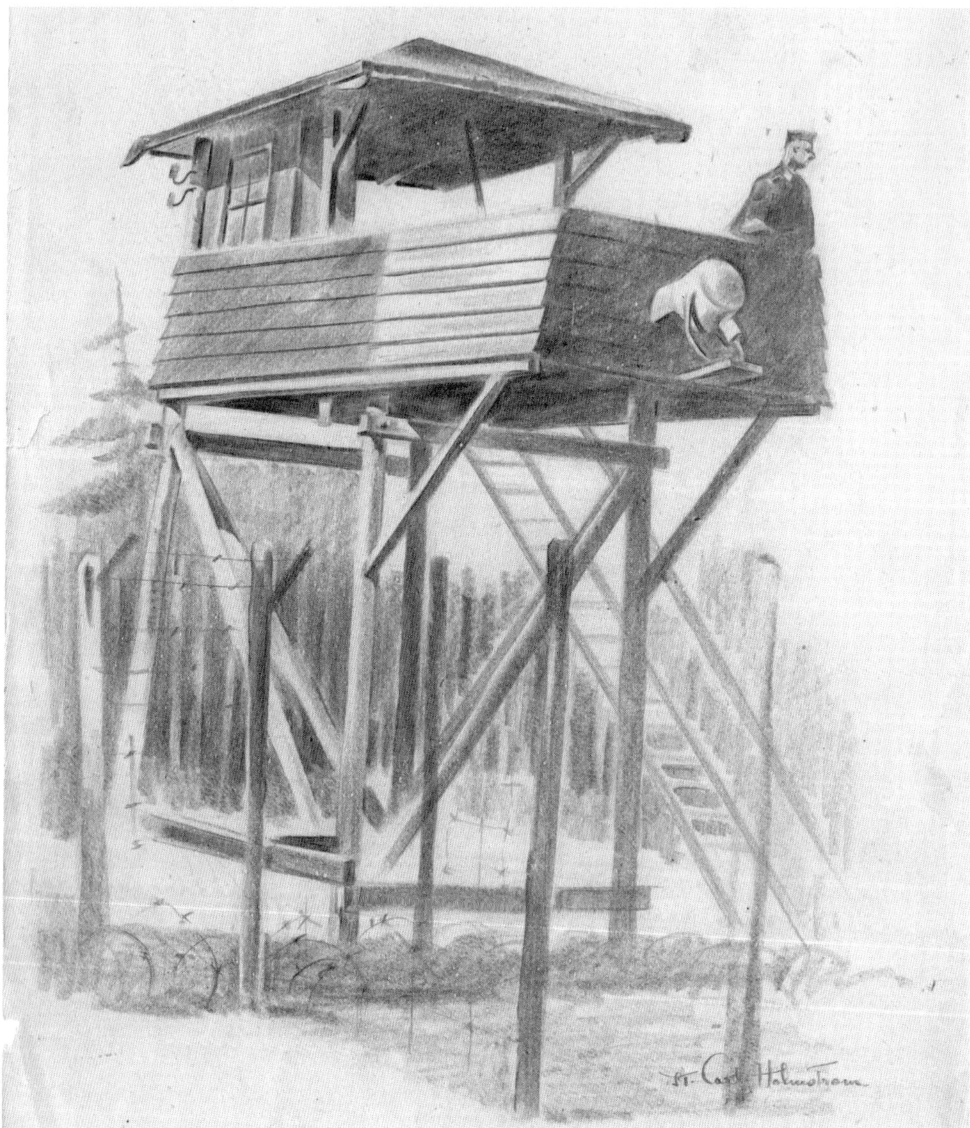

Strollers Patrol Barbed Wire

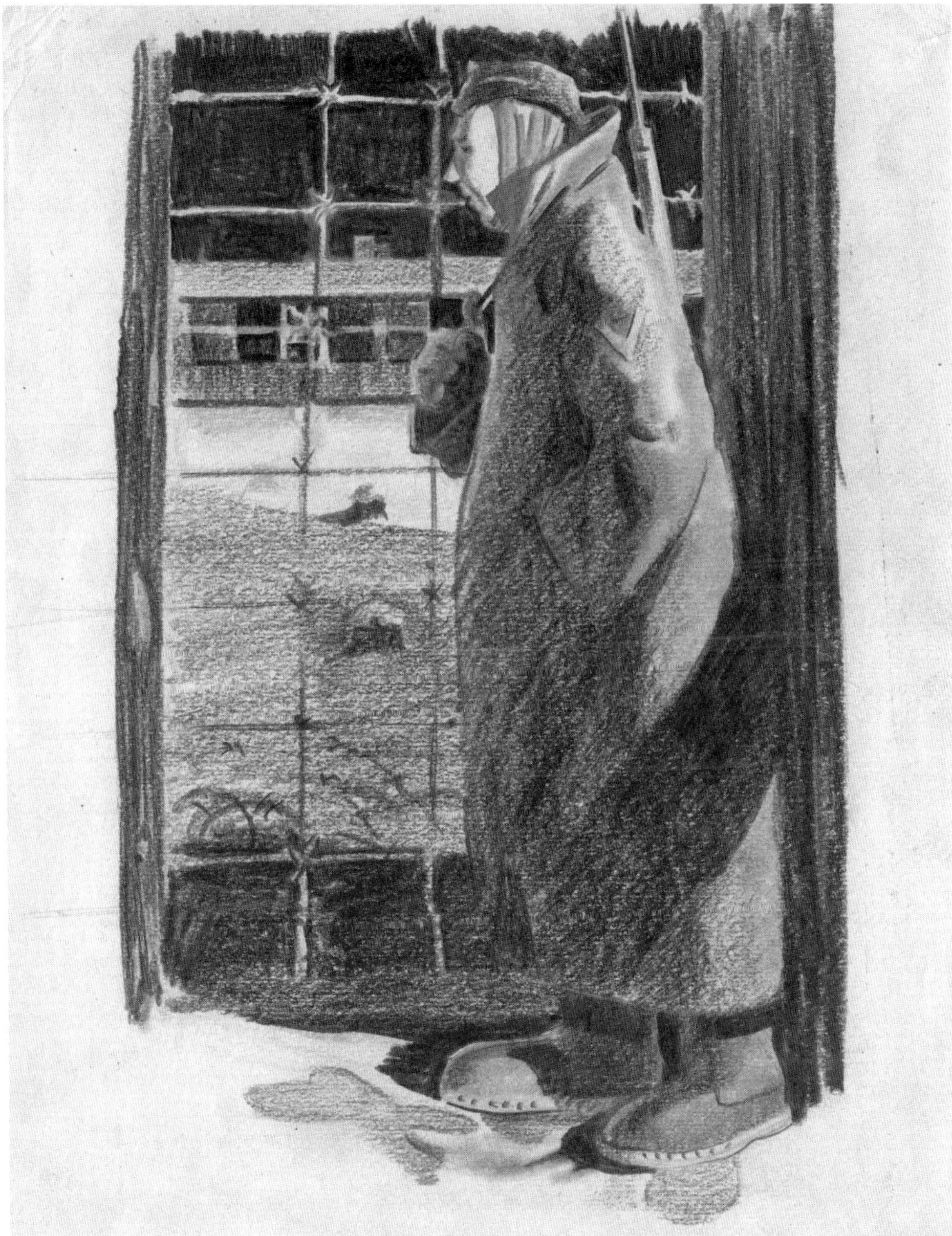

Strollers, resembling monsters in their winter boots, patrolled the barbed wire. The boots, consisting of heavy felt nailed to wooden shoes, were worn as overshoes and left distinctive prints in the snow.

The camp personnel were composed of non-flying Luftwaffe officers and enlisted personnel who were generally not qualified for front-line duty. Many were old and uneducated. Most spoke no English. They were constantly rotated out of camp. As with all the other German personnel in the camp, the guards understood that if they failed in their duties, they could expect to be sent to the Eastern Front, a fate considered synonymous with death.

Ferrets and Weasels

The men who worked inside the compounds at Stalag Luft III for the Germans were called 'ferrets' or 'weasels'. They could be easily spotted because of their dark blue utility coveralls designed to withstand their work under, around and inside the barracks and other buildings.

One officer and six NCO ferrets were assigned to each compound and they paraded among the prisoners from dawn to dusk, probing anything and everywhere. They could enter rooms unannounced, listen at windows, hide under floors or inside the roofs and search or arrest anyone they thought looked suspicious.

Equipped with metal probes, they searched for the bright yellow sand indicating that a tunnel was in progress, or an English-speaking ferret would lie concealed under a hut listening for careless talk. There is evidence to suggest that when a tunnel was detected by the guards or ferrets, it was allowed to continue without intervention until it appeared to be near completion. Then, the ferrets would pounce, driving heavy trucks around the compound to collapse the tunnels.

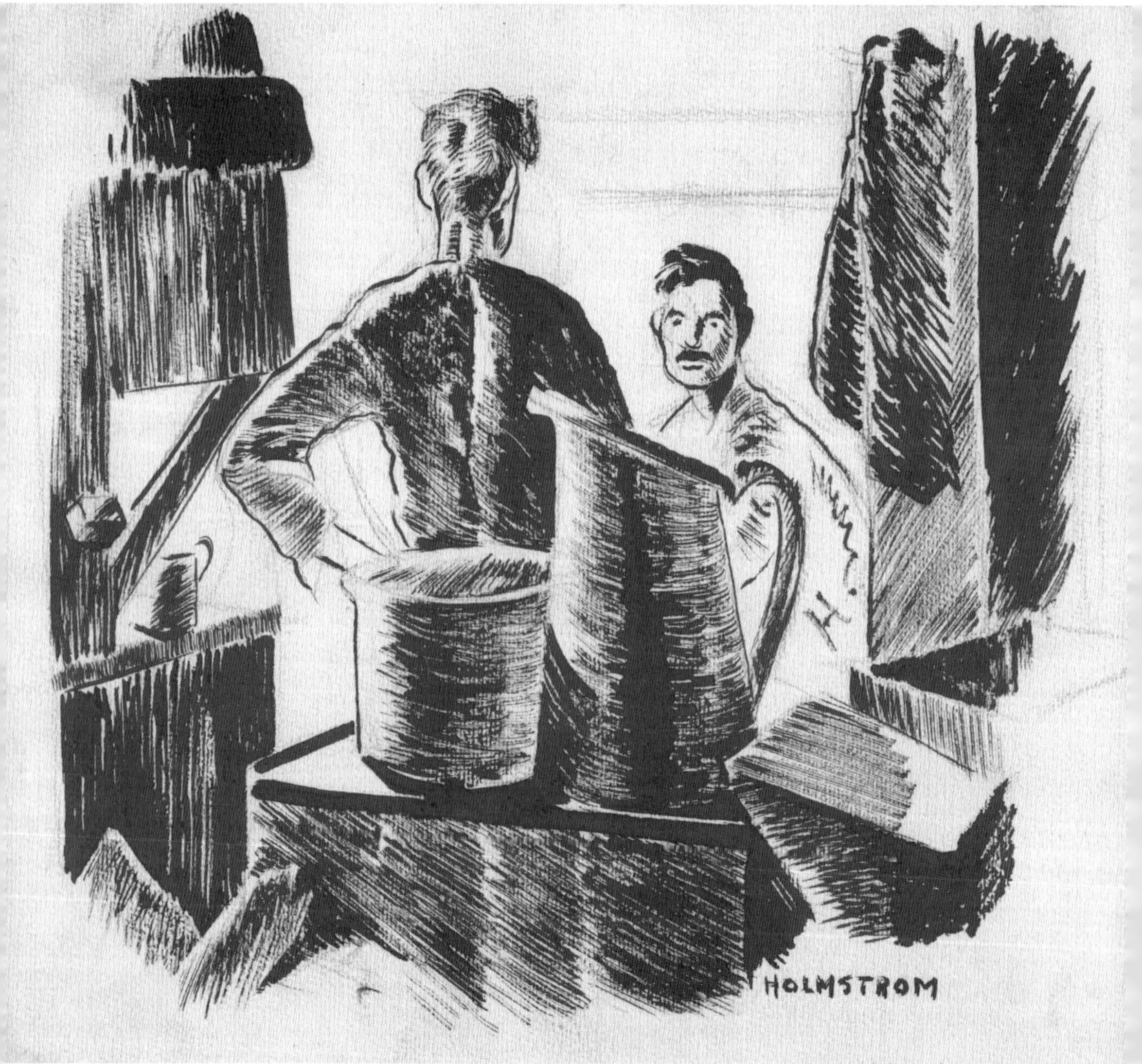

Guard Dogs: *Wachhunds*

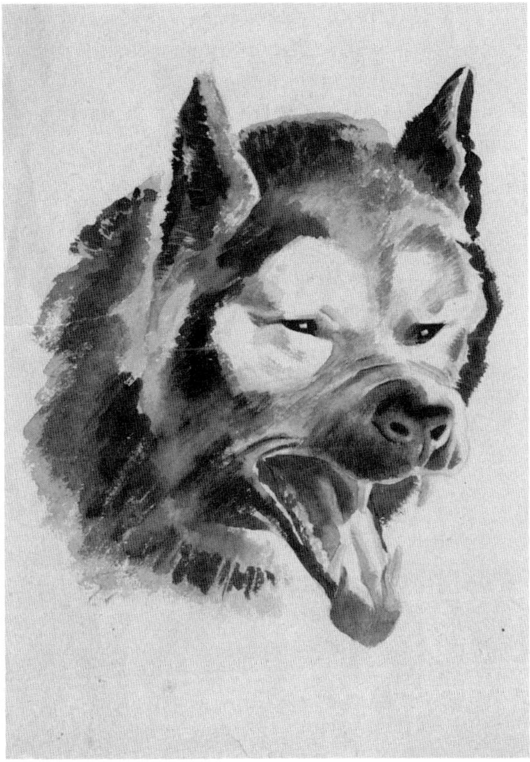

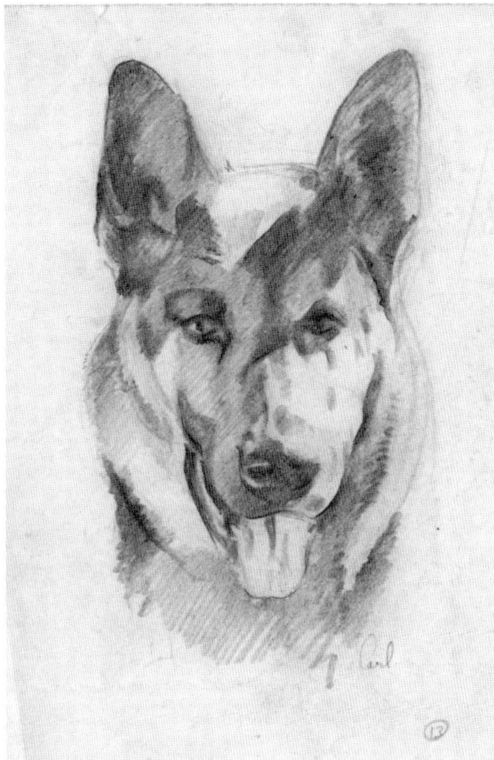

The guard dogs at Stalag Luft III were not typically friendly dogs. They were taken on the Evacuation March in 1945 and upon a few occasions became friendly with Kriegies who gave them food.

German Shepherds and Doberman Pinschers were sentry dogs, known to the prisoners as *Wachhunds.* They were let loose each night to prowl around the camp, discouraging escape attempts. The barracks were locked up at the same time each night and their wooden shutters were closed. The dogs' presence made it very dangerous to be out at night after lock-up. Even the commandant of the camp feared the dogs.

The German name *Hundeführer* means guard with dogs or dog-handler. The German military dogs were used for security duty in wooded areas, transport of the wounded and messenger service. The English and Americans only began their war dog programmes after seeing the amazing performance of the German dogs.

The Infamous 52-Mile Forced Evacuation March

Map of the 52-Mile Evacuation March

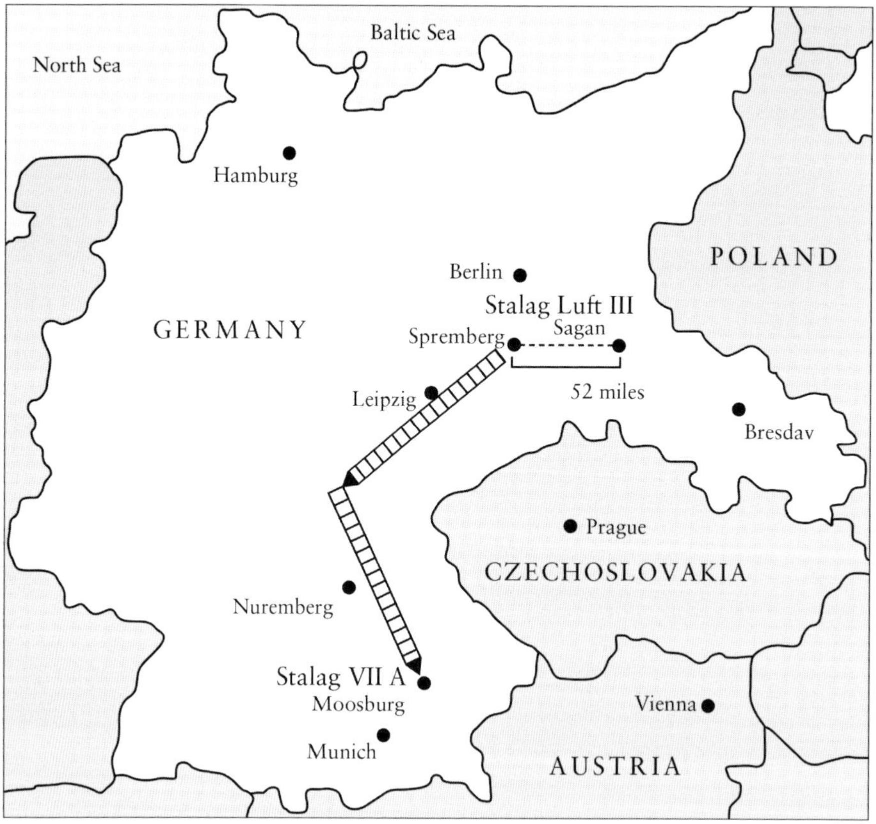

Evacuation marches across Germany were a series of forced marches during the final stages of the Second World War. More than 80,000 PoWs were forced to march westward across Poland, Czechoslovakia and Germany near the end of the war. The marches have been called various names: 'Death March', 'The Long March', and 'The Shoeleather Express', but most survivors just said, 'The March'.

As the Soviet army was advancing westward, the Nazis made the decision to evacuate the PoW camps to prevent the liberation of the prisoners by the Russians. Stalag Luft III was no exception. PoWs from that camp marched to Spremberg, Germany, to board 40&8 (forty men or eight horses) box cars there. From there, the British PoWs went north and the American PoWs went south, most going to Stalag VII-A in Moosburg, Germany. West Compound and infirm PoWs from Stalag Luft III went to Stalag XIII-D in Nuremberg before that group marched again to join fellow Stalag Luft III PoWs for liberation in Moosburg.

Packed and Ready to Go

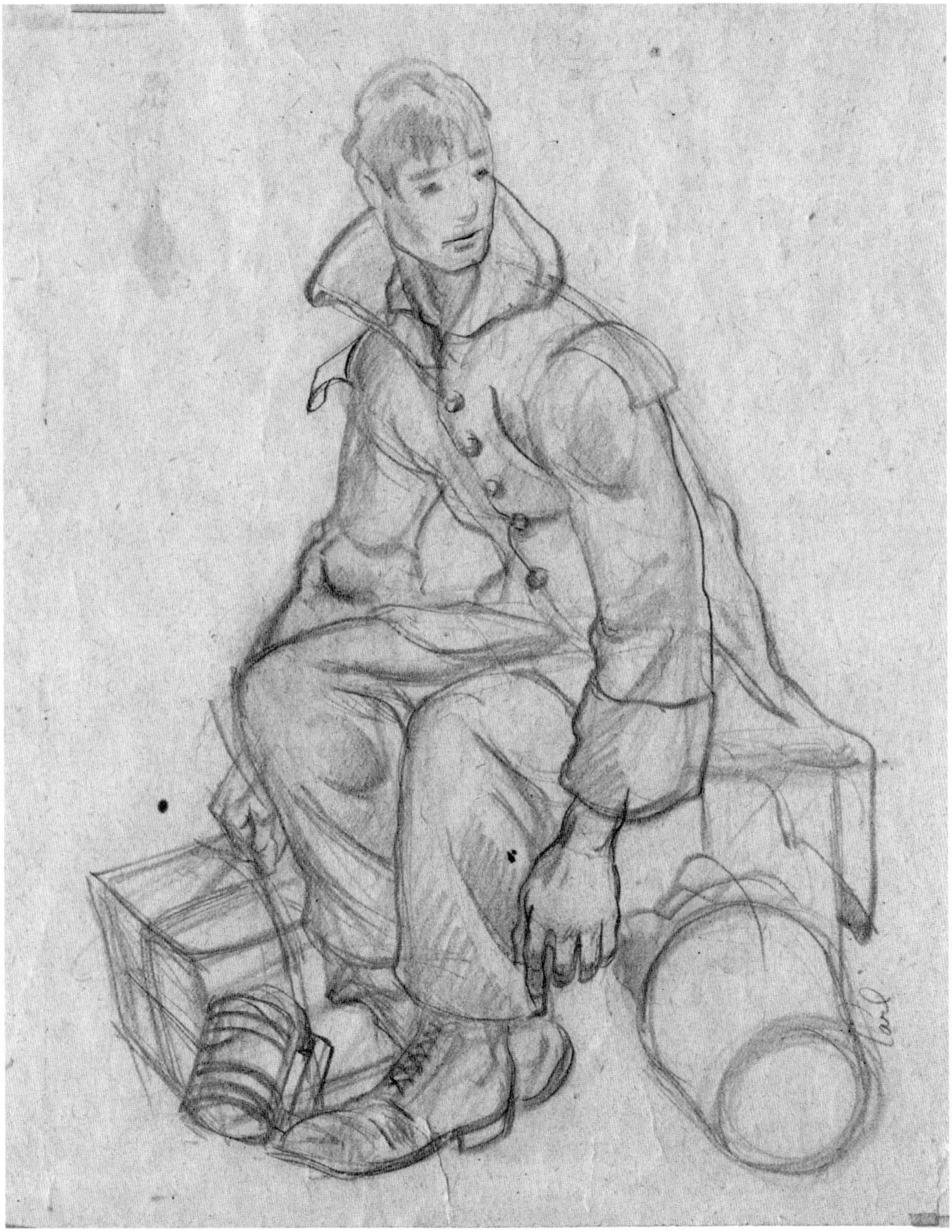

Weeks before the rumoured evacuation, Kriegies sewed packs and built sleds. They walked the circuit, a walking path in the camp, as commanded by their senior block commanders to ready themselves for a potential march. On 27 January 1945, the Kriegies were alerted at 9.00 pm and given a thirty-minute allowance to pack their food and belongings, only what they could carry, and establish a formation at the gate. Most belongings had to be left behind.

The Forced Evacuation March Begins

In the barracks, bedrolls had to be repacked with available food and limited belongings. The men cleaned out cupboards and 'bashed' what food could not be carried. They were careful to destroy anything that might be of value to the Germans. Barracks 104, from which the Great Escape tunnel had been dug, was set on fire by the British, sending smoke and flames into the frigid night. After two more hours waiting in the cold, the forced evacuation of Stalag Luft III began when Carl, along with all of South Compound, left at 11.00 pm. The march was conducted contrary to Article Seven of the Geneva Convention, which specified that prisoners of war could not be marched more than 12.5 miles per day. South Compound men covered 34.5 miles in twenty-seven hours with one six-hour stop in barns in Gros Selten before arriving in Muskau, where they spent two days in factories before continuing on the next day and night. On the final day, they marched from Graustein to Spremberg to board the cattle cars for the last leg of their torturous journey.

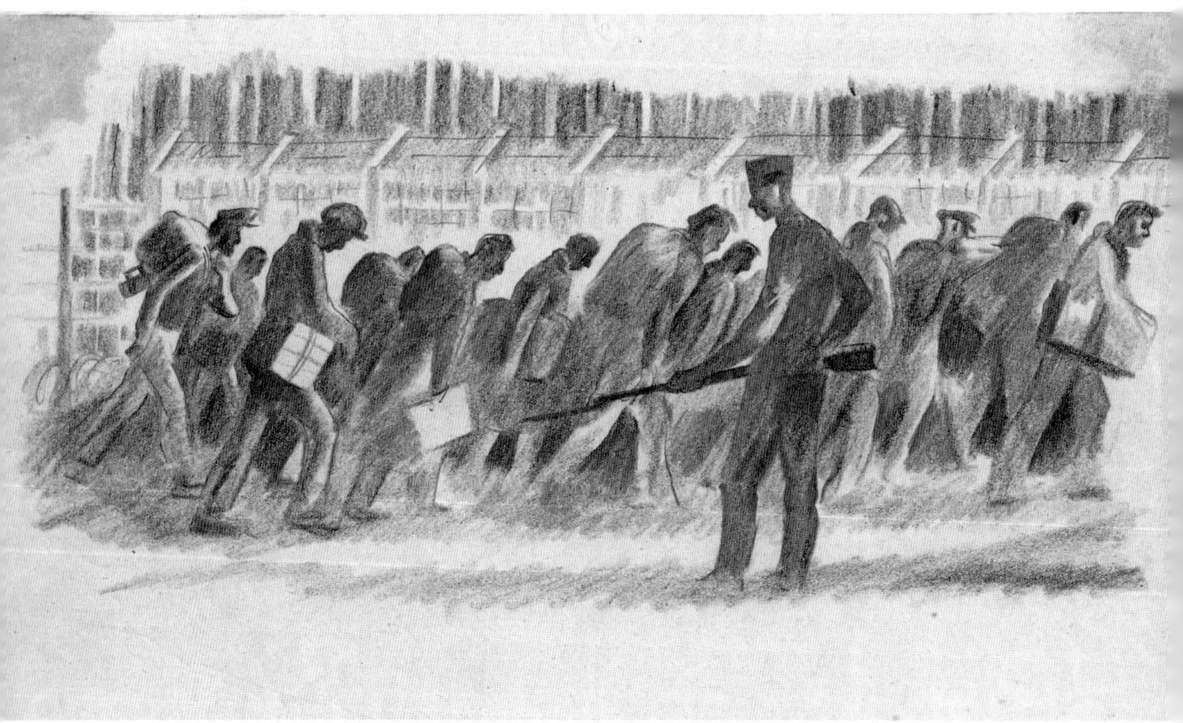

Blizzard Conditions

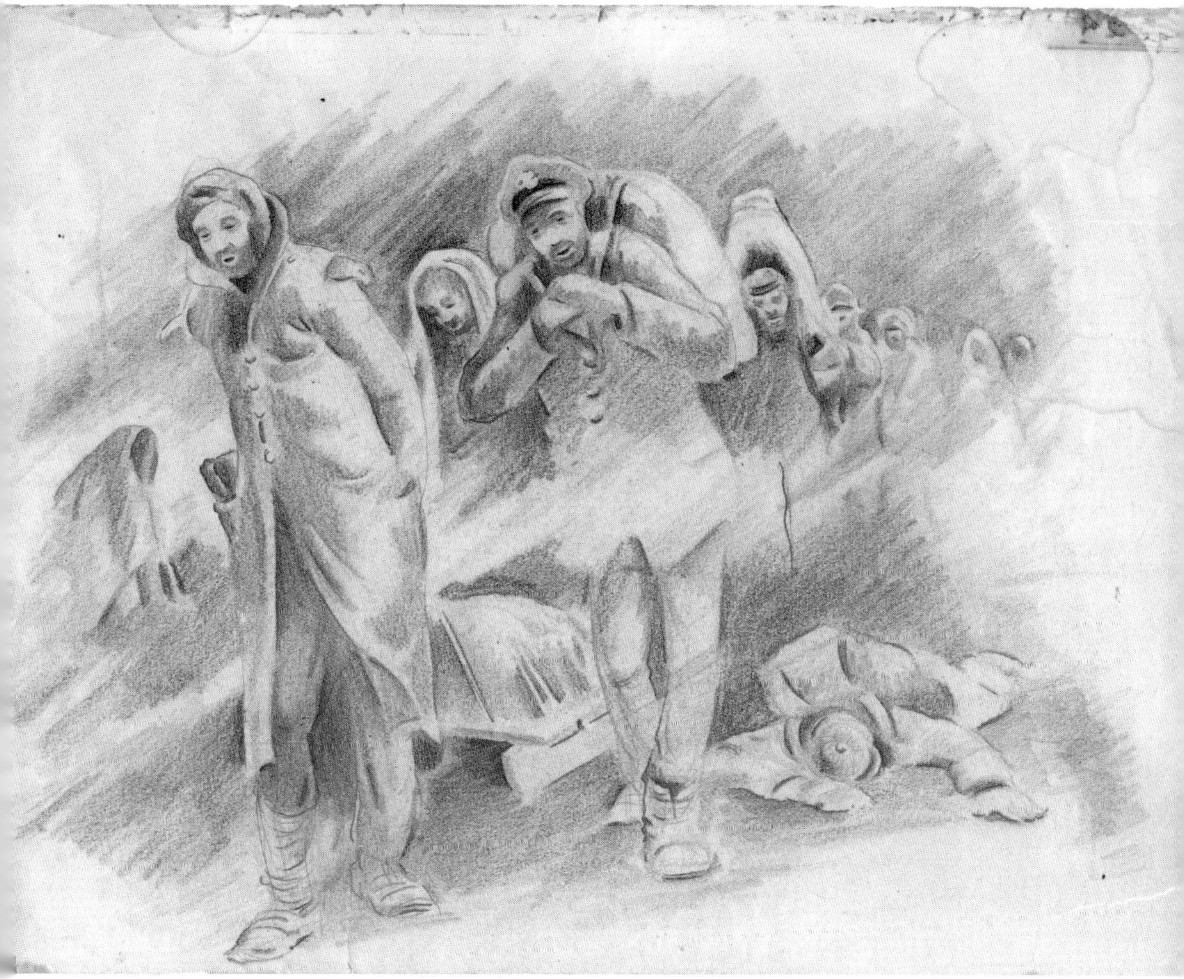

Days before leaving the camp, Russian guns were finally heard in the distance ending years of imprisonment for many of the PoWs. Many of the British had been confined for over five years. Some 10,000 prisoners were evacuated from Stalag Luft III as the Russians moved in from the east. 6in of snow had accumulated, enabling the men to pull the sleds they had made.

The temperature at the time of departure was determined to be 16°F with wind creating blizzard conditions and fierce wind chill factors. Ice formed on eyelids and moustaches. Exposed flesh was covered as best as the men could manage as they pushed against the unforgiving elements. Blisters, stiffened backs and legs and the pain of frostbitten feet and hands plagued many men.

Overcoat and Newspapers for Warmth

Layers of clothes were worn by the Kriegies and newspaper-reinforced German-issued wool blankets were wrapped around their hunched shoulders. Their overcoat pockets were filled with margarine to grease their shoes and lips. The frozen margarine was bitten off alternatively with hunks of German black bread when available. Sugar cubes and raisins from Red Cross parcels also filled pockets. Canned goods were difficult to carry, but the men brought along their cans of SPAM.

As cold and exhaustion set in, men pulled out everything they could not carry. Many belongings taken on the march had to be discarded along the way due to excessive weight. Much of the artwork from camp never came home. Extra shoes, clothing and souvenirs that had been saved for so long were dumped on the side of the road. Even cans of margarine, the only protective balm they had, were discarded.

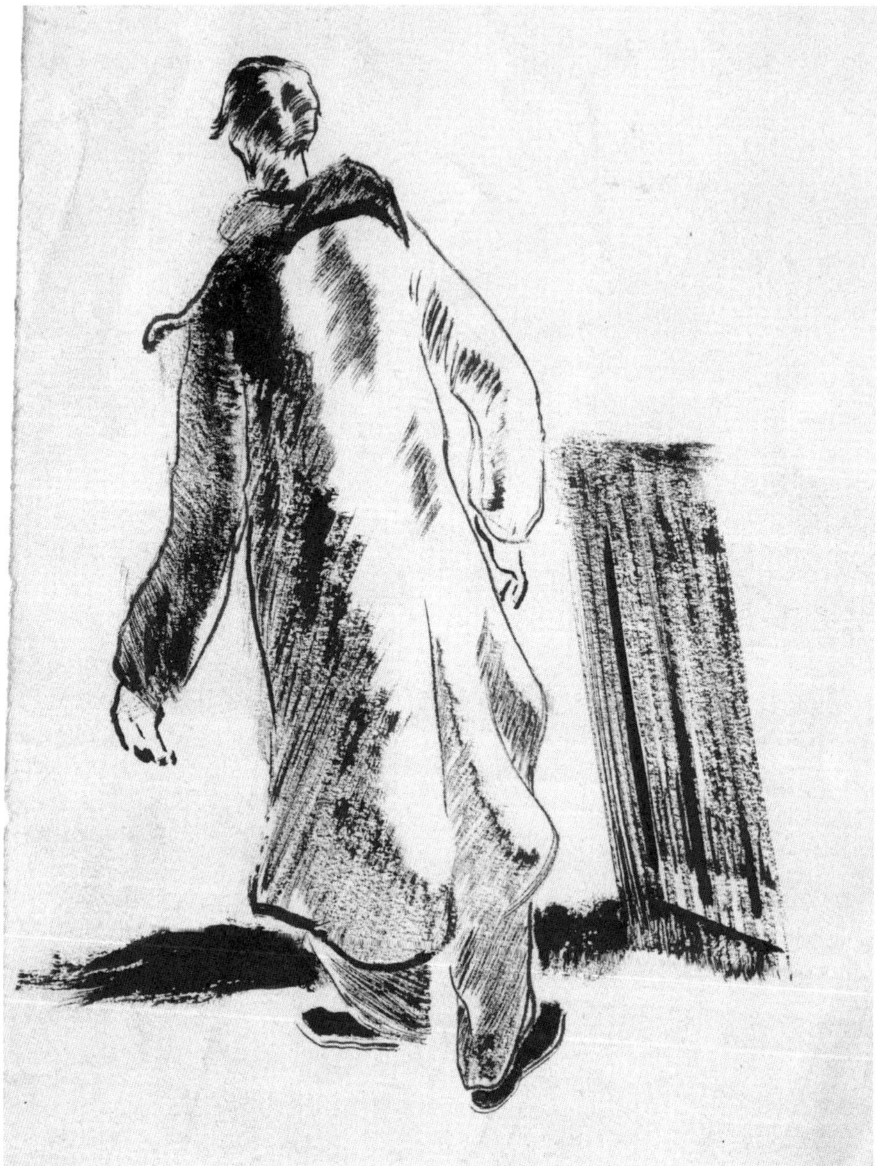

Varied Views of the Evacuation March

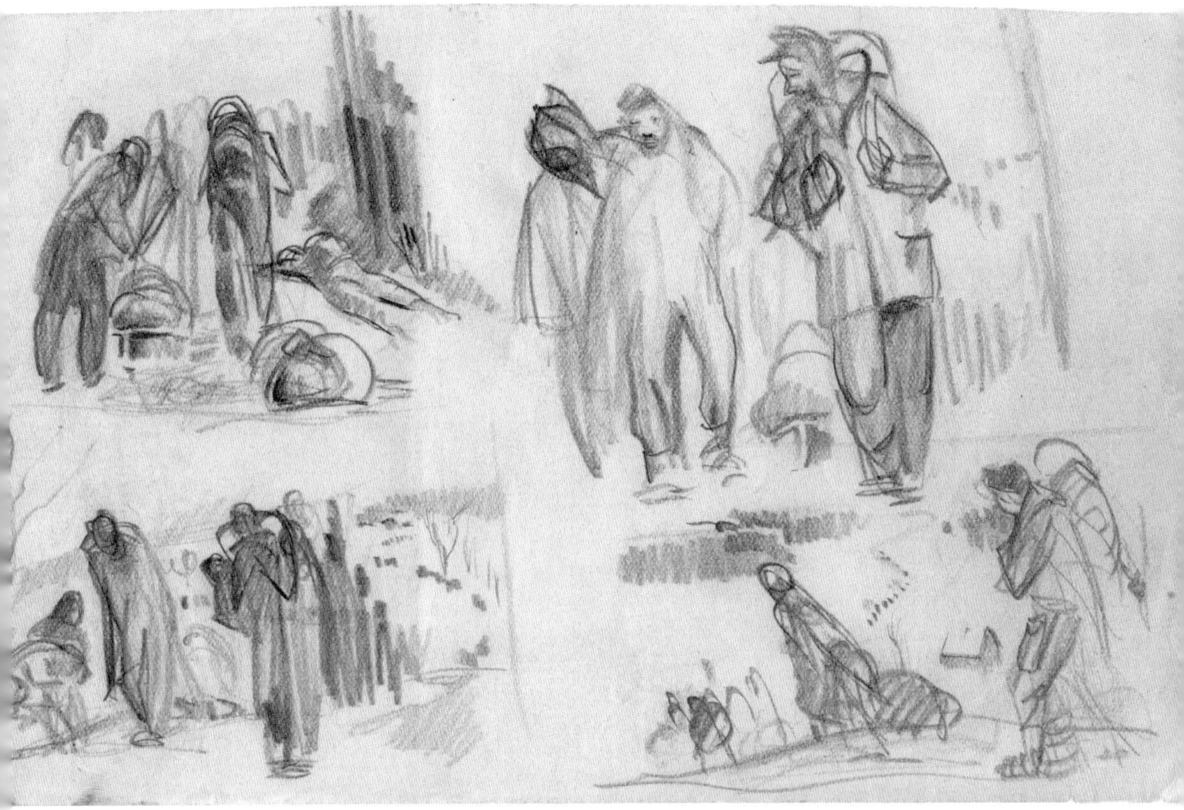

The harsh weather took its toll on the already-weakened PoWs. Men dropped at the side of the road from fatigue and cold. Every man that was able helped the man next to him. Men who fell were encouraged to get up and come along or get in the wagon that followed the column. Men ready to give up were supported by their fellow prisoners as falling to the ground in the snow and not getting up again would mean freezing to death.

It was the general impression that anyone who lagged behind would be shot, but the guards themselves were older men who were in worse condition than the prisoners. PoWs often carried the rifles of the older unfit guards who marched in deeper snow at the side of the roads.

Into the Frozen Night

During the 'Forced March', the Kriegies marched out of Stalag Luft III at measured intervals, leaving every few hours, with the British leaving early in the morning of the next day. Their long column, usually five men abreast, twisted over hills and along the banks of frozen streams. They passed freshly-dug one-man foxholes, roadblocks and tank emplacements.

Every hour or two, the long column stopped for about ten minutes. It was difficult to sit on the ground without becoming frozen to the spot. When stopping for rest, frozen prisoners burned cherished letters, artwork and journals to stay warm and to lighten their loads. Backpacks became too heavy to carry, and every ounce of pressure on pack straps dug into tired, aching shoulders.

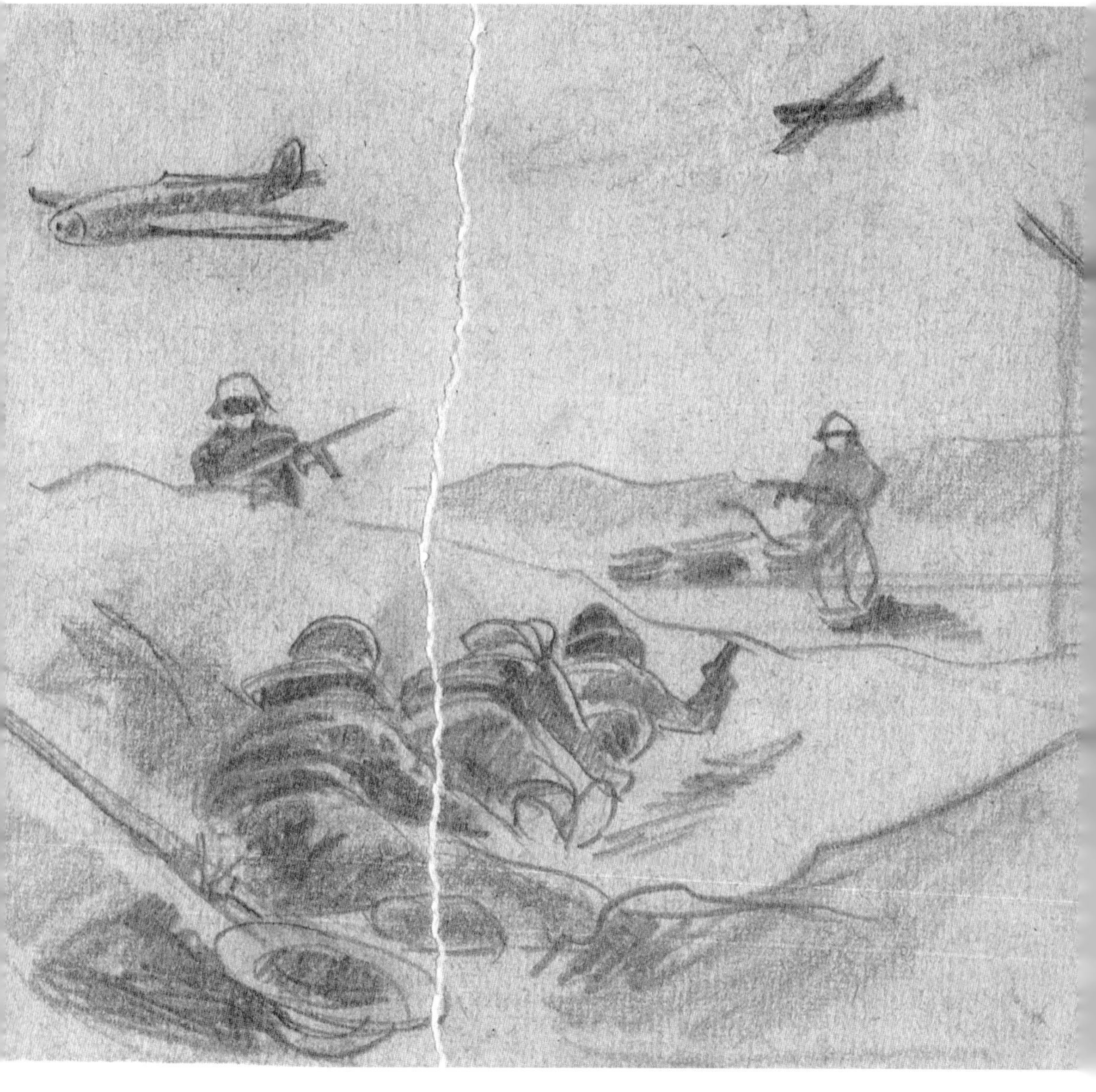

Caravans of Fleeing Refugees

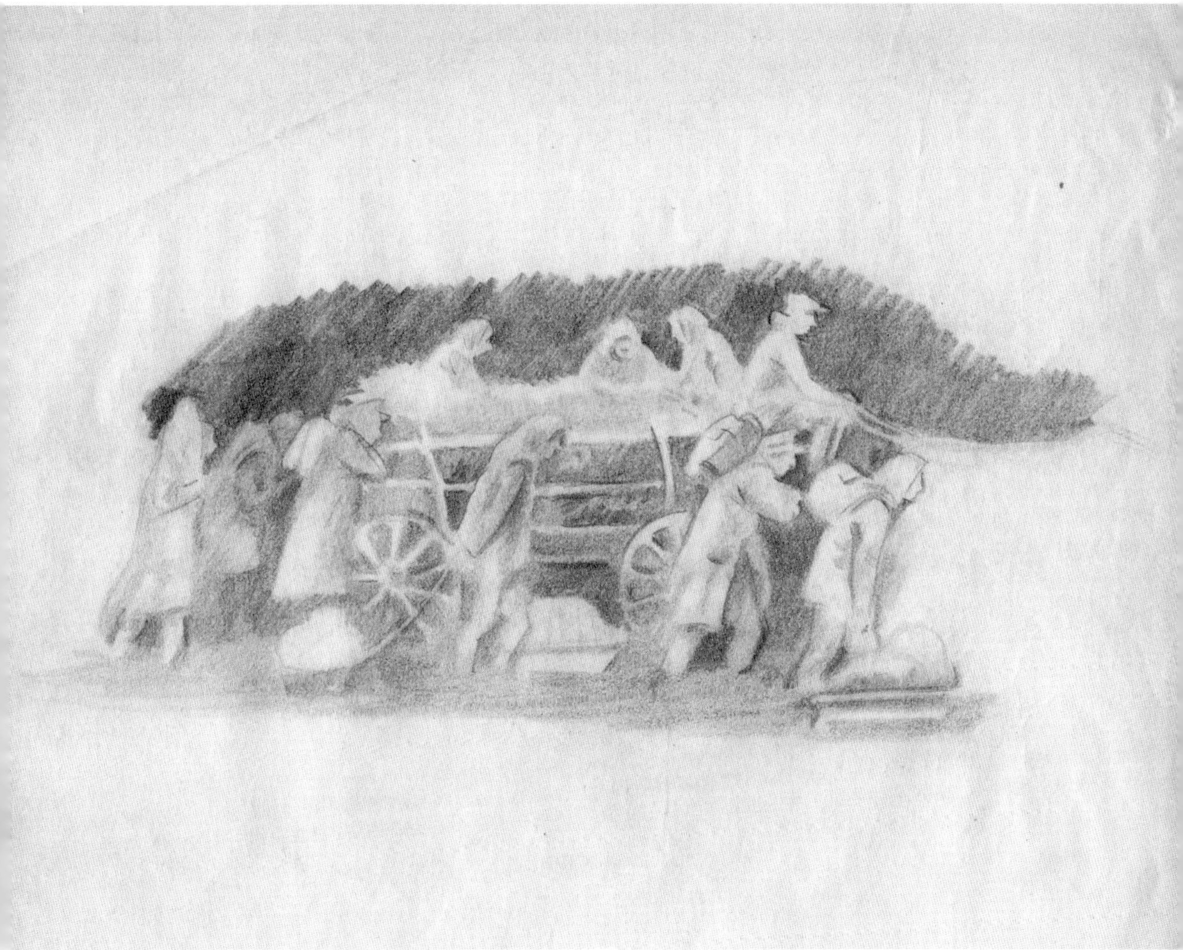

Long remembered by Stalag Luft III Kriegies were the caravans of refugees fleeing along the road with them. Fear of the Russians emptied a mass of humanity onto the same roads. These desperate and panicked refugees fled from their homes hoping to escape retribution from the invading Russians.

They were mostly old men, women and children, drawn in creaky carts by emaciated horses. One Kriegie stopped to give his gloves to a crying little German girl. Others gave chocolate bars to the hungry children on the road, and they often pushed wagons with frozen wheels out of ditches. Both groups had to move aside when German Wehrmacht troops, dressed in white, came through on their way to the east to meet the Russians.

The Germans had made no plans for provisions on the long march so the prisoners mostly ate the food in their bedrolls and backpacks. They bartered for additional food and water along the way with many friendly Germans. The prisoners from South Compound were pressed to keep moving with only brief rest stops as they tamped down the snow and set a path for the compounds that followed. Had they not moved rapidly, the advancing Russian troops might have overtaken them, something feared by the Germans.

Heading Towards Spremberg and Box Cars

After days of a gruelling march, sleeping in barns and factories along the way, the long ribbon of Kriegies arrived in Spremberg. The men boarded the 40&8 box cars, fifty to sixty men to a car, without the benefit of the cars having been cleaned out after livestock had been removed. The men of all compounds except West endured a horrendous three-day, one-night ride before arriving at Stalag VIIA in Moosburg, Germany. Men from West Compound went from Spremberg directly to Stalag XIIID in Nuremberg.

Food distribution was sporadic and many cars got nothing. There were no windows, and the only ventilation or light came through cracks in the cars' wooden sides or from a small vent at the top corner of each car. Not all men could sit or stand at the same time so the men changed position every hour. With only one waste bucket per box car, the filth and stench were unbearable. After 72 hours in the cars, with only a few short stops, South Compound, the first to arrive, pulled into Moosburg in the late afternoon of 2 February 1945. They were not allowed out of the box cars until the next morning, even though they pounded on the doors.

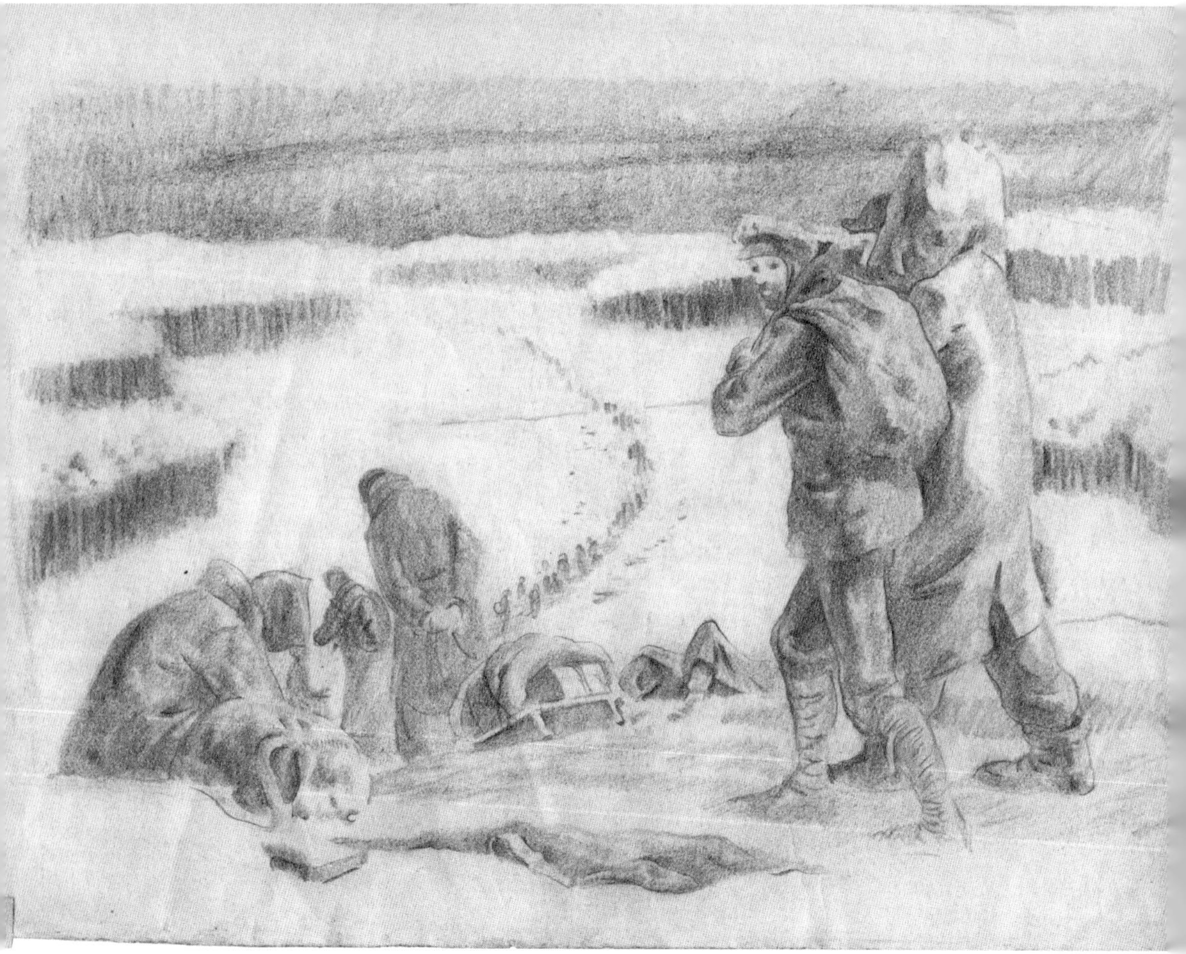

Moosburg and Liberation

Carl and Fellow PoWs at Nuremberg

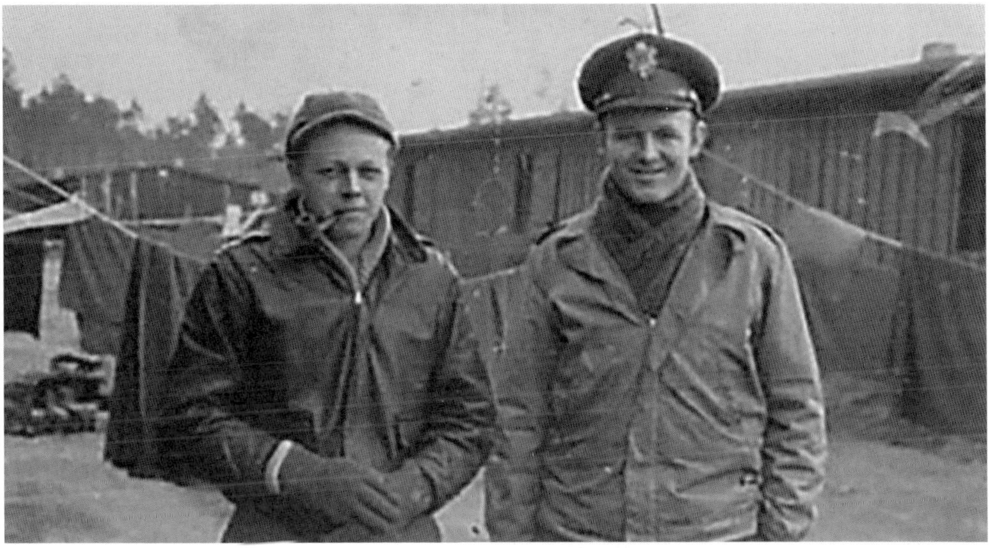

Ordinarily, Carl would not have gone to Nuremberg, but when the men of South Compound reached the factory town of Muskau earlier in the march, Carl had fallen ill. West Compound arrived at the factory after South Compound had departed. West Compound later took Carl and the remaining ill men from South Compound with them on the 40&8 box cars in Spremberg, arriving at Nuremberg, Stalag XIII-D, instead of Moosburg, Stalag VII-A. Stalag XIII-D was too close to the centre of town that was bombed day and night, and the barracks shook. After three months, the entire camp was evacuated on 4 April and for a second time, the men were on a march. It would take about two weeks to join the other PoWs from Stalag Luft III in Moosburg, Germany, where they would all be liberated together three weeks later. The weather for this springtime march was much better, but they were strafed one time along the way by friendly fire.

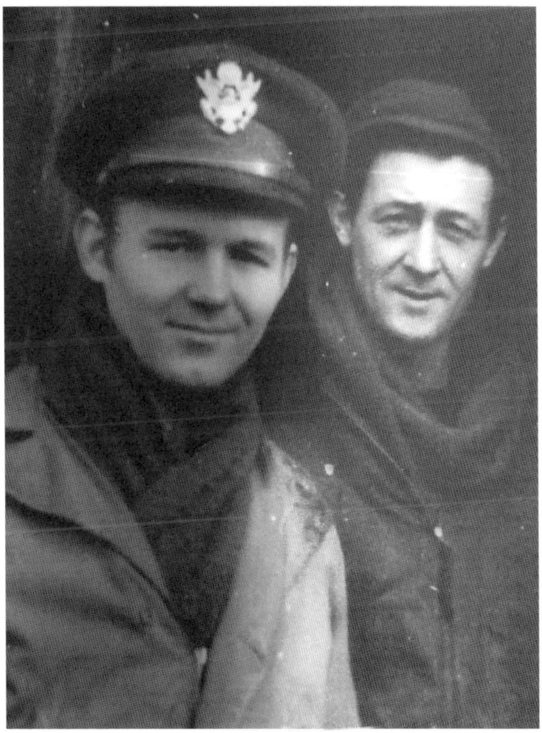

Rats, Mice, Bedbugs, Lice and Fleas at Stalag VII-A

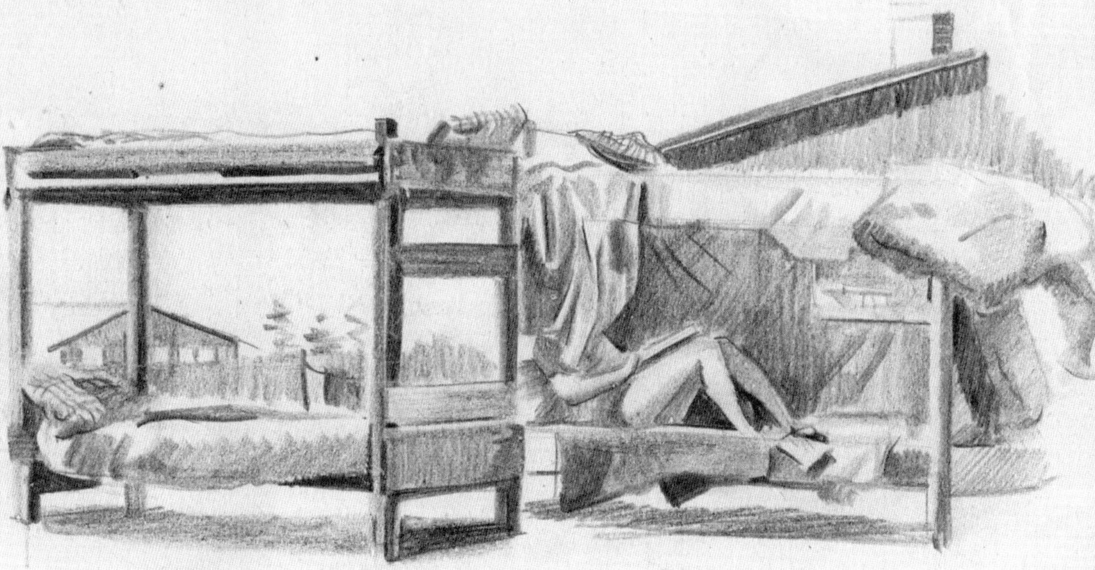

Stalag VII-A, 70 miles north-west of Munich, was an overcrowded camp with deplorable conditions with more prisoners arriving every day.

In spite of the Germans' best efforts, latrines overflowed and garbage accumulated faster than it could be carried away. Rats, mice, bedbugs, lice and fleas were everywhere and no adequate disinfectants or anti-vermin powders were distributed. The stench in the camp was overpowering.

Hungry men, who had been steadfast in battle and through the continual deprivation of the prison camps, became crestfallen and discouraged. Parts of the camp became unsafe to enter and a desperate 'every man for himself' air was apparent.

Tent Camps at Stalag VII-A

The men from Stalag Luft III's South Compound chose to live out their days of confinement in huge white tents in the corner of the camp. The five large tents set up by the Germans proved to be insufficient and prisoners slept outside. Crude lean-tos were hastily constructed. Kriegies lived in the primitive, improvised shelters for weeks to avoid overcrowding and the infestation of biting bugs in the barracks. One water tap and pump were used per 400 men.

Inadequate nutrition sapped the men's strength. Allied bombing of the roads and railways caused delays in the delivery of Red Cross food parcels, bringing many to the brink of starvation while air-raids continued, and men sat outside and watched. At no time, day or night, was the air free of increasing numbers of Allied planes.

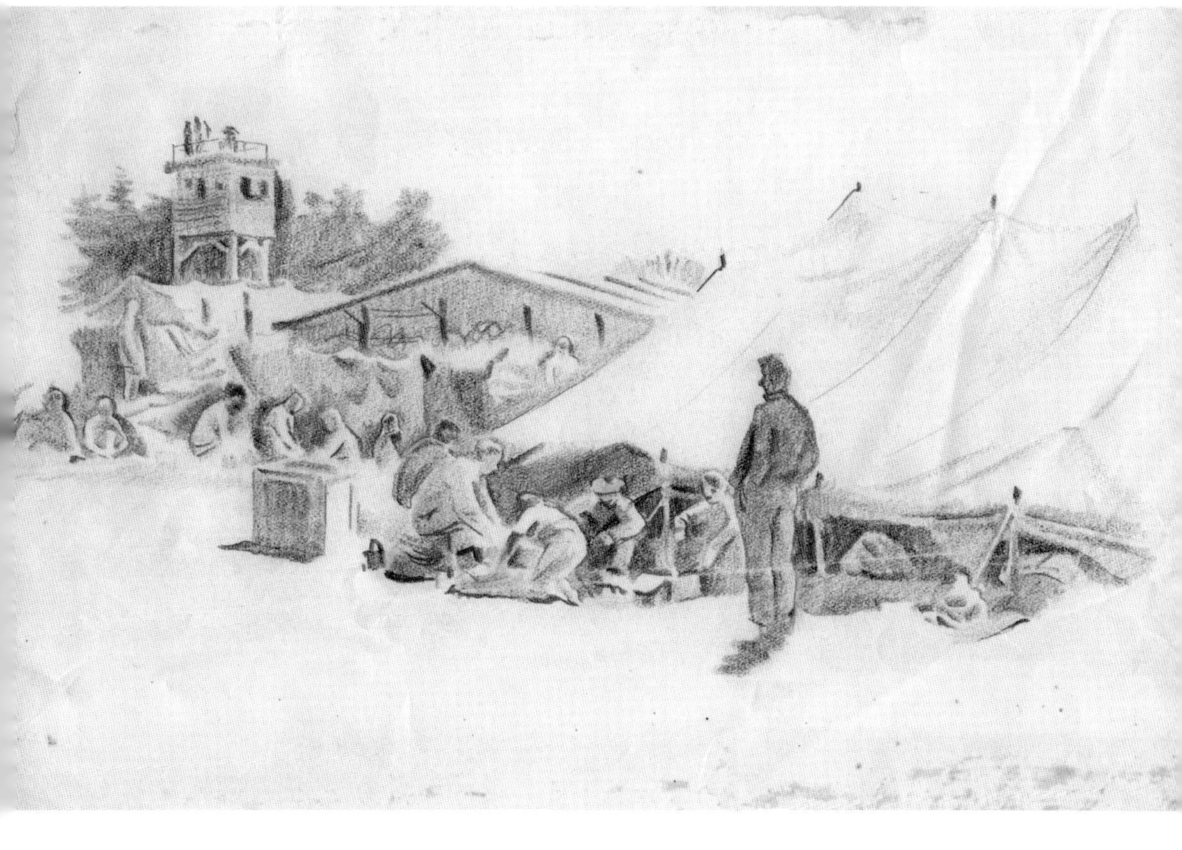

Overcrowding at Stalag VII-A

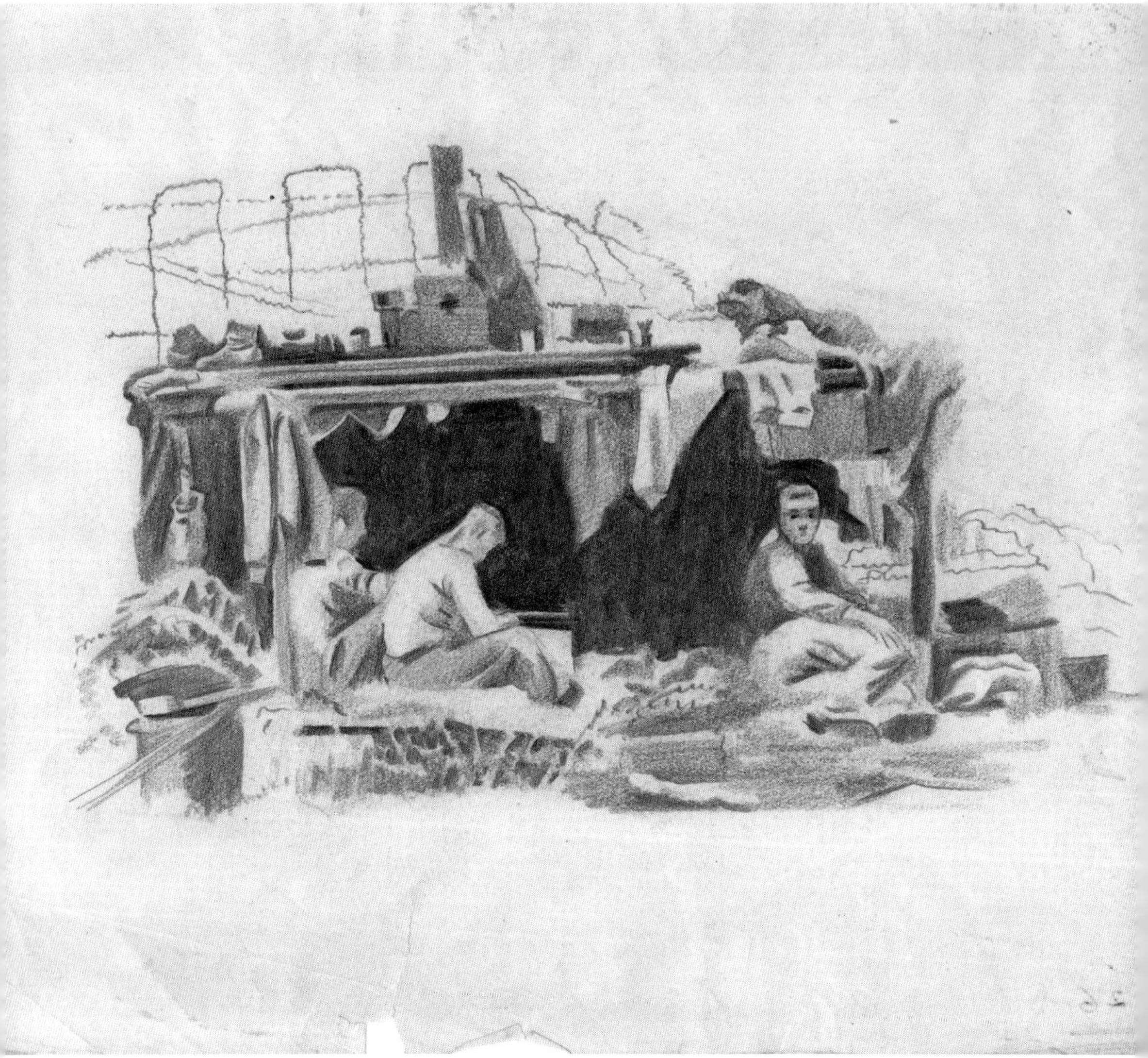

Initially, the Wehrmacht camp held 3,000 prisoners, but the number of men of every nationality soon increased that number to more than 120,000. Crowded conditions, lack of fuel for the stoves, lack of food and an abysmal lack of sanitation facilities increased the prisoners' susceptibility to disease, especially dysentery and pneumonia. Their bodies were livid with the bites of the fleas, ticks and bedbugs. The danger of epidemics arose, but prisoners could do little to change their living conditions.

Many men thought of escaping during these last days of the war. They frequently heard rumours that Hitler intended to use them as hostages for better truce terms, or to kill them outright. In mid-April 1945, Senior American Officers (SAOs) were ordered to prepare the men for another march south. Using a clandestine radio, the officers heard a news broadcast from Luxemburg indicating that the Allies had reached an agreement with Germany and no more Allied or German prisoners would be moved from their present locations. The officers informed the Germans, and no prisoners were moved.

Cooking on our 'Kriegie Burners'

Carl is shown here cooking on a 'Kriegie burner'. They were often called either smokeless cookers or cookless smokers. The burners were used primarily at VIIA in Moosburg.

These were made with the KLIM condensed milk tin to which was added a small fan that was turned manually. With this system it was possible to produce maximum heat using the smallest quantity of wood or any in flammable rubbish found in the camp. The amount of smoke they produced was extreme, but they provided a means to cook outside and prepare food quickly.

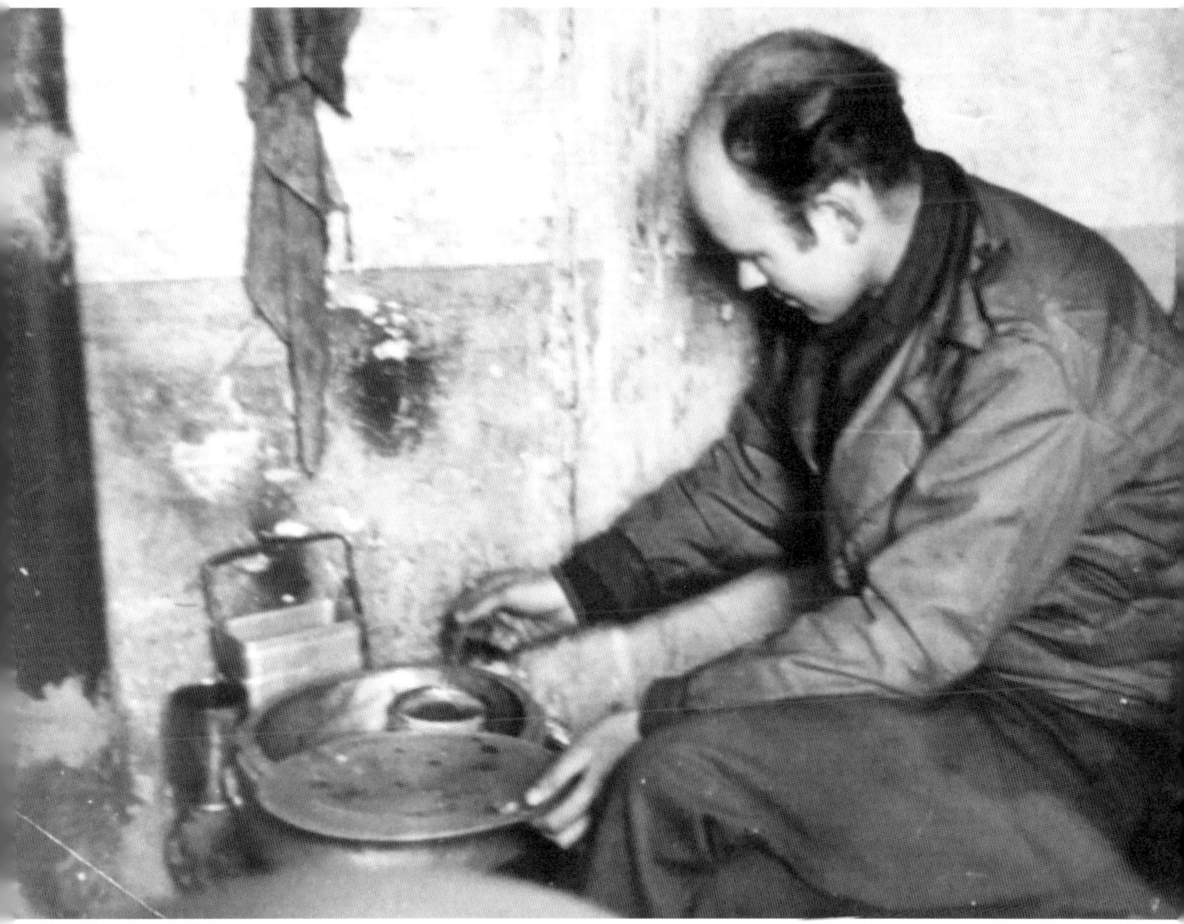

Negotiations for Surrender

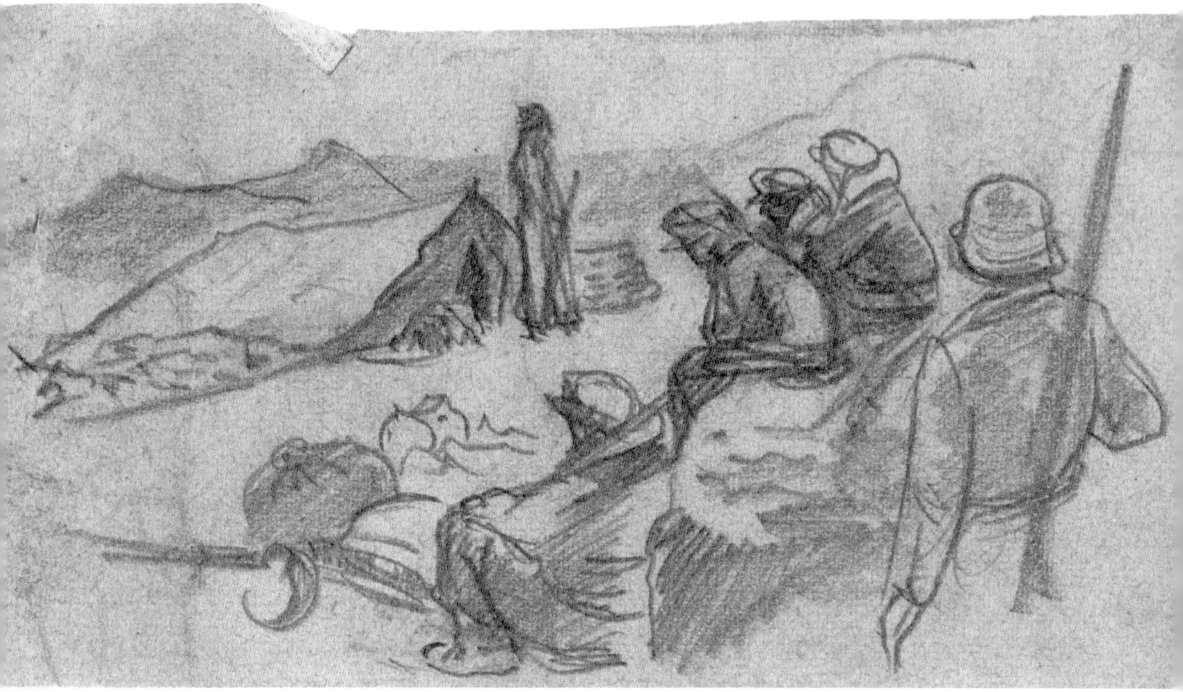

On 28 April 1945, many German guards quietly left the camp in trucks during the night leaving only a skeleton force behind. The remaining acting commandant had been negotiating with General Patton's army that day for a peaceful surrender, but the proposal was rejected outright. A senior PoW officer who had been included in the negotiations returned early in the morning and warned the PoWs to take cover. Hours later, artillery shells flew into the camp as PoWs ran for shelter in the barracks. SS troops in the area demanded loyalty from the remaining guards, killing those who refused.

The PoWs heard the familiar sound of Sherman tanks approaching across a field. The American 14th Armored Infantry Division of the US Third Army engaged the resisting SS troops in a fairly short skirmish. When it was over on 29 April 1945, the American flag flew over the city of Moosburg, and replaced the Nazi flag on the camp flagpole. Jubilant men knew that they were going home.

Liberation!

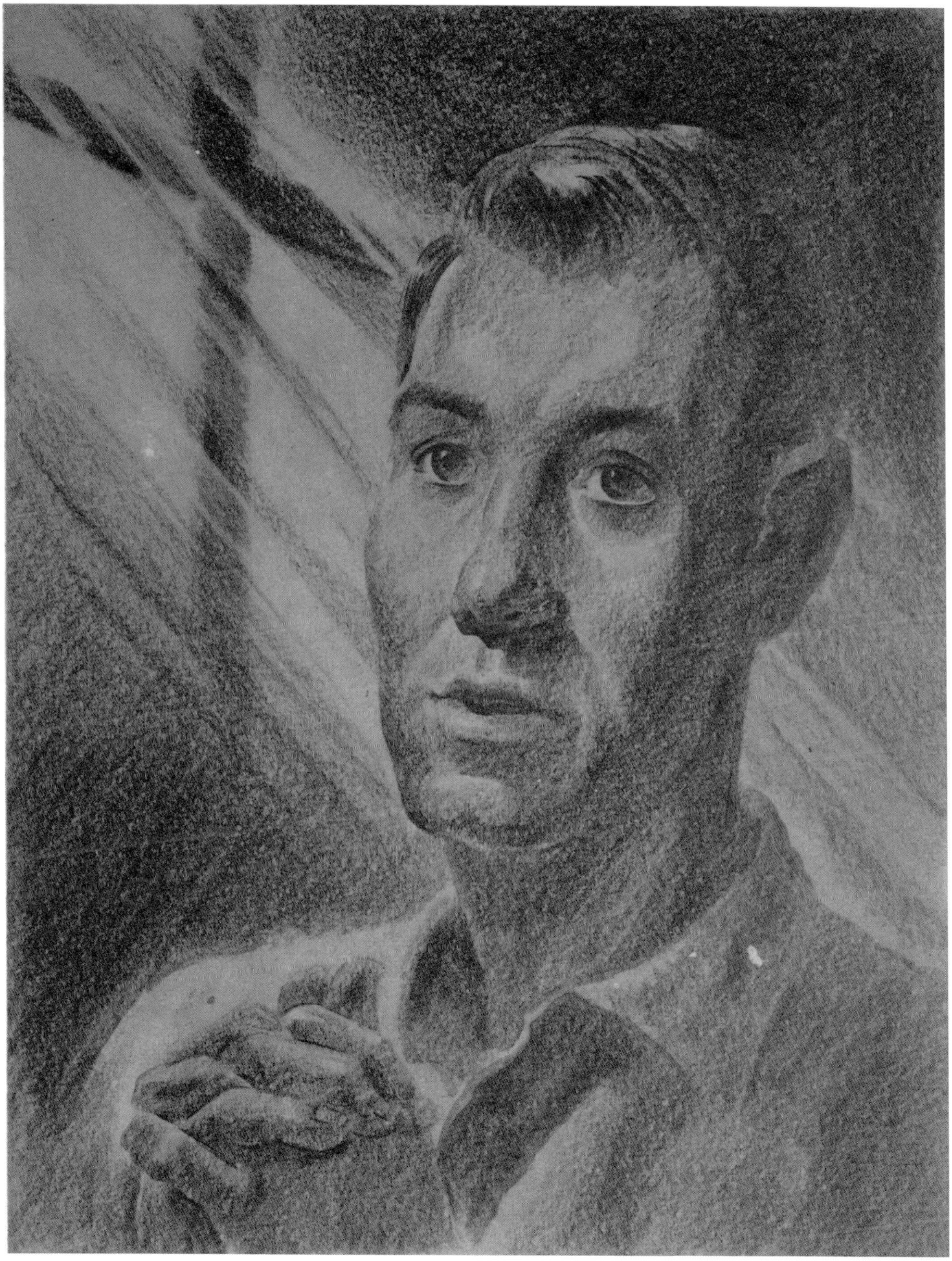

The time for which many PoWs had waited, some for as long as five years, finally came. Others more fortunate had measured their time in months. To all, however, it was the answer to their prayers. Yet it meant the parting of many friends; bonds cemented under conditions that proved a man's worth. It became more than generosity when one shared his only crust of bread with a comrade when he himself was hungry.

The war had ended, and the time to recall the humorous phases of the adventure had arrived.

Life After Liberation

Many of the German towns through which Carl Holmstrom passed on his AWOL way home were, in his words, 'pretty well messed up, and Nuremberg and Frankfurt just weren't there anymore'. The civilians Lieutenant Holmstrom saw along the way met him and his friend with varying attitudes. 'Some were arrogant – some looked beaten. But the guards in the camps were mostly fairly decent. We used to exchange cigarettes and soap with the civilians, which they never had, for food, especially eggs which we'd eat right on the march.'

After reaching Frankfurt, he flew to Paris, arriving on 7 May 1945, the day before V-E Day. 'That was quite a night,' he said, smiling and reminiscing. 'A lot of the fellows had just gotten back from the front, and everyone was feeling pretty good.' Carl and his fellow AWOL friend finally managed to get themselves on an early ship list in Le Havre, France, near Camp Lucky Strike, and arrived in New York after a rough Atlantic crossing. The convoys of liberty ships were escorted even after the war as German U-boats still patrolled the area, some possibly feeling vengeful and others not getting the word that the war was over. High seas and dense fog often made the journey more difficult and dangerous.

As his ship eventually passed the Statue of Liberty and tugboats in the New York harbour spouted streams of water in welcome, bands on the shore played patriotic songs, and mobs of people waved and yelled. Carl was overcome with emotion. He still had his drawings under his arm and would never forget his Kriegie days. His incredible artwork, a constant companion through the cold and the imprisonment and the danger, would be a constant reminder.

In a newspaper interview, Carl said:

> The Germans gave us very little food – one-seventh of a loaf of black bread a day, a couple of potatoes, cabbage, and maybe some margarine. They gave us blood sausage and fish cheese – stuff so vile most of the boys wouldn't eat it. So the Red Cross parcels came in fine – though near the end we didn't get any. The Russian prisoners had a tough time, mostly because they didn't have any Red Cross to help them. We threw food and cigarettes over the wire to them and did it make the Germans mad!

After the war, Carl had an urgent need to publish a book about his experiences and many of his PoW friends encouraged him to create a book about their experiences using his drawings. He tried to get a book of his pictures published post-war, but every publisher he visited in New York turned him down, even though Walter Winchell compared him to the famous Second World War artist Bill Mauldin and the Smithsonian Institute wanted his drawings. 'At that time, people were tired of war tales, and he was not a salesman,' Mrs Holmstrom said. 'He didn't want to split up the work. He thought it should go as a collection.'

On the advice of New York publishers, he returned to his wife's native Meriden, Connecticut, and took time off as a freelance artist to work on publishing a book of his drawings made while a prisoner of war for more than two years. He and his wife spent a year compiling his book. It contained more than fifty drawings with short texts explaining their background. At the time of its printing, he had more than 500 copies already ordered by fellow PoWs, their families and interested readers. Finally, they had 1,000 copies of his book, entitled *Kriegie Life*, published at their own expense by a Meriden printer. Books were sold in local bookstores or through the author.

Unlike any book that had been published about the PoW experience, the wide variety of the drawings gave the reader a vivid picture of life as an Army Air Corps PoW shot down over the war-torn skies of Europe and Africa, of which little information had previously been available. How the prisoners' ingenuity helped them to convert limited materials into the necessities of life had not been explored before. Although the daily routine was monotonous, one learned through his unique book that humorous moments were to be found, even during the blackest days. The 'Daily Life' section illustrated universal moments experienced by each PoW in the massive camp from the routine daily duties to a variety of recreational opportunities. For the first time, readers could see sketches of the Germans who worked in the camp. They could identify with the activities so accurately portrayed by Holmstrom that would be forever etched on their minds.

Sadly, many more scenes, more than 100 sketched in the camp, are lost to time. On the long marches and box car rides from camp to camp, it was hard to carry large bundles. Starving and weakened men, who could no longer carry much weight on their backs or who had frostbitten hands, were forced to part with precious letters, pictures, log books and portraits. Carl was no exception:

> While on the Forced March, I threw one of my bundles away before I realized my portraits were in it. They only gave us thirty minutes' warning before we left, and I left many of my portraits behind. Forty of my drawings I sent home via the Red Cross, but some never got here. I have about 200 left.

Carl returned from the war in June 1945 and accepted employment with the Tower Studios in New York City as a commercial artist. He met and married Frances Jourdan in New York City, New York, where he worked briefly as a commercial artist. She was a former WAVE lieutenant and was the first woman to join the WAVES in Connecticut.

The couple moved to Cheshire, Connecticut, where they lived most of their lives and had four children. Carl continued his art career as a commercial artist doing freelance advertising work and creating many portraits in pastels and tempers until he retired. He passed away in August 1979. After his death, his wife donated his collection of drawings from his PoW experience and his scrapbook of newspaper clippings and political cartoons from German newspapers to the US Army Heritage and Education Center at Carlisle Barracks, Carlisle, Pennsylvania. She did not leave the collection to their children as 'to me they're something that belong in a museum. This institute is a place for researchers.'

'It was Carl's art that helped him endure the harsh conditions, the boredom and the uncertainty,' Mrs Holmstrom said of his prison experiences. 'Carl never did dwell on his time as a PoW. He always told us the humorous stories. He often spoke of the soldier who spent days collecting solder from cans in the garbage to make a little statue.'

That eye for detail, never missing anything in the camp, translated to the passion he brought to his artwork. Carl Holmstrom was a first-hand eyewitness of the horrors of the Second World War. He found himself trying to make the best of his horrendous fate, but he found possibility and promise in a grim prisoner of war camp that aided in not only his survival but that of his new friends. He spent the rest of his life trying to make sense of it all. 'Hitler must have had lots of people behind him, not just a few thousand, or he never could have gotten where he did,' he said in a post-war analysis. 'The civilians couldn't have helped but knew what was going on in the prison and concentration camps. We saw Jews in the slave labor battalions being beaten outside of our camp. The problem of Germany? I don't know,' he said, shaking his head. 'It's all pretty complex.'

Fortunately, the book you hold in your hands provides the insights of a talented man willing to share his unique place in history to remind us all that our freedom is precious and was earned by those willing to sacrifice all to fight for it. Such a man was Carl Holmstrom. His history in art lives on.

Susan Holmstrom Kohnowich
Daughter of Second Lieutenant Carl Holmstrom, PoW #221

Assorted Colour Drawings

Flight Lieutenant Henry A. Picard: Biography

Flight Lieutenant Henri A. Picard was born in Brussels, Belgium, on 17 April 1916. He was attached to the Belgian 350 Squadron RAF, flying a Spitfire VB. His victories, as well as his brilliant general ability, earned him the Croix de Guerre with two Palms, which he received on 21 July 1942. Shortly afterwards, on 27 August, he was reported missing from an air battle over the region of Abbeville, France. Picard's plane was shot down by a Focke-Wulf 190 fighter plane, and he had to bail out over the sea.

Although seriously wounded in one leg, he succeeded in climbing into his inflated dinghy, but his trials were by no means over. He drifted for five days and six nights in his tiny raft, buffeted by two storms and suffering from his wound as well as from hunger and thirst. Finally, when he was almost delirious and utterly exhausted, his dinghy was washed ashore on the French coast, and he fell into German hands. He became a prisoner of war on 2 September 1942. After recovery from his leg wound, he was sent to Stalag Luft III in Sagan, Germany.

During the preparation for the Great Escape, Henri was part of the team of Flight Lieutenant Walenn, who copied real identity papers and passes. He became one of the seventy-six who escaped through Tunnel Harry during the Great Escape on the night of 24/25 March 1944. Henri Picard was recaptured at Scheidemuhl, Germany, and murdered on 29 March 1944 by *Hauptsturmführer* Reinhold Burchardt from the Danzig Gestapo. Picard was cremated at Danzig.

It was believed that Picard, travelling with PoW Gordon Brettell, had been trying to make it back to Belgium. *Hauptsturmführer* Burchardt was traced in 1948 and sentenced to death, but later had his sentence commuted to twenty-one years imprisonment.

Portrait of Second Lieutenant Carl Holmstrom by Henry A Picard

Drawn by Belgian officer Flight Lieutenant Henry Picard, who was one of fifty murdered by the Nazi SS after an attempt to escape from Stalag Luft III during 'the Great Escape'.

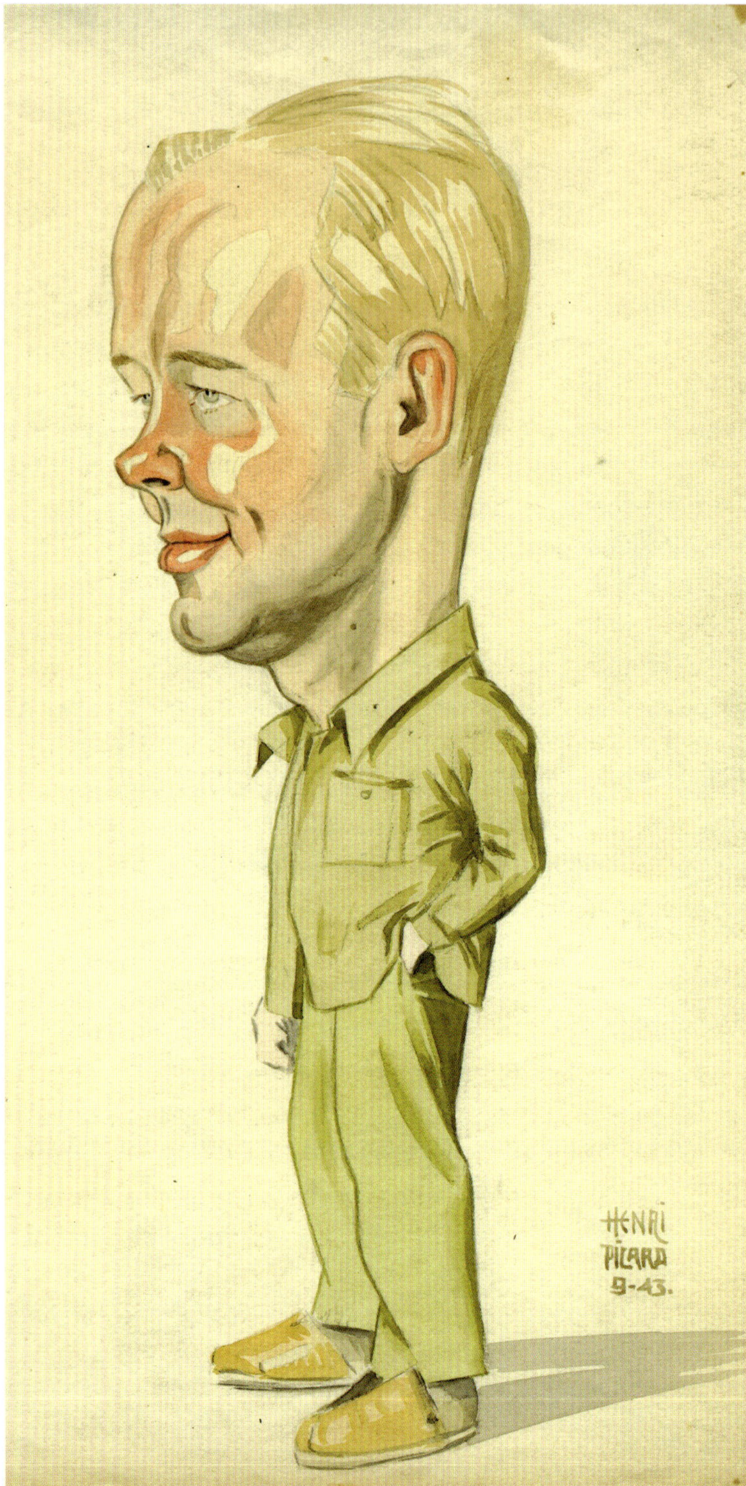

Bird's Eye View of Oflag XXI-B

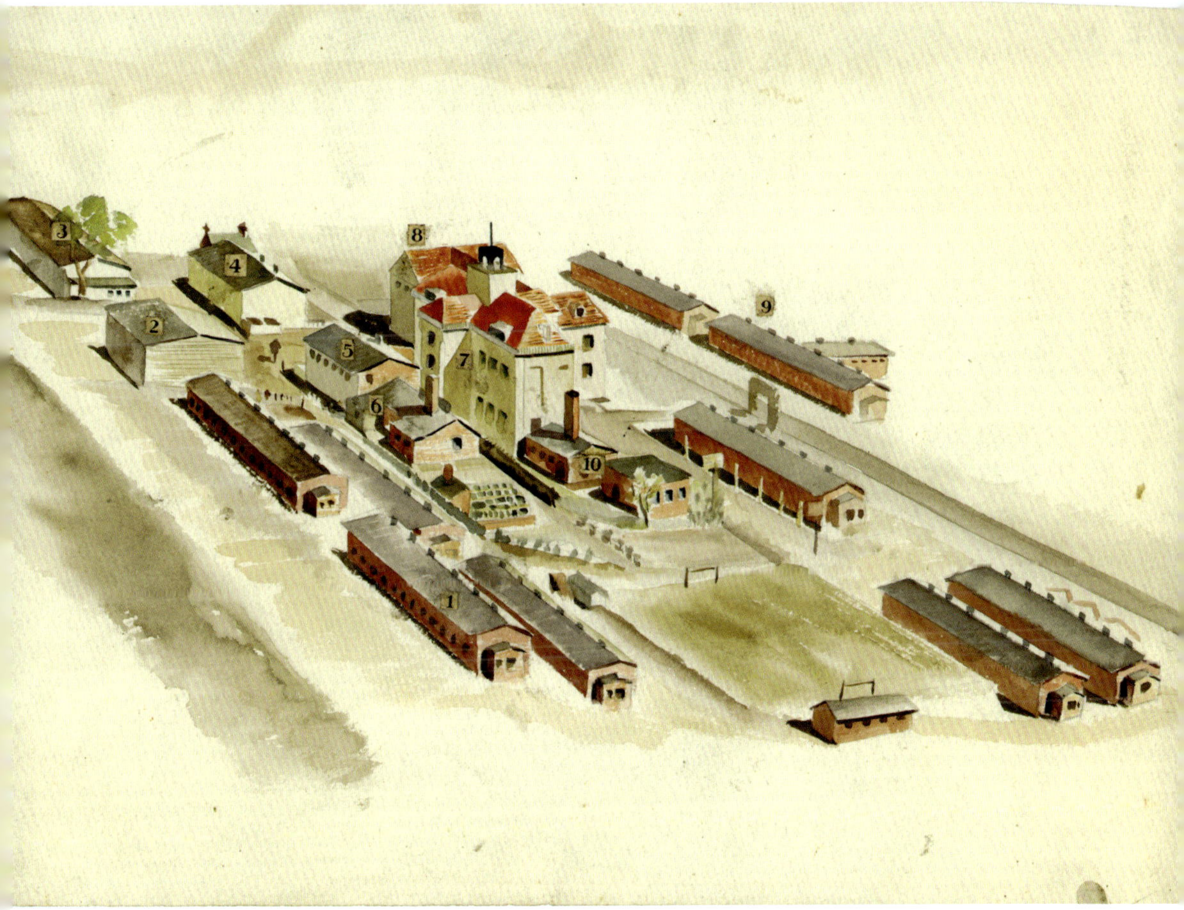

Goon boxes and barbed wire fences were not included in this picture to avoid confiscation of the pictures by the Germans. The camp buildings were (1) barracks, (2) British orderlies, (3) linen and utensil store, (4) cobbler, (5) tin stores, (6) cook house and 'Foodacco' (trading post where items could be exchanged), (7) hospital, (8) library and theatre, (9) administration building and cooler. The building for senior officers (10) is on the right and showers on the left side.

Hospital at Oflag XXI-B

The hospital's cupola was the highest reachable point in the camp. The hospital was comparatively well-heated, although still slightly uncomfortable.

The library in the 'White House' was the warmest room in the camp, mostly because of the number of PoWs who gathered there, not because of the heating system.

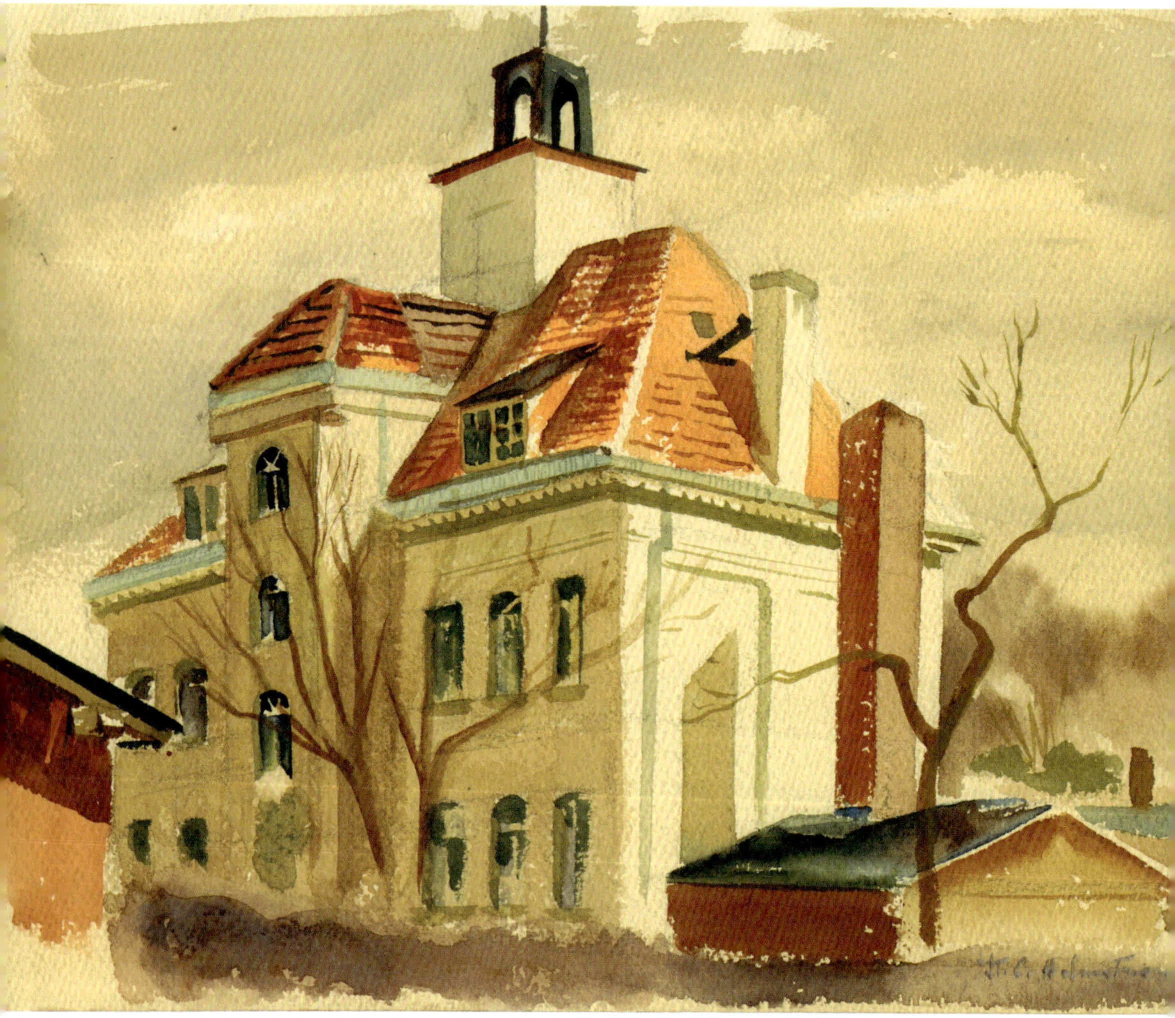

'There I Was' Cartoon by Second Lieutenant Joseph B. Boyle

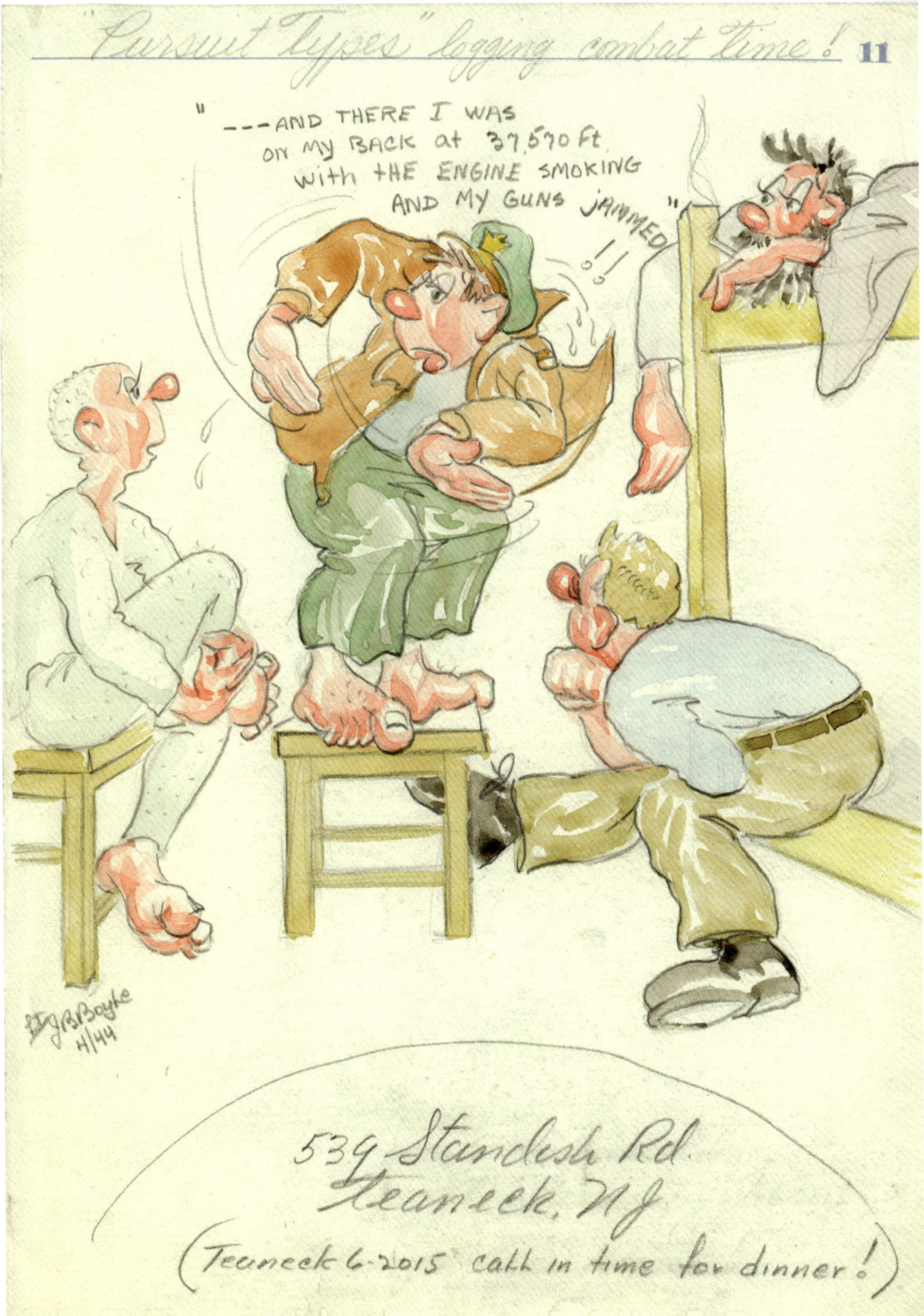

(*Courtesy of Rick Grice, son of Charles (Dick) Grice, grandson of Joe Boyle*)

Shower Room and Cobbler Shop at Stalag Luft III

Stalag Luft III was two years old before the building shown here was constructed as a shower room and cobbler shop, but for nine months lacked the equipment necessary for its operation. It took so long to get the shower hut working that many men went for more than a year without a hot shower.

The prisoners had to settle for hose and punched-can devices or sponge baths. Since the water table at Sagan was about 300ft, the water was extremely cold. Few men stayed under the sprinkler buckets attached to the spigots for more than a minute or two.

Shaving was a difficult chore. There were few razor blades available and obtaining hot water was always a problem. Eventually, prisoners were allowed two minutes' use of hot water per week. Many men stopped shaving to best utilize the short washing time.

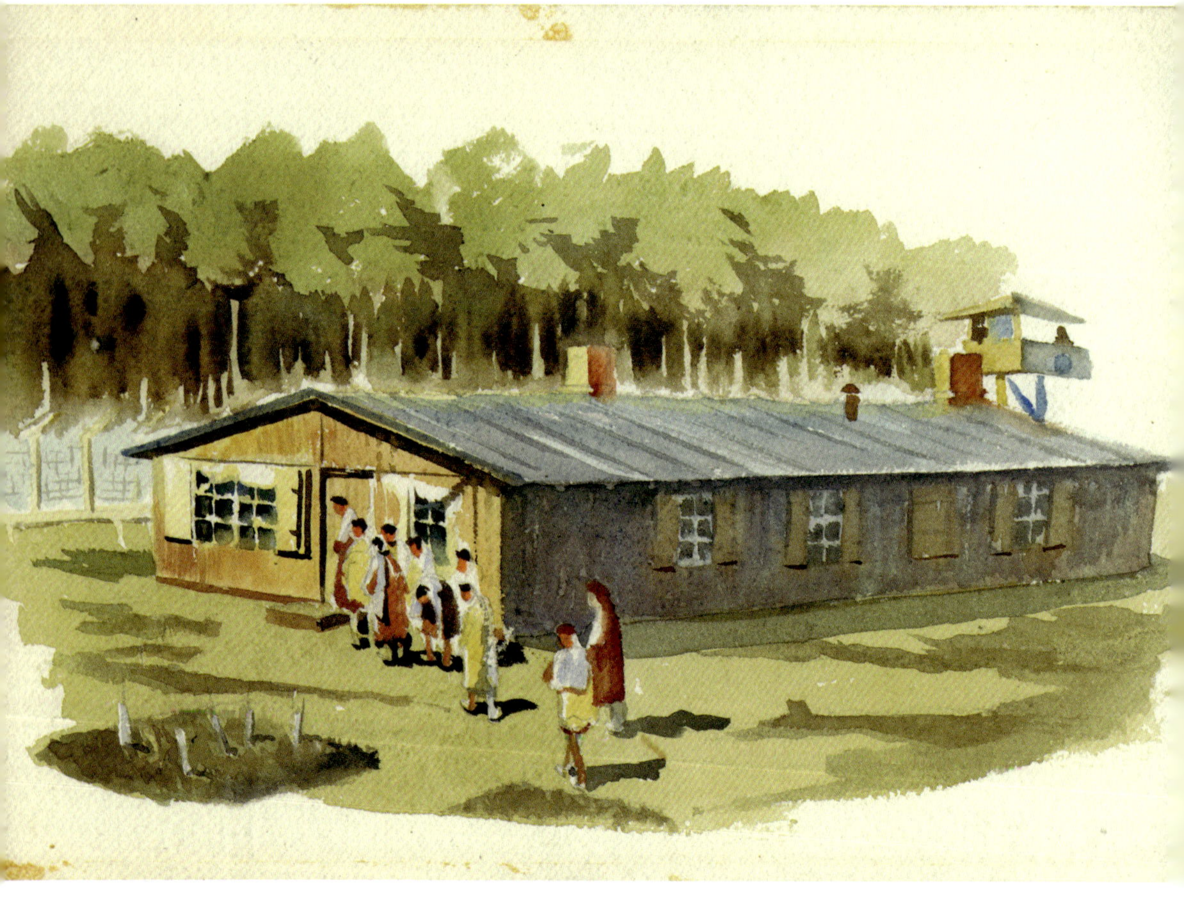

Prison Camp Latrine at Stalag Luft III

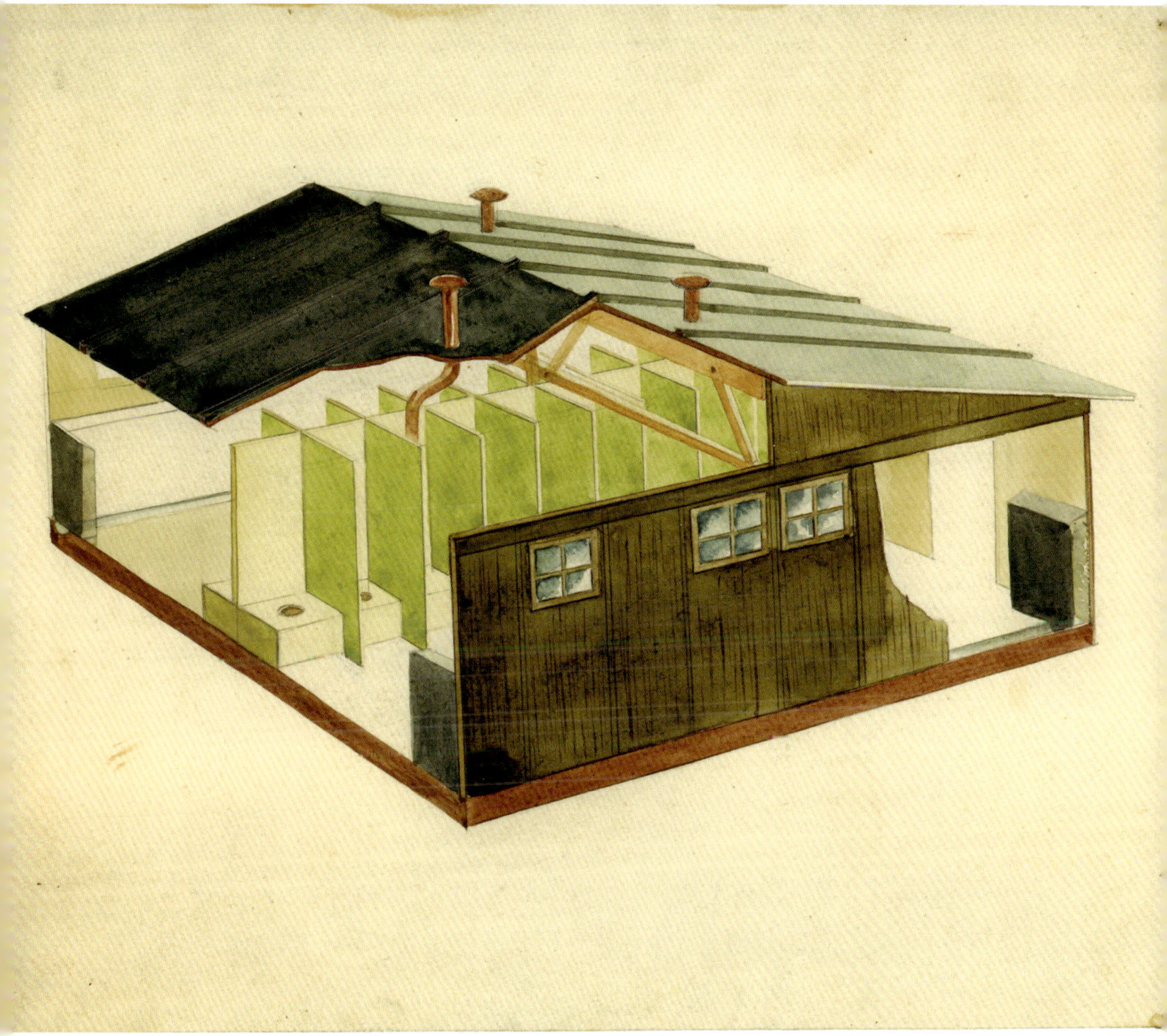

Stalag Luft III was constructed on sandy areas cleared of vegetation to prevent tunnelling. Each latrine contained twenty seats and an accumulation pit underneath. The pits were seldom emptied on schedule, and early on the latrine huts had not been properly sealed off on the outside. Consequently, this caused a foul odor around the area. Millions of flies bred and swarmed about and slugs crawled out of the latrines. Impetigo and dysentery were rampant.

Roll Call or *Appell*

Each day at Stalag Luft III began and ended with *Appell,* when all prisoners were counted by the Germans. Attired in a variety of made-over uniforms, the Kriegies looked more like hobos than soldiers.

If the final numbers did not correspond with the rosters, it could mean standing out in all weathers for hours. It was not unusual to stand for hours when the count was incorrect because a prisoner was asleep in his sack. Often a second roll-call was necessary. These roll-calls became a convenient time for guards to make periodic searches of the barracks for evidence of escape activities.

Appell was usually held twice a day, but when an escape had occurred or the Germans thought that one was about to occur, three or sometimes four *Appells* were held throughout the day and during the night. During bad weather and at night, the count was taken in the barracks by individual rooms. The Germans also conducted frequent and thorough searches of the barracks. Usually, the search was the result of someone or something having aroused German suspicions.

A memorable 'hardware' *Appell* happened on 27 March 1944 after seventy-six British officers escaped from North Compound. The Germans retaliated by getting those in South Compound out for extra *Appell* counts:

> We believed two roll-calls a day were plenty and showed it by milling around about while the Germans tried to take a count. They dismissed us in anger only to come back with a small army, carrying everything but German 88s guns which earned its reputation as the best overall gun of the war because of its accuracy, lethality and versatility, and German 105 guns, similar to the American 105mm howitzer. With this heavily armed force tactically placed at our backs, daring us to move, needless to say, they got a count.

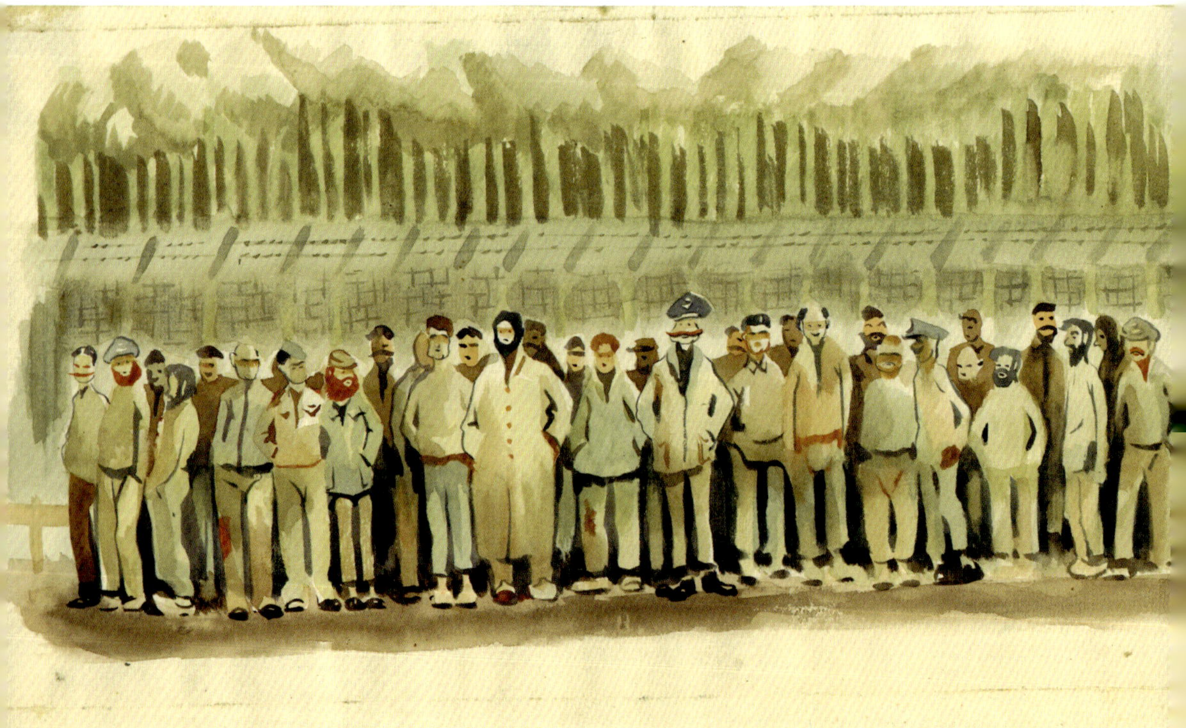

Lunch and Tea Time at Stalag Luft III

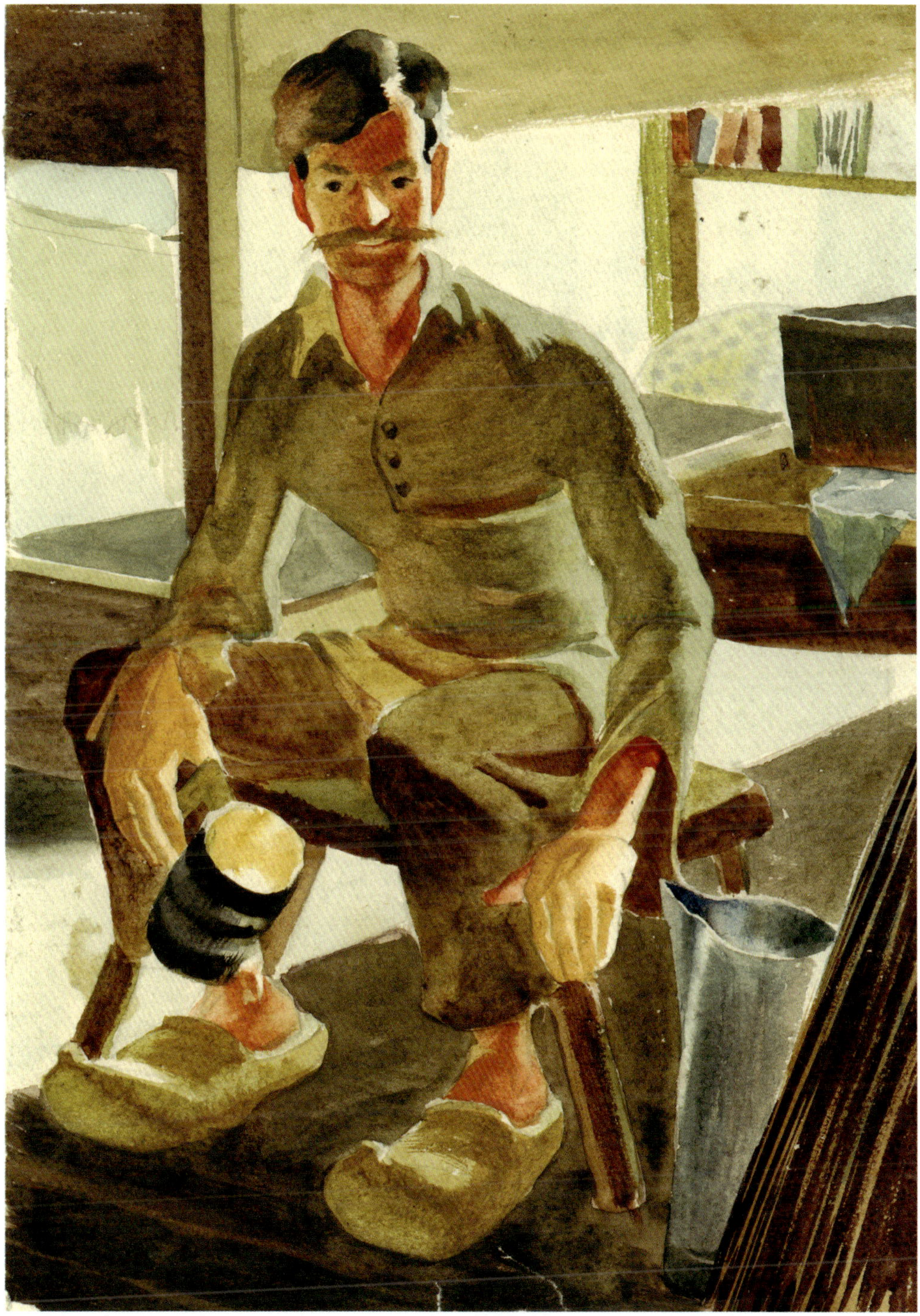

Lunch at Stalag Luft III, as supplied by the Germans, consisted of two or three potatoes and some 'Green Death soup': 'We would eat the soup but save the potatoes for the evening meal.' At tea time, there would be another slice of black bread and ersatz jam.

Cooking in Our Barracks at Stalag Luft III

Once food was prepared, it often took an hour to divide it equitably. All roommates watched the process for fairness so that no one was short-changed. The man cutting and dividing was always the last to choose his portion.

The barracks had a small, shared kitchen, but they were not in individual rooms.

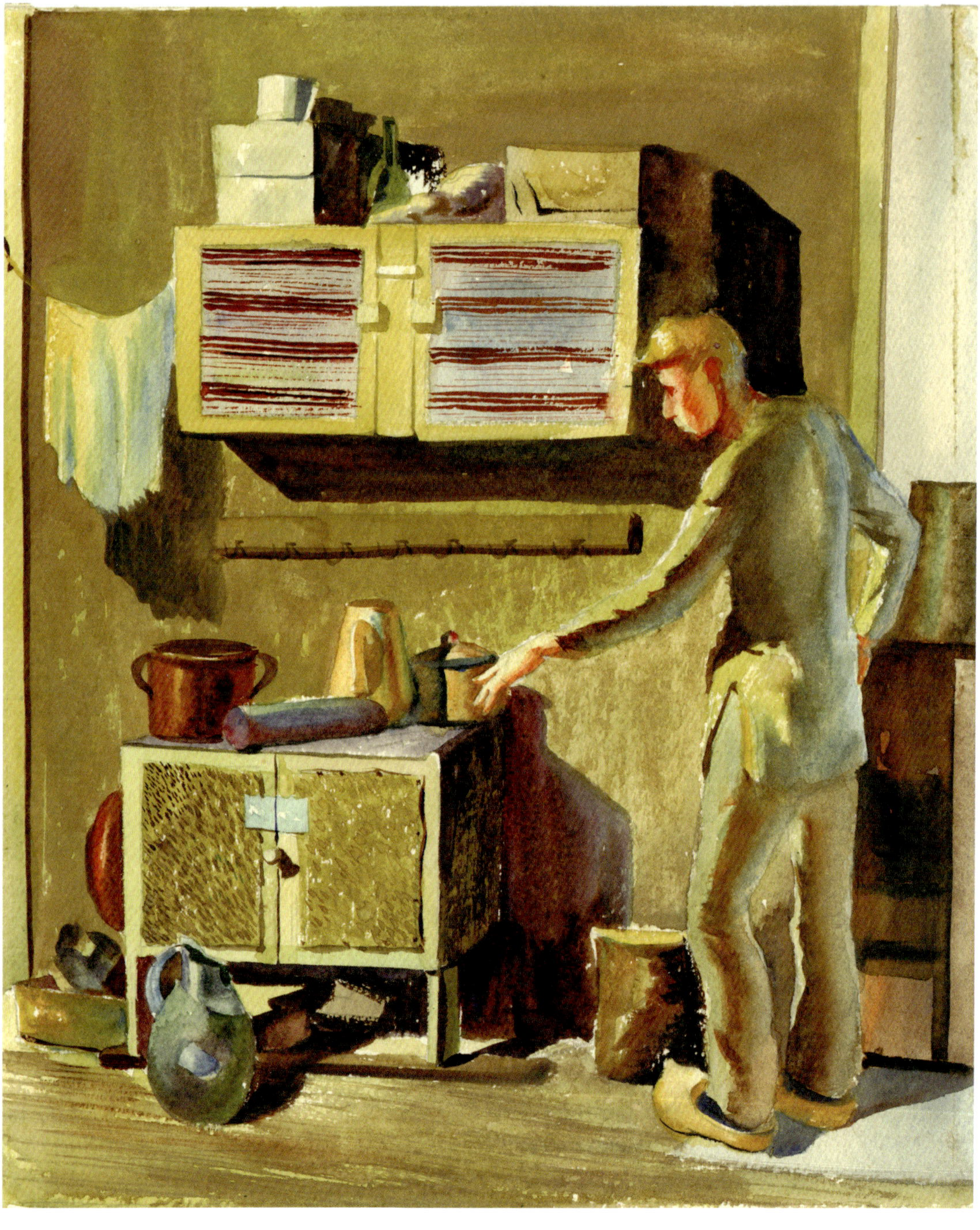

Latrines and Kohlrabi

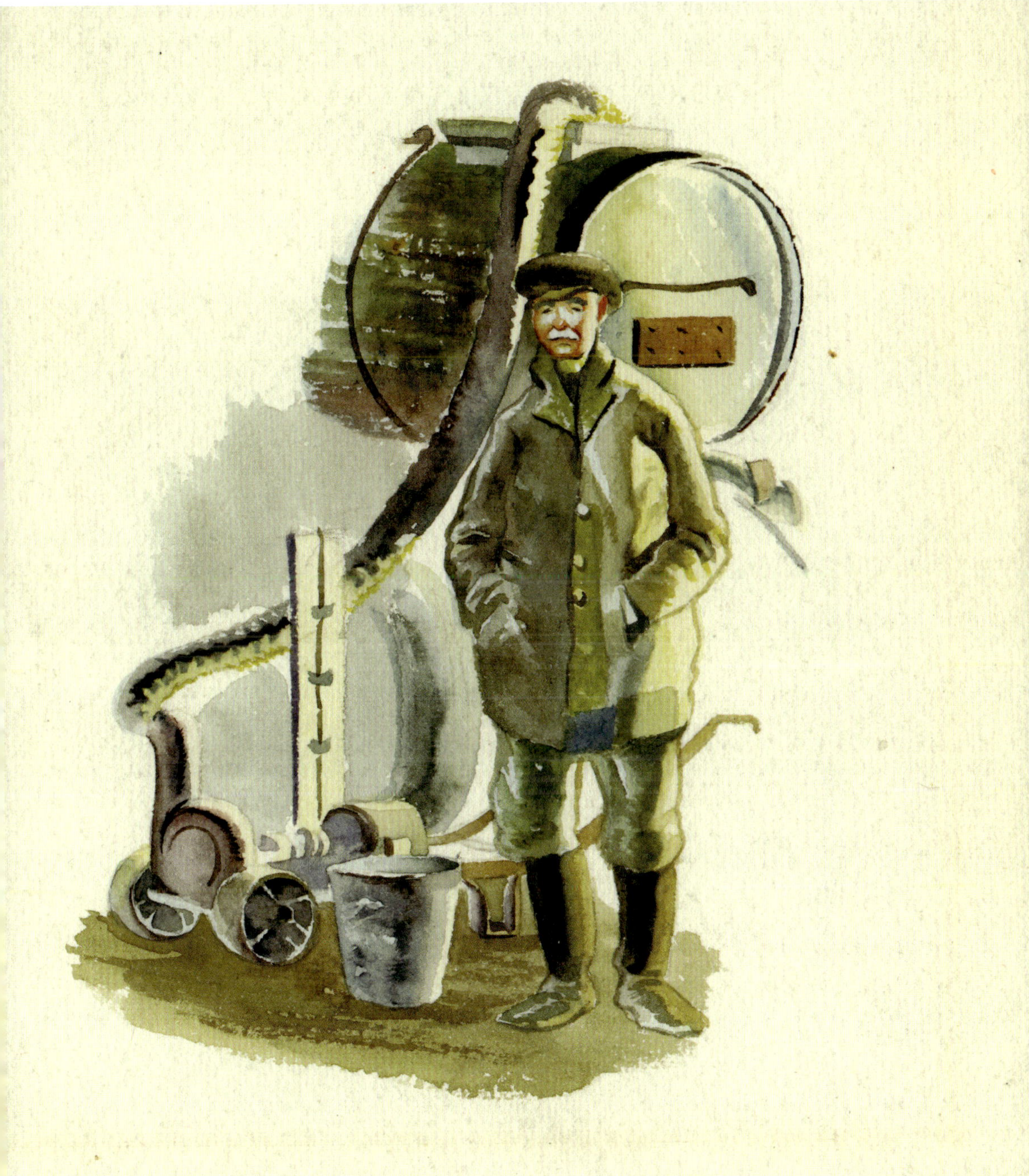

When the Honey Wagon entered camp at Stalag Luft III, windows of barracks would be forcibly slammed shut, and Kriegies downwind of the aborts moved to the opposite side to avoid the nauseating smell. Kohlrabi, the universally disliked vegetable, was a cross between cabbage and turnips. Its woody pulp made it inedible. Kriegies often threw the kohlrabi down the aborts until the Germans threatened to close them.

Honey Wagon Crew at Work at Stalag Luft III

The Honey Wagon man brought assistants to help with the odious task of pumping out the latrines. Once a week, the contents of the pit were hand-pumped into a horse-drawn "honey wagon" for removal from the camp. The honey wagon's Polish driver, Franciszek Lewandowski, used the waste as fertilizer on his pig farm. It was not inconceivable for a tunnel to be started in the abort.

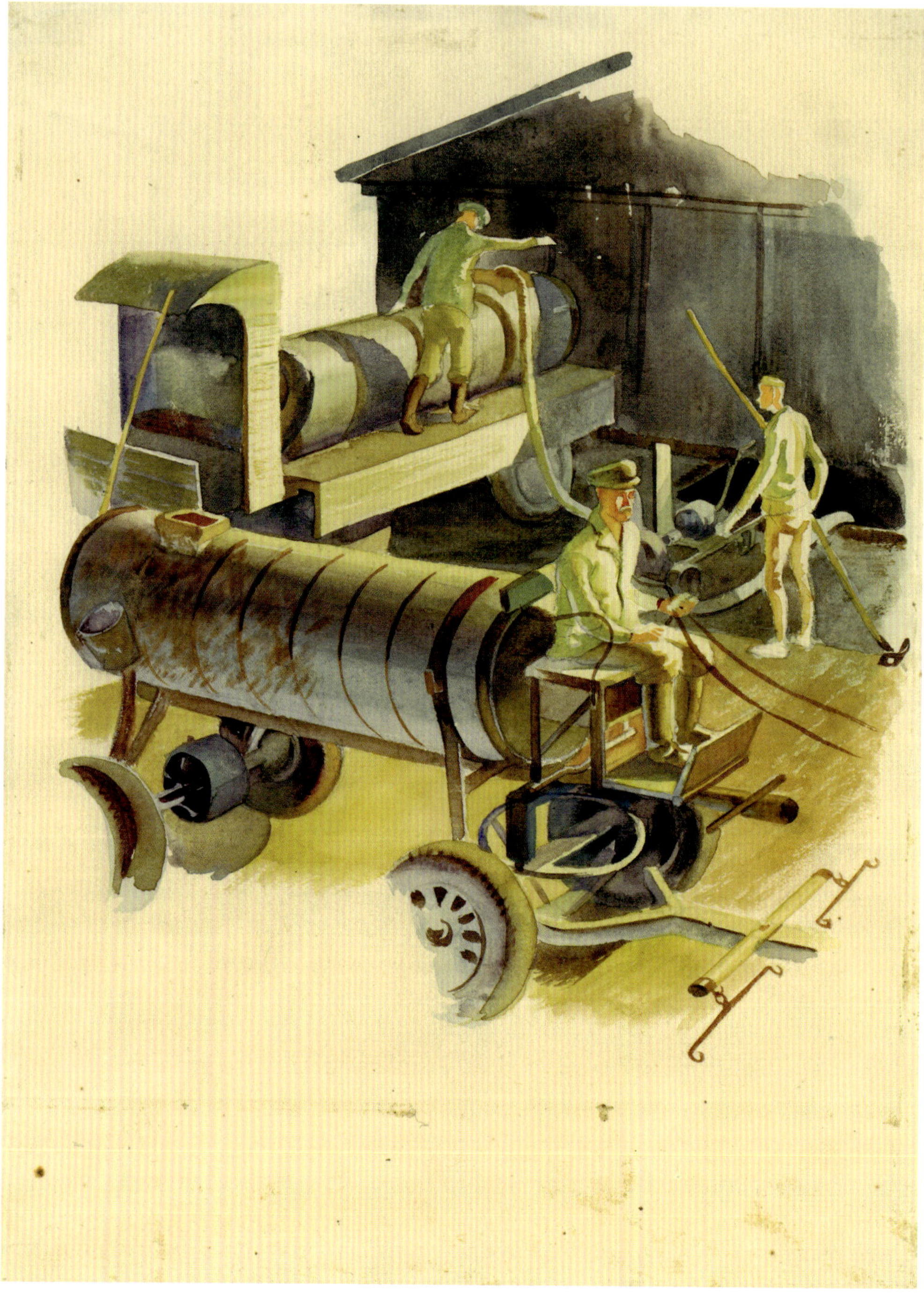

Goon Boxes, Barbed Wire and Searchlights

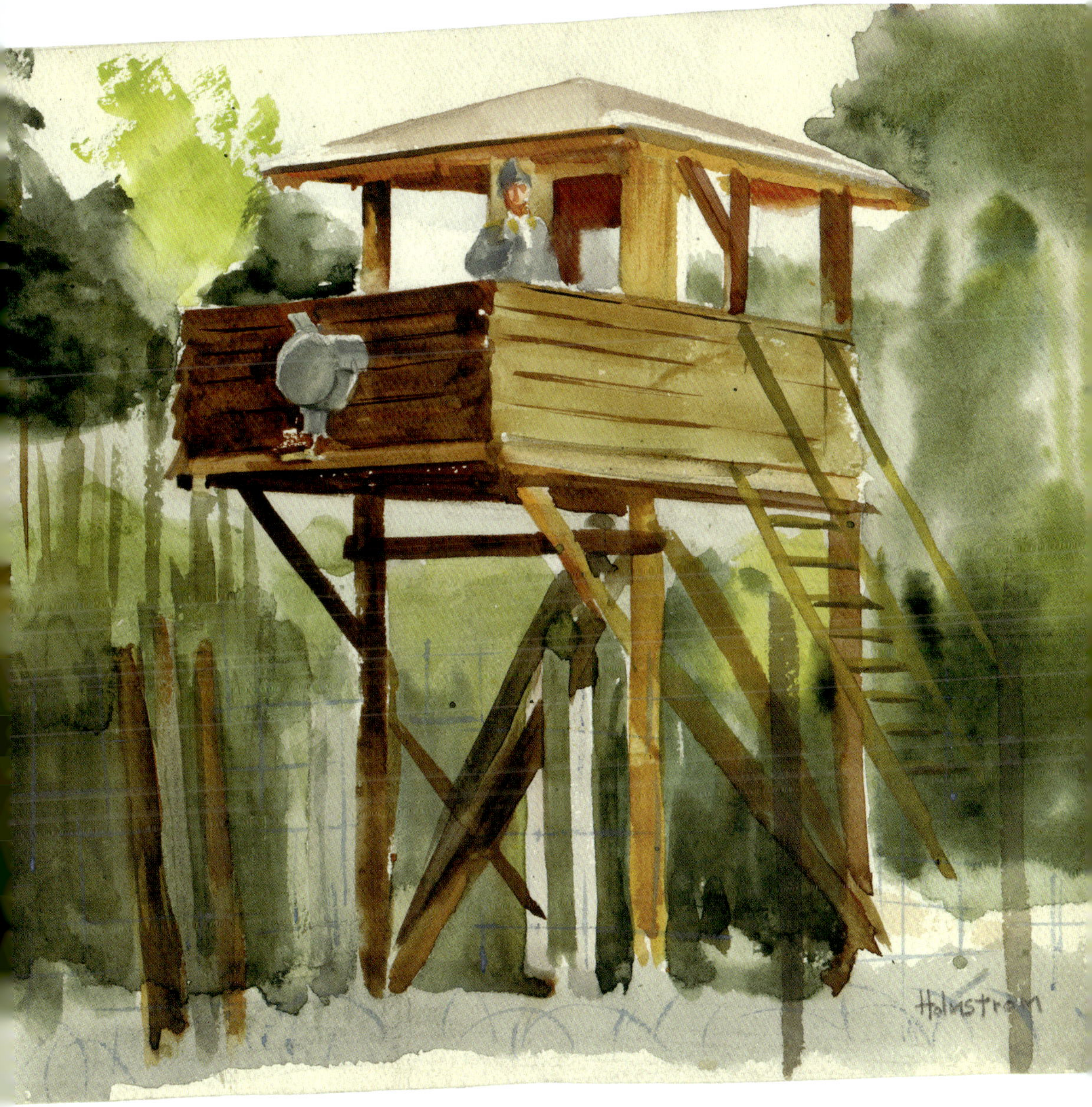

Two fences of barbed wire plus goon boxes enclosed the Stalag Luft III camp. The area accessible to prisoners ended with a guard rail 20ft inside the barbed wire fence, not to be crossed. Goon boxes were about 20ft away from buildings. Large searchlights in the goon boxes swept across the camp each night as guard dogs ran loose in the compounds. Besides the guards in the towers, there were so-called German 'ferrets' and 'weasels' who checked beneath the raised barracks with poles to detect escape activities.

Unknown PoW Portrait #1

This is one of two portraits that Carl Holmstrom had mounted behind his desk when he was working at home so it had special meaning to him. The identity of the person is unknown.

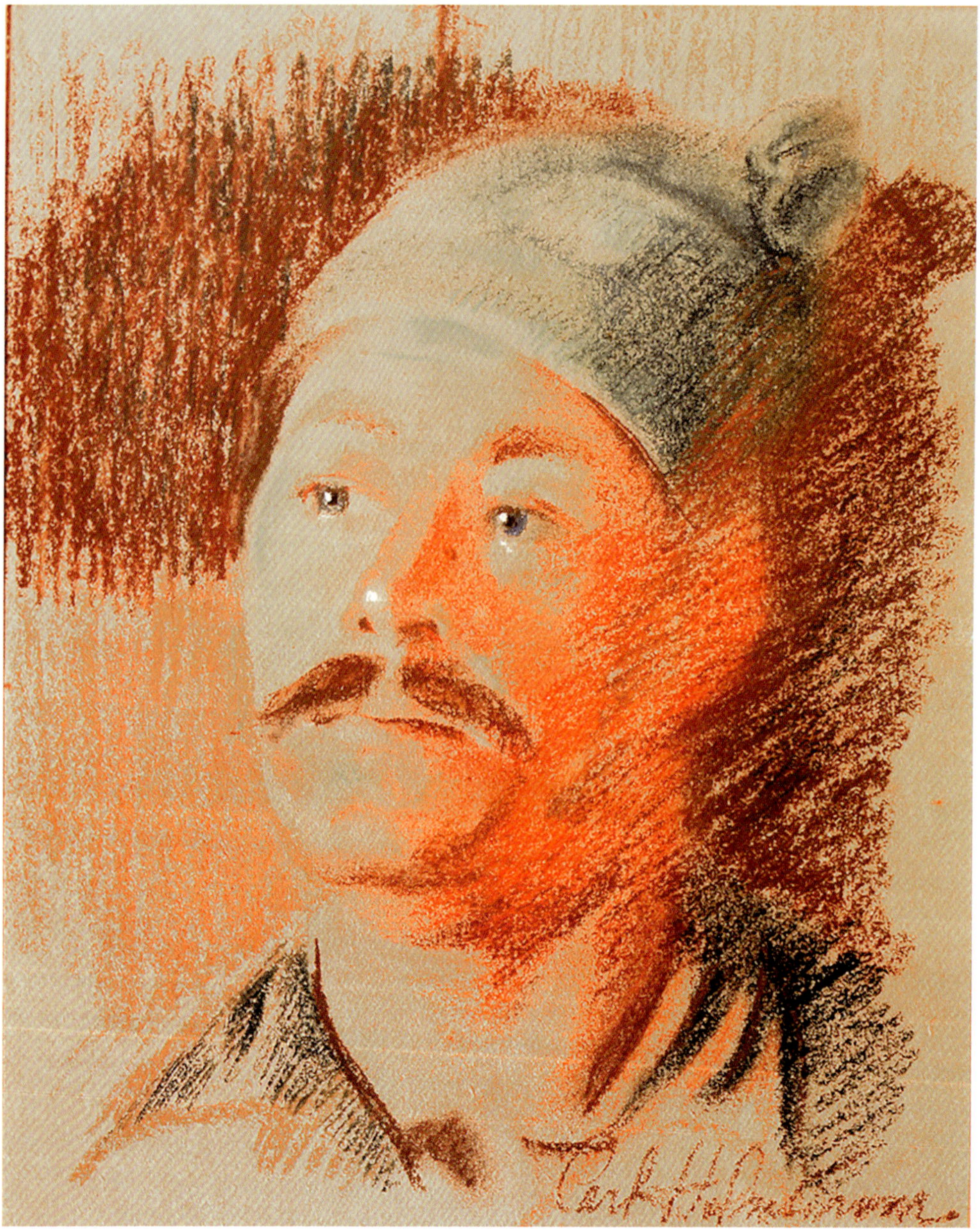

Unknown PoW Portrait #2

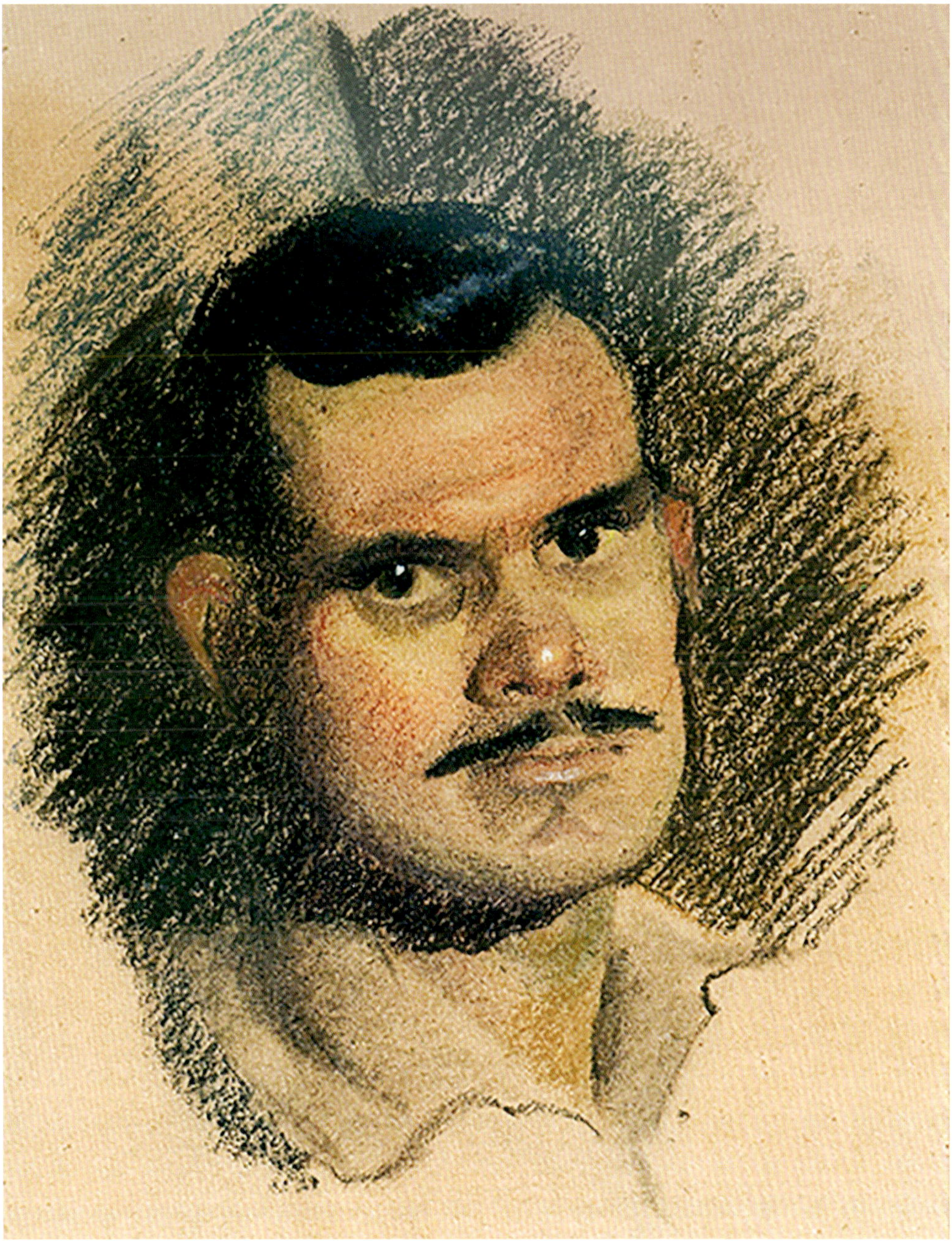

This is the second of two portraits that Carl Holmstrom had mounted behind his desk when he was working at home so it also had some special meaning to him. The identity of this person is also unknown.

Second Lieutenant William E. 'Bill' Gravins, Jr., Richmond, Virginia, USA

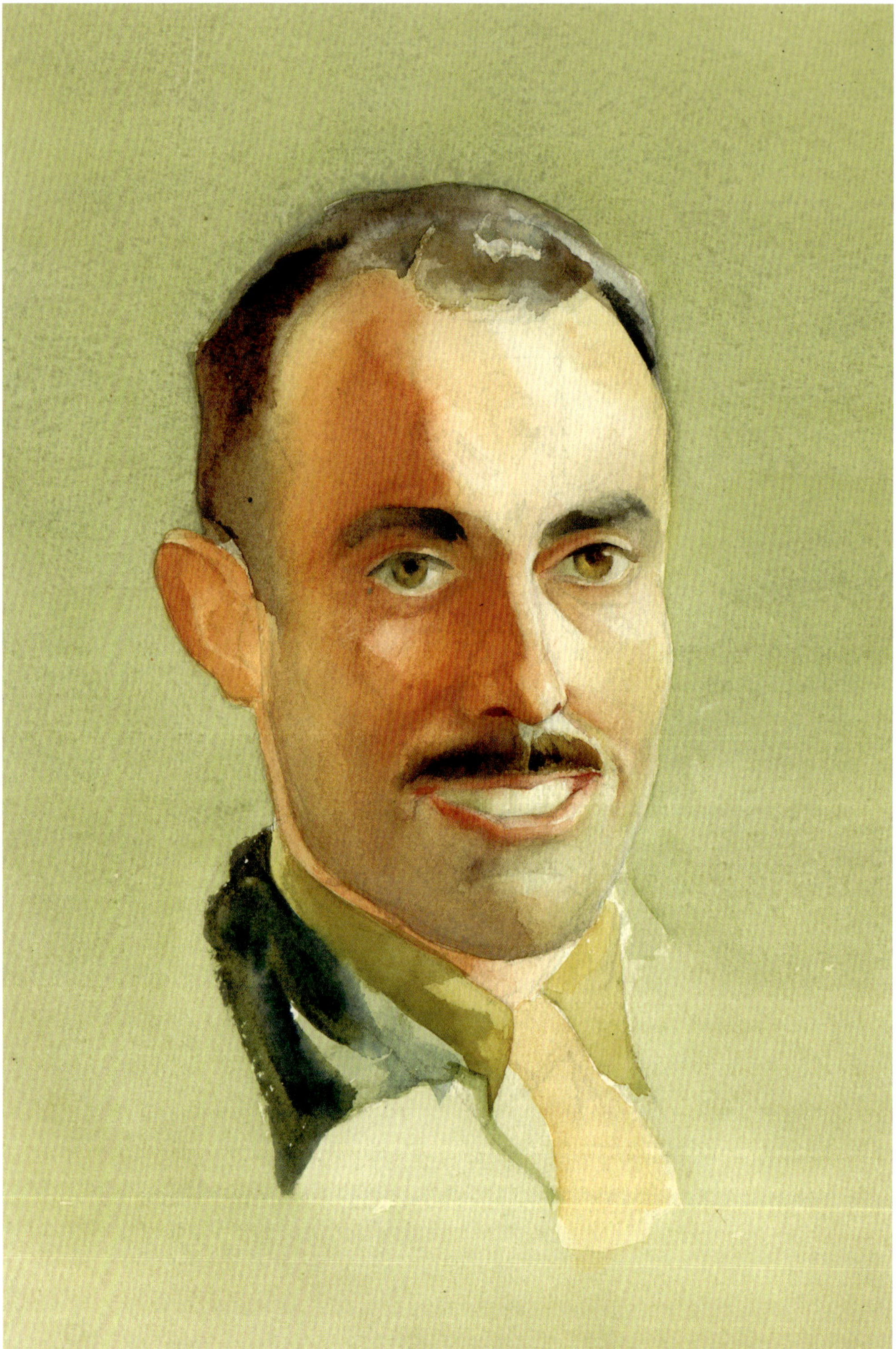

Second Lieutenant William E. 'Bill' Gravins was a B-17 bombardier from Richmond, Virginia. He was shot down on his first mission on 15 May 1943 by a Focke-Wulf 190 fighter plane. He ditched 80 miles west of Heligoland, Germany, and remained in a dinghy for twenty hours before being picked up by a German patrol boat. He was bombing the dock installation in Wilhelmshaven, Germany. Gravins was interrogated at Dulag Luft in Oberursel, Germany, and sent to Stalag Luft III to South Compound, barracks #134, room 3.

'Bill passed out shoe polish, toothbrushes and powder, and orders for books on the German army. He bought up about everything the German merchants would sell.'

Quote from *Clipped Wings*

Portraits of PoWs

Second Lieutenant Carl H. Holmstrom,
Branford, Connecticut, USA

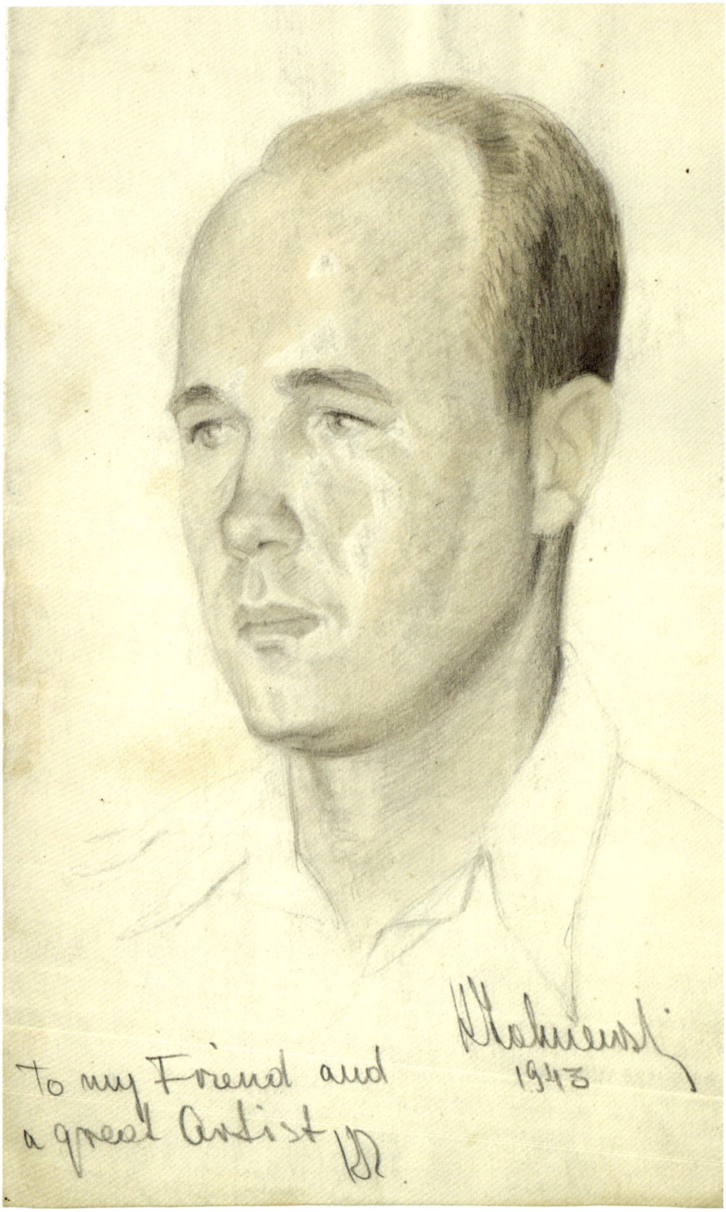

Carl's arrival at Stalag Luft III provided him with an opportunity to meet and sketch many other prisoners of war. Even though two members of his B-17 crew, Henry Keller and Cliff Pearson, wanted him in their combine at the new camp, it was filled, so he ended up rooming with some fellows he met on his own purge. Little did he know at the time that long after the war his sketches would become so cherished by those he had drawn. Fortunately, the YMCA provided some artistic materials so he was able to complete the sketches seen here:

> When artistically bent, Kriegies, who wanted drawing materials, stood in line in front of the canteen window where Second Lieutenant Carl Holmstrom would issue paper and pencils. Holmstrom was the executive officer who handled all the arts and crafts supplies for the camp and the forgers. Almost every man devised some means to keep his hands and mind occupied. Some who had never drawn a curved line took pin-up photos from German magazines, squared and lined off the pictures, ruled the walls of their room with congruent squares and made crayon murals that surprised themselves and astonished visitors.
>
> Quote from *Clipped Wings*

As an accomplished artist, he illustrated camp life in stunning detail. He sketched what he saw, but his speciality was portraits, which covered the gamut from the lowest German worker in the camp to the senior officers. His talent for drawing was appreciated by all in the area. After the war, Walter Winchell, in his newspaper column, wrote about Carl's artistic talent.

Holmstrom received the following awards and decorations: the American Campaign Medal, European-African-Middle Eastern Campaign Medal, Second World War Victory Medal and one Bronze Star. He was the author of *Kriegie Life*, a picture diary of his PoW experience.

Carl died in August 1979. The portrait of him was done by an unknown artist at the camp.

Second Lieutenant Daniel J. Barberis, North Bergen, New Jersey, USA

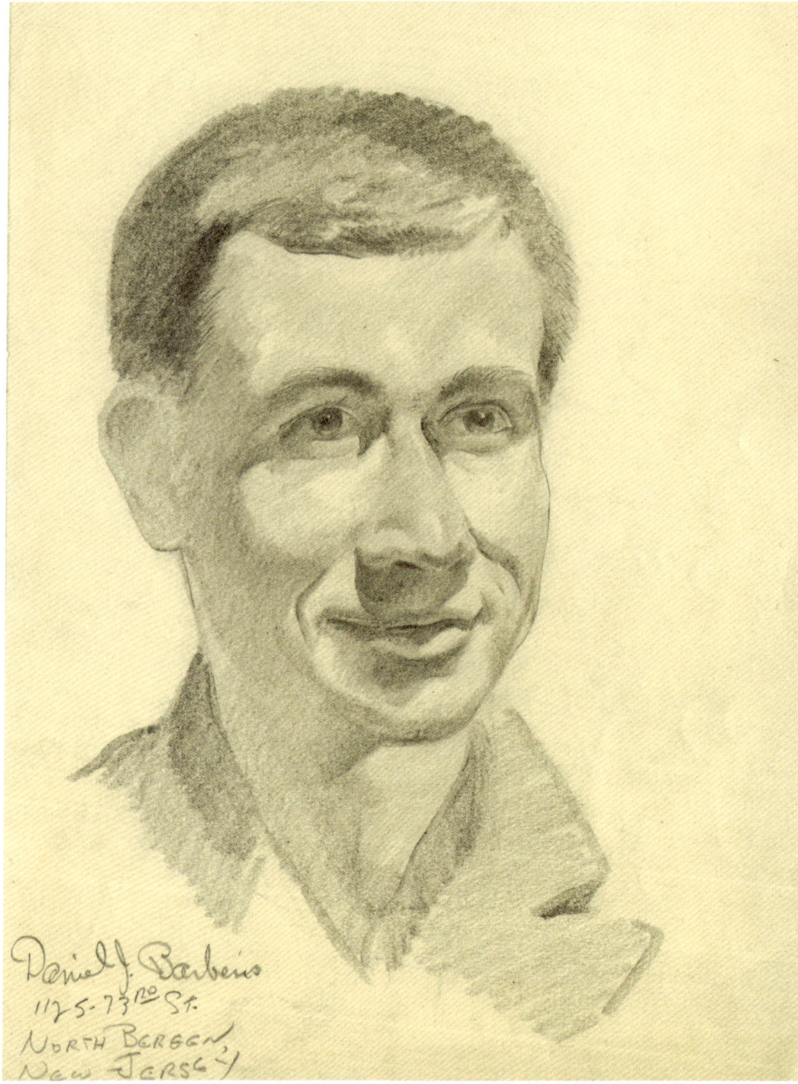

Second Lieutenant Daniel J. Barberis from North Bergen, New Jersey, was a B-17 navigator. He was shot down on 28 July 1943 and taken to Dulag Luft, arriving on 3 August 1943 at Stalag Luft III where he lived in South Compound. Before ditching in the North Sea, Daniel was part of an Eighth Air Force bomber crew that destroyed eleven Nazi fighters in one raid.

He was shot down by fighters on his eighteenth mission as he bombed an aircraft factory in Kassel, Germany, bailing out and landing 30 miles east of Hamburg. He was captured immediately by the Home Guard.

Barberis received the following awards and decorations: the European-African-Middle Eastern Theatre Campaign Ribbon, Air Medal with two Oak Leaf Clusters, the Purple Heart and the American Defense Service Medal.

After the Second World War, he moved to Vermont, married and had two sons. He worked in the lithographic trade in North Bennington, Vermont. He was an avid cyclist and was known for his beautiful gardens and fresh vegetables.

Second Lieutenant William J. Billig, South Miami, Florida, USA

Second Lieutenant William J. Billig from South Miami, Florida, was a B-26 pilot. He was shot down on 3 October 1942 when he crash-landed on the beach near Vlissingen, Holland. He was held for two and a half years in Stalag Luft III in South Compound and Stalag VII-A.

He was a member of the Escape Committee, forger of papers and was a code user, 'C.U.', sending and receiving coded messages for a top-secret military intelligence operation.

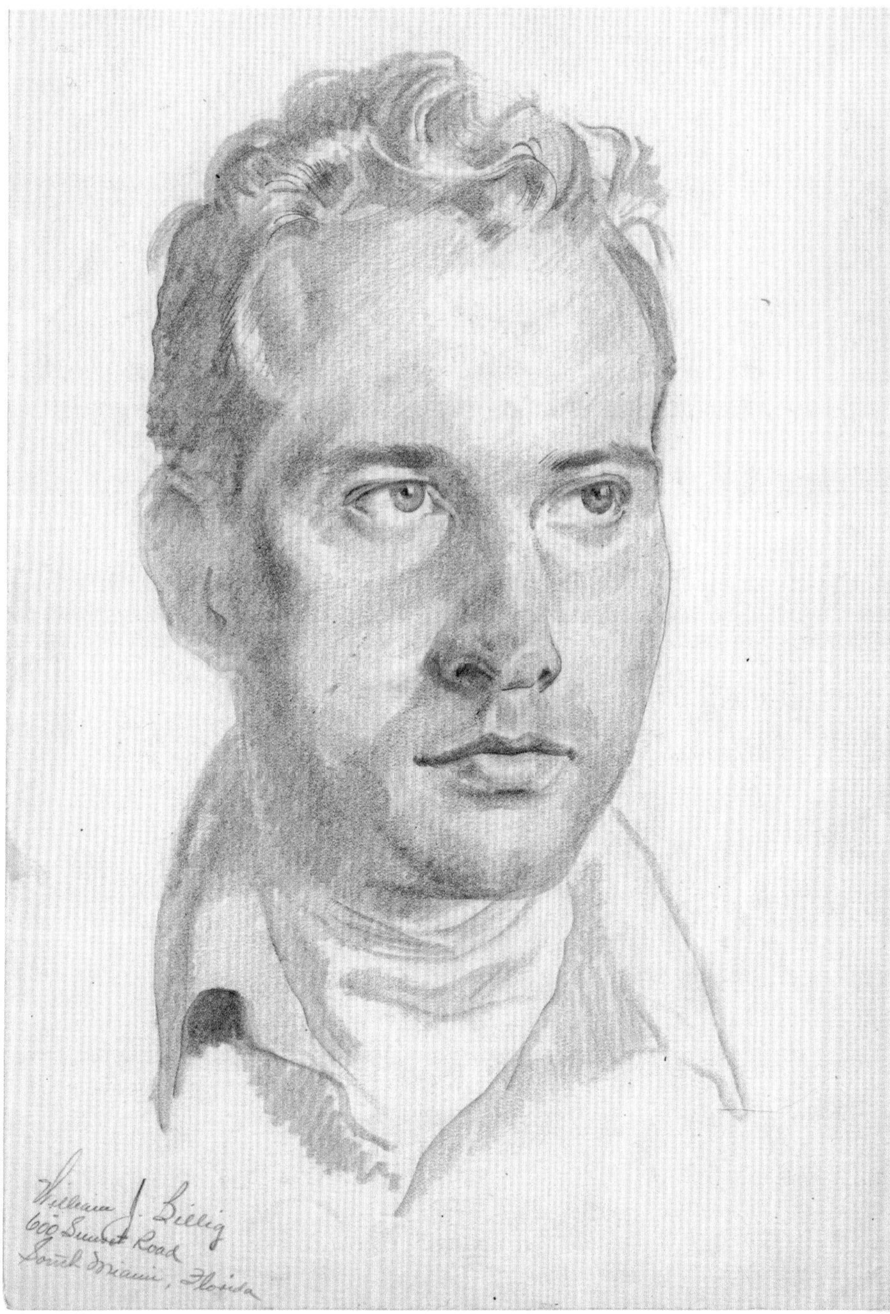

Second Lieutenant Joseph B. 'Joe' Boyle, Teaneck, New Jersey, USA

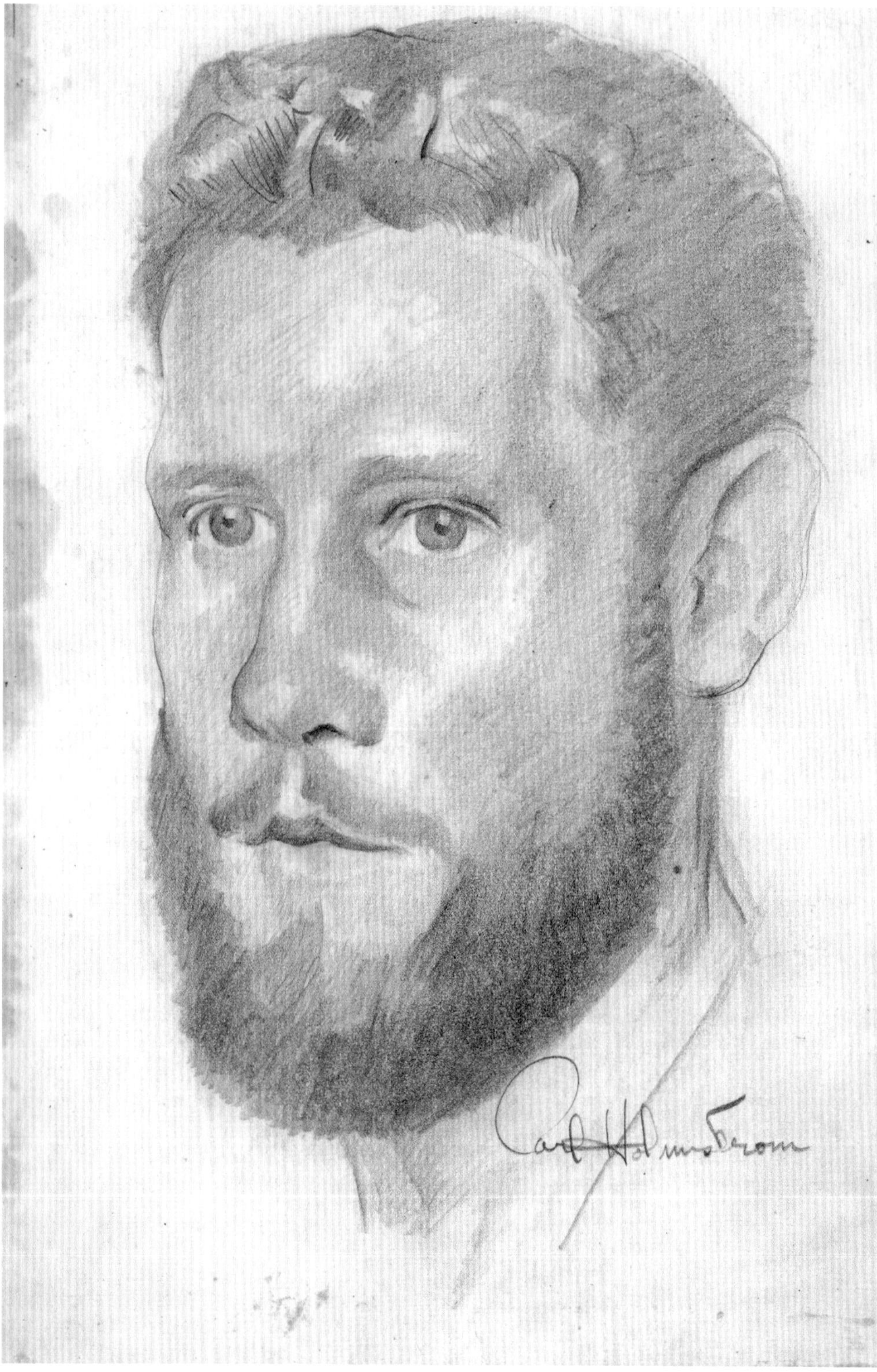

Second Lieutenant Joseph B. 'Joe' Boyle from Teaneck, New Jersey, earned a Bachelor's Degree in Business Administration from Lehigh University in 1939. He joined the Eighth Air Force, 308th Bomber Group and was a B-17 co-pilot who flew fifteen bombing missions. He was shot down on 17 May 1943 while on a return run from bombing the submarine pens at Lorient, France.

Boyle's plane, 'Dry Martini and the Cocktail Kids', set a record for the most German fighters (ten) shot down by a bomber on a single mission on a raid to bomb the Renault works near Paris. After his capture, he was interrogated at Dulag Luft and transferred to Stalag Luft III.

During his imprisonment he became creative, writing poetry and drawing cartoons, many of which were humorous, revolving around his capture and internment. He was a popular cartoonist of camp life, and a poet who wrote *The Ribbons We Will Wear* and *And Who Shall Judge*. His famous quote was 'Oh, drab the days and slow to pass within this barbed wire fence.' During Stalag Luft III's 4th of July celebration, Boyle played the part of Paul Revere, sitting on a horse made up of two fellow PoWs as they ran through the camp calling 'The British are coming!' This scene was duplicated in the movie *The Great Escape*.

During his imprisonment, he lost 40lb. Boyle was awarded the Distinguished Flying Cross and a Purple Heart. After the Second World War, he returned to the carpet and furniture business and operated his own stores in northern New Jersey. He married, had three children and was a lifelong tennis player and golfer, enjoying both sports into his 80s.

His family said that whenever it was Memorial Day he would say: 'I think of my buddies who can't go to Memorial Day with their children.' Another of the things he spoke about was his concern for civilians who might have been killed or wounded in his crew's raid. He was relieved to know later that the Germans evacuated most of them from the city and those in his crew who were left behind would be in shelters with their captors.

Among the poems written by Boyle, his family felt that the following one best reflects his internment and thoughts of the future:

> The fate we share as prisoners is drab and often grim,
> Existing on such scanty fare as Reich-bread, spuds and Klim.
> Beds and books and little else, to fill Time's flapping sail.
> She makes or loses headway all, depending on the mail.
> Oh! Drab the days and slow to pass, with this barbed wire fence,
> When all the joys of living are still in the future tense.
> So here's to happy days ahead when you and I are free
> To look back on this interlude and call it history.

Lieutenant Colonel Albert P. 'Bub' Clark, San Antonio, Texas, USA

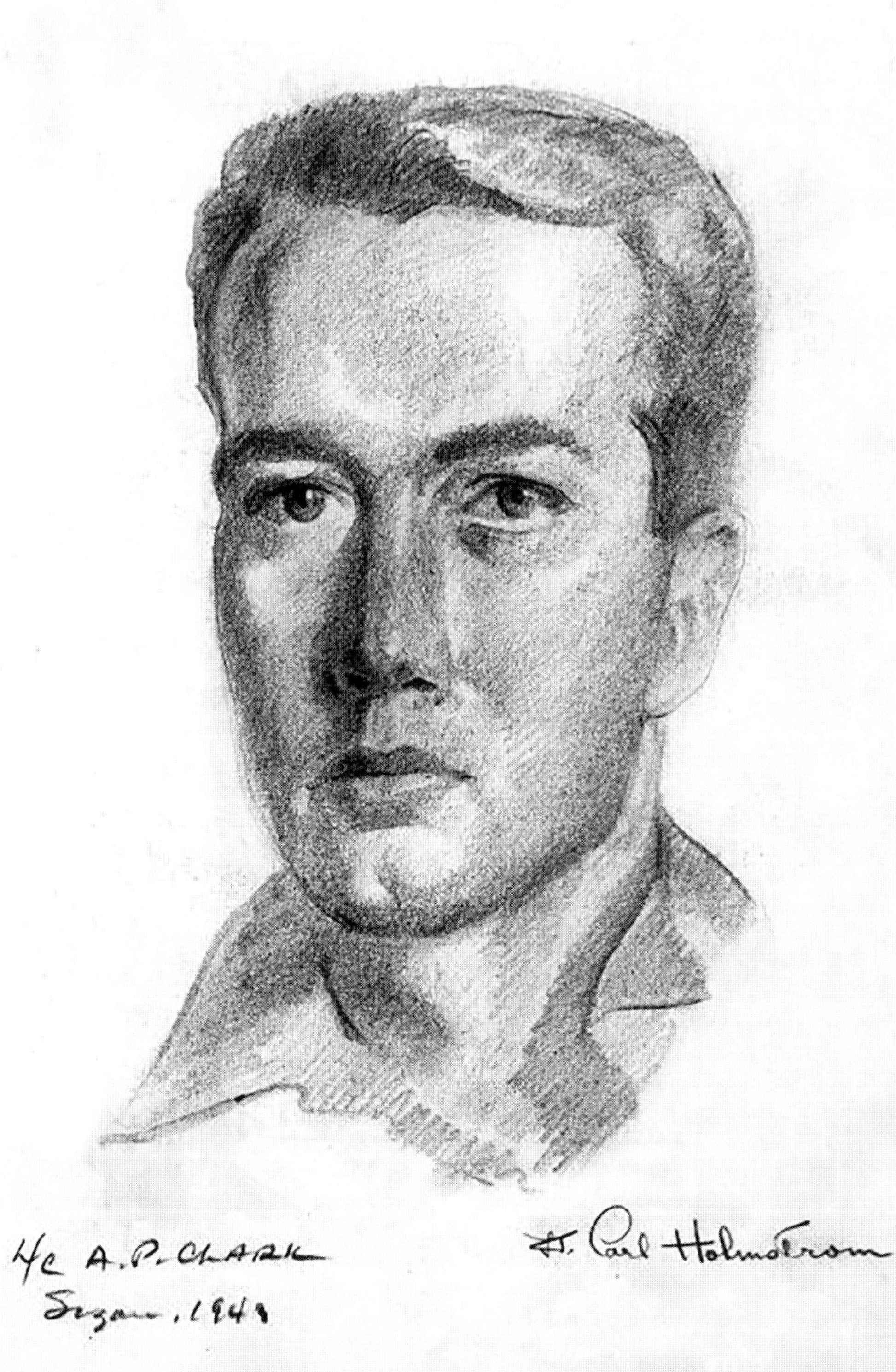

Lieutenant Colonel Albert P. 'Bub' Clark from San Antonio, Texas, was a West Point graduate and fighter pilot. In 1942, he was second-in-command of the 31st Fighter Group, the first American fighter unit in the European Theatre of Operations during the Second World War. He was shot down over Abbeville, France, on 26 July 1942 while flying a Spitfire. He crash-landed 8 miles south of Cape Gris-Nez, France, was taken to Dulag Luft for interrogation and transferred to Stalag Luft III, living in many compounds. At just 28, he was one of the youngest lieutenant colonels in Stalag Luft III.

Clark was the first USAAF fighter pilot taken prisoner of war in Germany and was initially held in North Compound with the RAF prisoners. He was imprisoned for thirty-three months at Stalag Luft III, and while there he was a manager of the acquisition and hiding of supplies surrounding what would later come to be known as 'the Great Escape'. While imprisoned, he was the head of security, 'Big S', during the planning of the Great Escape and was Senior American Officer there. Clark had a clandestine camera with which he captured some of the only known images of life inside Stalag Luft III.

He would prove to be a rock to his men throughout their ordeals and a role model for young men who were tested to their limits. Loyal to his men, he would stay with them through each emotional trial and even sacrifice his own early return after liberation to 'close the gate' at Stalag VII-A in Moosburg after being assured that each of his men was safely headed home.

After the war, he married, had three children and continued his military career, progressing through key staff assignments with Tactical Air Command, Continental Air Command and Air Defense Command prior to a tour of duty at Headquarters US Air Force. His next assignment was as Chief, US Military Training Mission to Saudi Arabia.

He was Director of Military Personnel at Headquarters US Air Force for four years beginning in 1959, and was then assigned to Okinawa as commander of the 313th Air Division. In August 1965 he was named Vice Commander of the Tactical Air Command. He assumed duties as Commander of Air University in August 1968, and in August 1970 he was appointed superintendent of the US Air Force Academy. He retired from the Air Force on 1 August 1974.

Clark received the following awards and decorations: Air Force Distinguished Service Medal, Legion of Merit with Oak Leaf Cluster, Purple Heart, Air Medal and the Air Force Commendation Medal.

(*Courtesy of US Air Force Academy McDermott Library SMS 329*)

Second Lieutenant Jack W. Daniel, Humble, Texas, USA

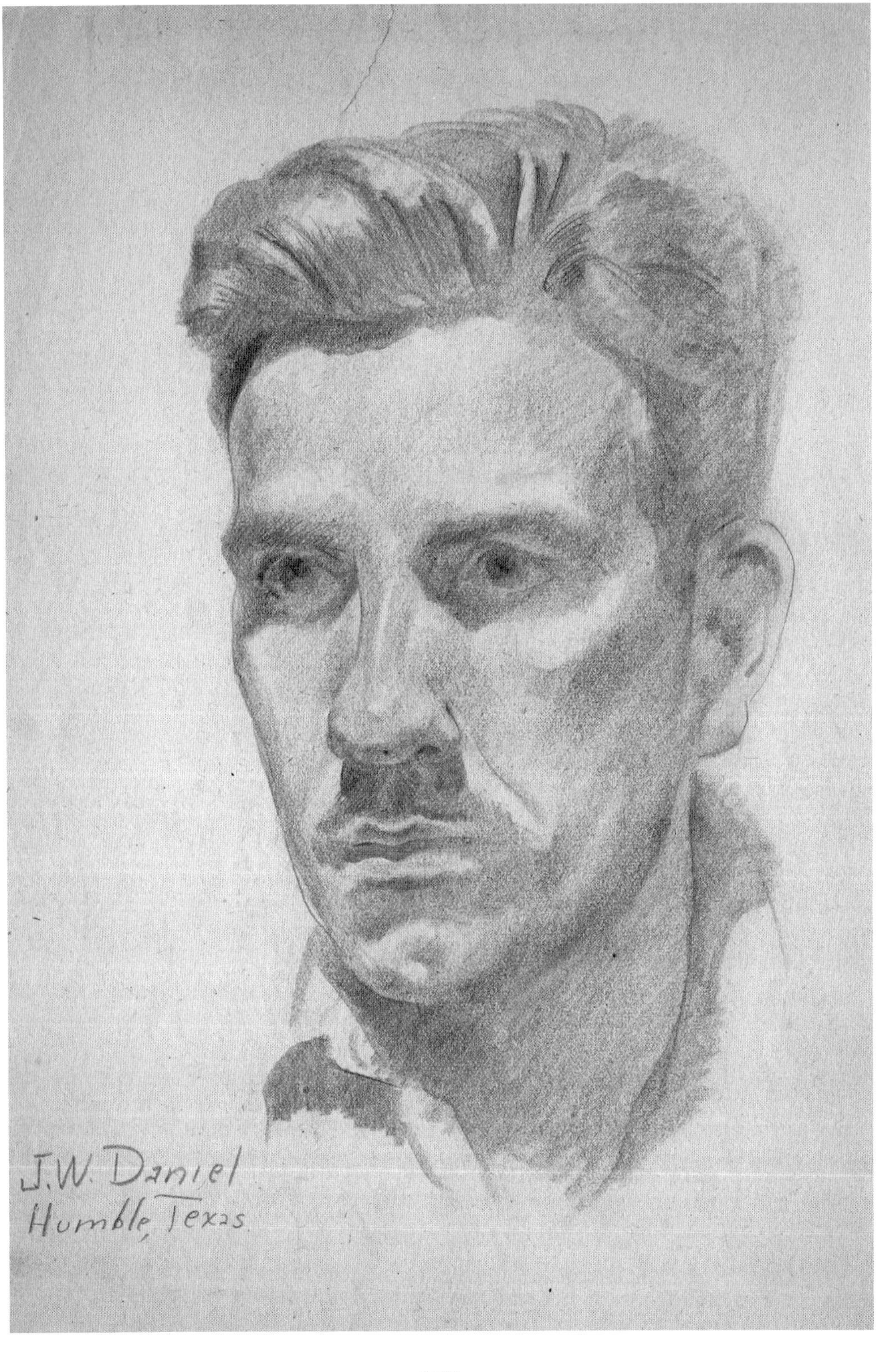

Second Lieutenant Jack W. Daniel from Humble, Texas, was a B-17 pilot shot down on his third mission on 26 July 1943 and was taken to Stalag Luft III on 12 August 1943. He was placed in South Compound, barracks 133, room 3. He was hospitalized at Hohemark, Dulag Luft, from 28 July to 6 August 1943.

He was promoted to first lieutenant on 5 January 1944. Daniel's plane was shot down by a Messerschmitt 109 fighter plane. He bailed out, landing 30 miles east of Heligoland. He was captured by the Kriegsmarine, the navy of Nazi Germany. He suffered burns on his face and right hand when his plane exploded and broke in two at the bomb bay. He lost consciousness, regaining it in the radio room. He was bombing a rubber factory in Hanover, Germany.

Colonel John C. 'Bucky' Egan, Manitowoc, Wisconsin, USA

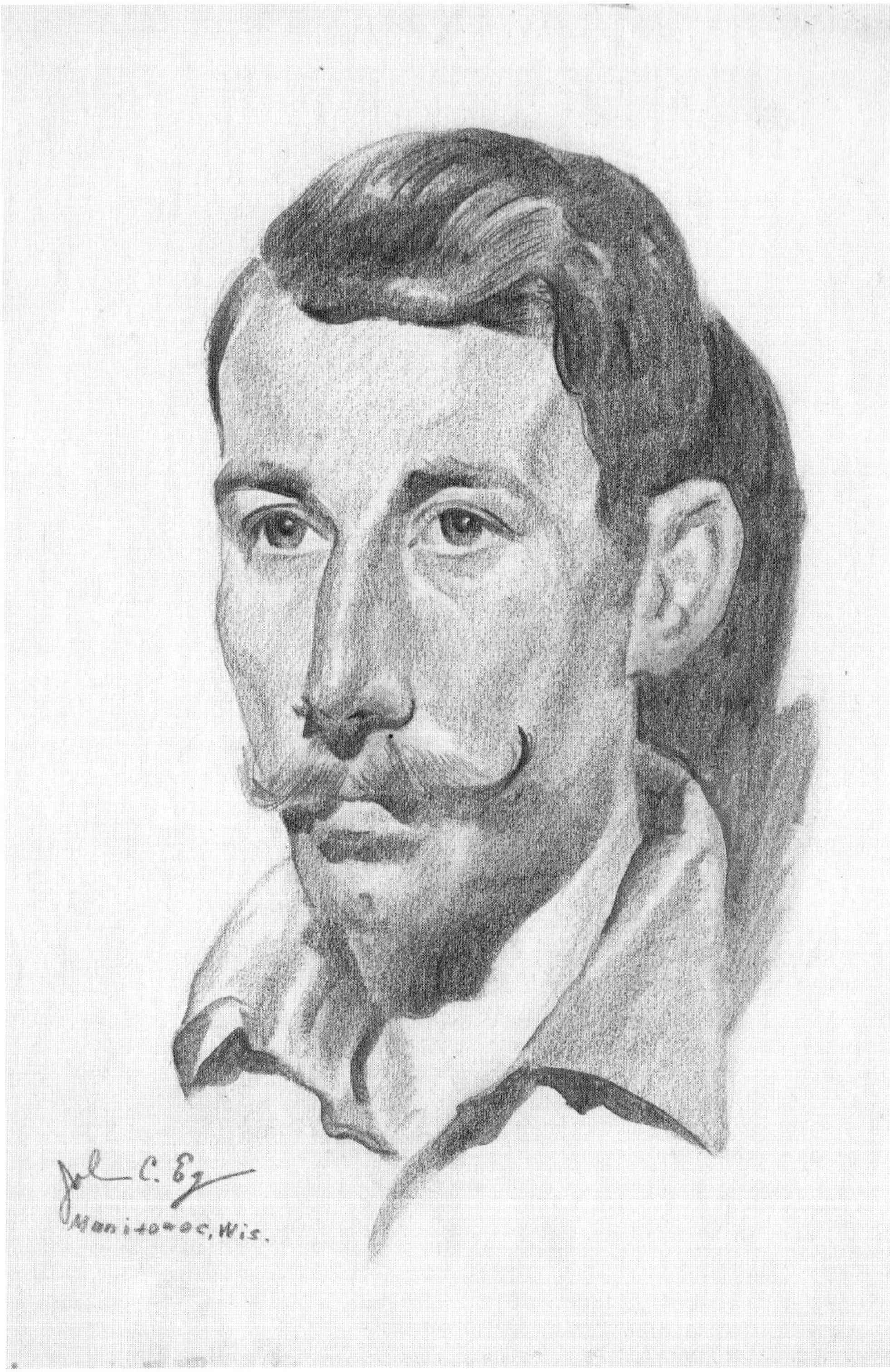

Colonel John C. 'Bucky' Egan from Manitowoc, Wisconsin, received a Bachelor of Science Degree from Georgetown University, Washington, D.C. He entered the US Army Air Force in March 1940. He flew the Münster mission on 10 November 1943 with the John Brady crew. He was one of three 'Buckies' with the 100th Bomb Group. This group was known as 'The Bloody 100th' as no other American unit sustained such heavy losses in the war.

Upon Egan's shooting down over Münster (he led the mission to avenge his friend, Gale Cleven, who was shot down two days earlier), he was sent to Stalag Luft III. When Egan arrived there, the first thing Cleven said to Egan was 'What the hell took you so long?' Egan replied: 'That's what I get for being sentimental!' Egan was Cleven's roommate in primary pilot training and they were squadron commanders in the same group, as well as roommates in the PoW camp.

Egan was shot down in France near the coast; he saw eight chutes and then his plane burst into flames. He was described as quick-witted and a very likeable individual. Egan loved his fleece-lined flying jacket and is seen wearing it in most pictures.

After the Second World War, he married and had two daughters. He continued his military service and was active in the Korean Conflict, the Far East and, in 1958, as a colonel, he was assigned duties in the headquarters of the USAF Chief's Policy Division, Directorate of Plans, DCS/Personnel. He died in April 1961 and was buried in Arlington National Cemetery with military honours.

Egan received the following awards and decorations: Distinguished Flying Cross, Air Medal with three Oak Leaf Clusters, Commendation Medal, Purple Heart, Distinguished Unit Citation, American Defense Service Medal, American Campaign Medal, European-African-Middle Eastern Campaign Medal, Second World War Victory Medal, National Defense Service Medal, United Nations Service Medal, Air Force Longevity Service Medal with three Bronze Oak Leaf Clusters, Korean Service Medal, China Service Medal and Korean Pilot Wings.

Second Lieutenant Don H. Eldridge, Chicago, Illinois, USA

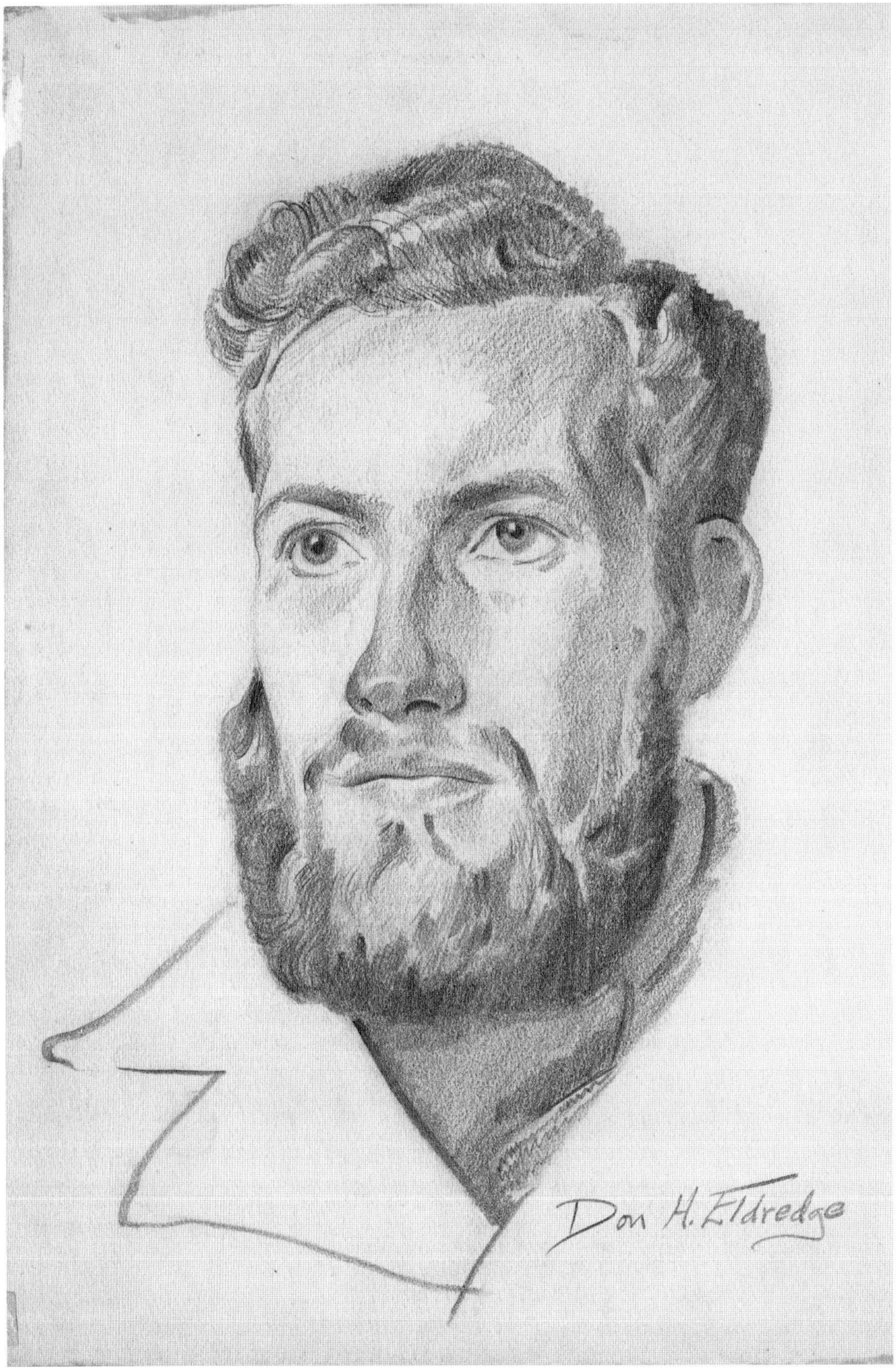

Second Lieutenant Don H. Eldridge from Chicago, Illinois, received his MBA from the University of Chicago. He served in the Army Air Corps as a B-17 pilot in the 306th Bomber Group. He was shot down on 8 November 1942 after successfully bombing submarine pens at La Pallice, France. He was a PoW for two and a half years at Stalag Luft III.

> Don H. Eldridge was a very fastidious guy. On word that they had ditched off Brest, people at our squadron joked, 'I'll bet Eldridge didn't get his feet wet!' They were right. Before the plane sank, Don stepped out the window onto the wing from the co-pilot's seat and into the life raft. One of his jobs at Stalag Luft III was to write and receive coded letters. On his recommendation, because of my newspaper background, I was taken into the program.
>
> Quote from Stalag Luft III
> PoW Joe Consolmagno

> We completed the camp theater in mid-February of 1944. It could seat 500 Kriegies, and we were very proud of our work. ...the room was always crowded with Kriegies and often Germans as well. The room was managed by Don Eldridge and Ed McMillian, and they put their hearts into providing the camp first-class facility (camp theater).
>
> Quote from *33 Months as a Prisoner of War in Stalag Luft III*
> by Lieutenant General A.P. Clark

After the war, he married and had five children. He retired after thirty-five years as a vice president of the Trade Division with the Rand-McNally Company. He died aged 88.

Second Lieutenant Paul Leo Fauerso, The Dalles, Oregon, USA

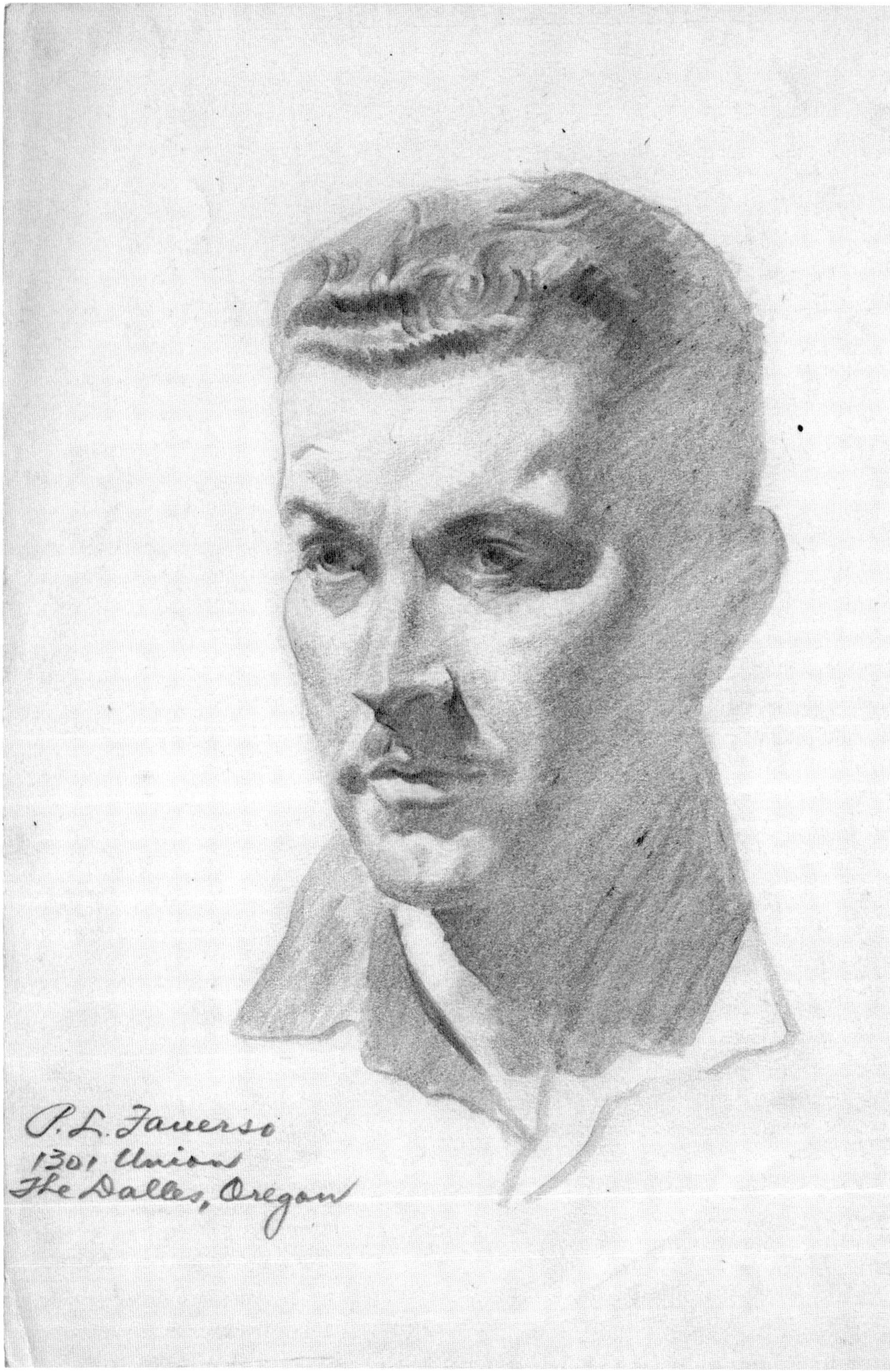

Second Lieutenant Paul Leo Fauerso from The Dalles, Oregon, was a navigator assigned to the 385th Bomber Group, 550th Squadron in 1943. He was on B-17F 'Grim Reaper' on 28 July 1943, his fifth mission, flying out of Great Ashfield, Suffolk, England. The plane was shot down 4 miles north-east of Herford, Germany. He bailed out but his parachute did not open at first. He hit the ground hard, breaking five ribs. 'I landed in a field, and when I came to, a 12-year-old boy with a bayonet was standing over me holding me captive.'

Fauerso was taken to the hospital in Bielefeld, Germany, on 28 July 1943. From there, he was taken to Dulag Luft for interrogation on 30 July 1943 and stayed there until 10 August 1943. He arrived at Stalag Luft III on 12 August 1943. He was PoW #1971, barrack 134, South Compound. Paul was the block representative for security. He sang in the Catholic choir and performed in Handel's *Messiah*, singing in his beautiful baritone voice.

On the forced evacuation march, he was so hungry that he picked up the discarded apple core of a German guard and ate it all, including a worm. Paul was liberated from Stalag VII-A in Moosburg on 29 April 1945.

After the war, he married and had two children. He joined a real estate and insurance company and later became its owner. He died on 24 March 1975, the thirty-first anniversary of 'the Great Escape'.

Second Lieutenant Francis J. Finnegan, Buffalo, New York, USA

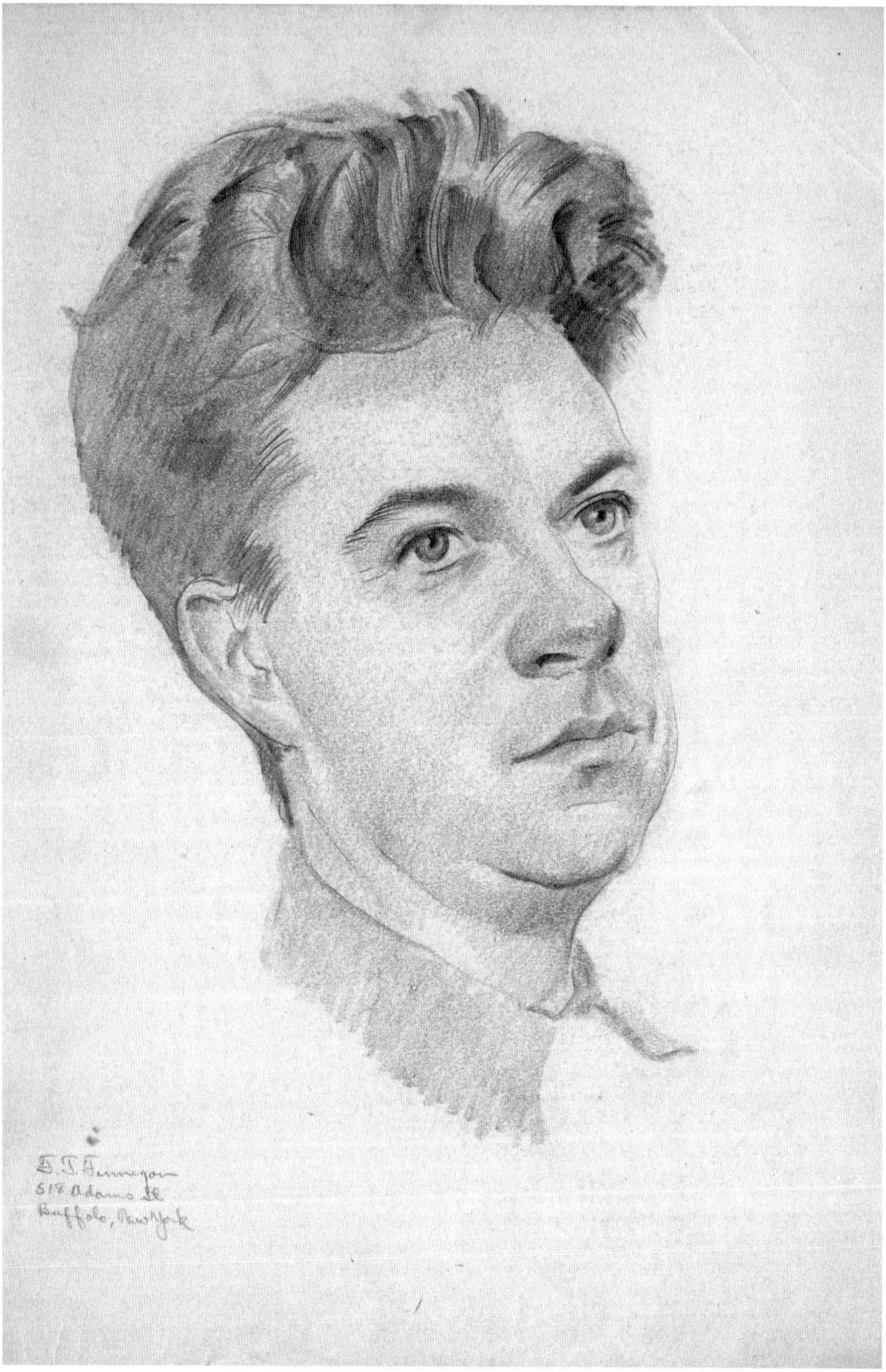

Second Lieutenant Francis J. 'Fran' Finnegan from Buffalo, New York, was a B-25 pilot with the 15th Bombardment Squadron. On his third mission, on 22 October 1942, his plane was attacked by fighters and also hit by flak (anti-aircraft fire). He crash-landed in the southern section of El Alamein, Egypt after bombing the aerodrome in El Daba, Egypt.

Finnegan was taken to Dulag Luft for interrogation, arriving at Stalag Luft III on 11 November 1942 where he headed up the code workers.

He and his crew (John Fitzpatrick, Ernie Sands, John Lindquist, Charles Woehrle, Jim Houser and Marshal Draper) were roommates who lived in South Compound, barracks 130, room 10 and stayed together on the 52-mile forced evacuation march in January 1945, sharing food and emotional support.

First Lieutenant Fred D. Gillogly, La Grange, Illinois, USA

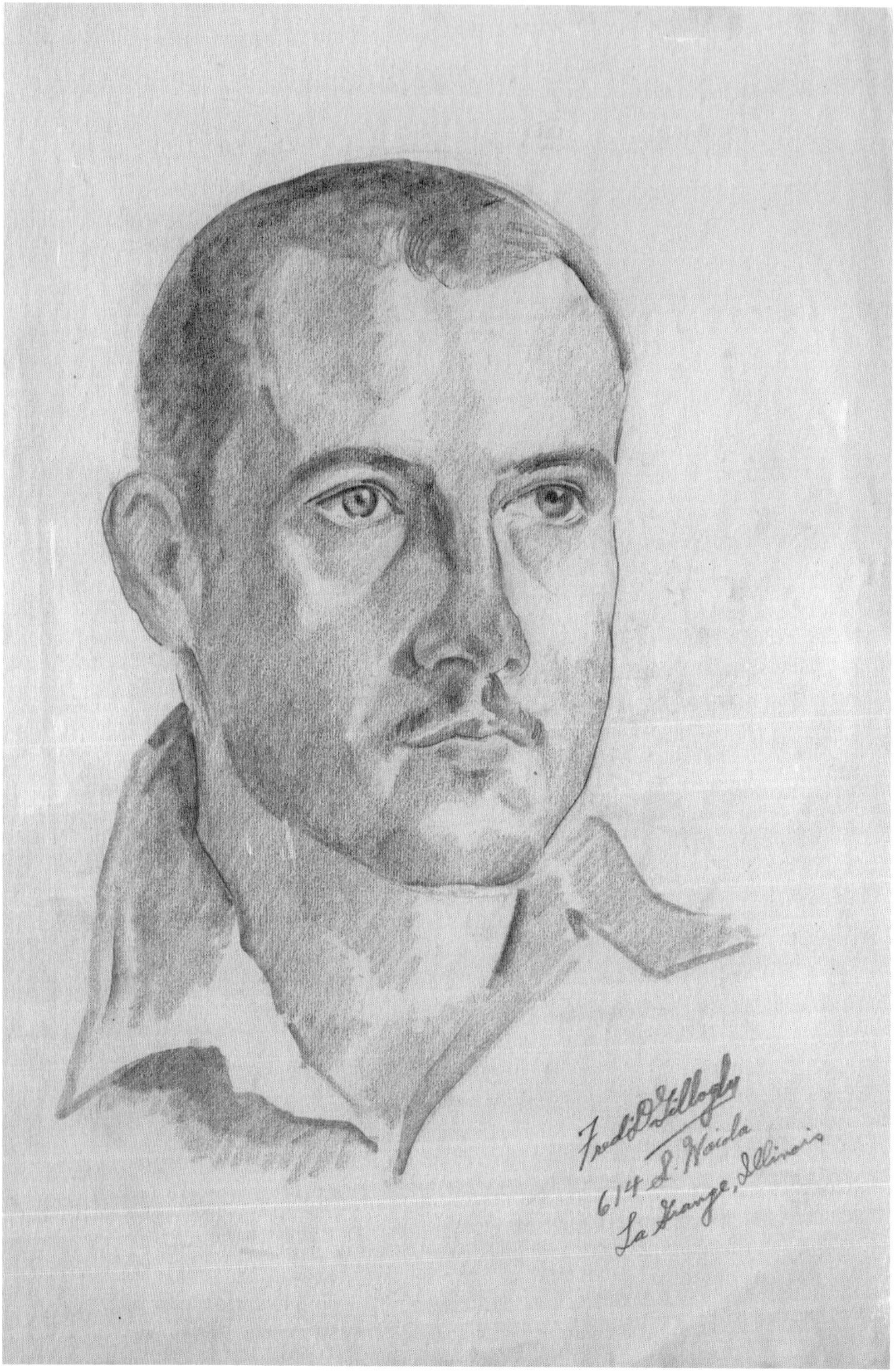

First Lieutenant Fred D. Gillogly from La Grange, Illinois, was a B-17 co-pilot with the 306th Bombardment Group 'The Reich Wreckers'. His assigned crew was Don Whipple (navigator), Carl Jones (bombardier) and John Brown (flight engineer/top turret gunner).

Gillogly was shot down on 26 April 1943 on his twenty-second mission by flak, Messerschmitt 109s and Focke-Wulf 190 fighter planes while bombing an aircraft factory in Bremen, Germany. He bailed out, landing 11 kilometres north of Oldenburg, Germany, and was captured immediately. He was taken to Dulag Luft and then to Stalag Luft III, South Compound, barracks 136, room 1, where he worked with intelligence writing coded letters:

> Following liberation, Fred and I, and Bob were pulled out of the ex-PoWs being herded to Camp Lucky Strike and diverted to Paris for debriefing on the code work. We spent eleven glorious days in off-limits liberated Paris awaiting air transport to Washington for further debriefing. On the plane home, we were the only American passengers. The others were Germans in civilian clothes, and we ignored each other.
>
> Quote from Stalag Luft III, PoW Joe Consolmagno

Colonel Charles 'Rojo' Goodrich, Augusta, Georgia, USA

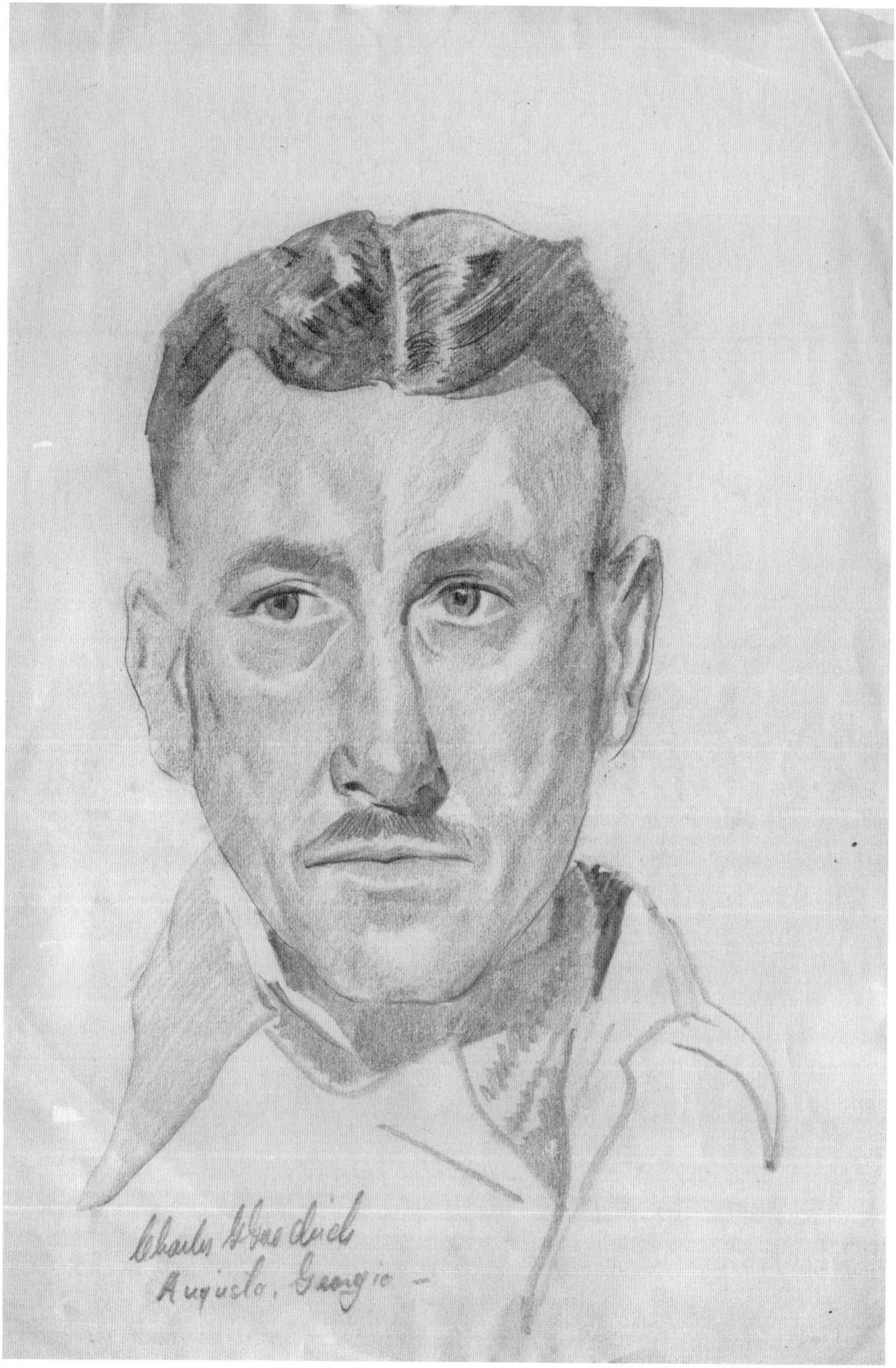

Colonel Charles 'Rojo' Goodrich, a red-headed pilot from Augusta, Georgia, was a graduate of the US Military Academy in 1929. He was the commanding officer of the 81st Bomber Squadron, 12th Bombardment Group and was shot down leading his light bomber group on a night mission over Benghazi, Libya, on 14 September 1942. He was severely injured as he went out of the top hatch of the plane above the pilot's cabin as the plane was on fire. He was severely injured with a torn shoulder, fractured spine and internal injuries requiring abdominal surgery. Goodrich was hospitalized in four facilities due to the extent of his injuries. He was treated at Mersa Matruh in the Mediterranean, at Freising, in Hohemark Hospital at Dulag Luft and at Oflag XXI-B.

As a full colonel, Goodrich automatically became the Senior American Officer when he arrived in the recently-opened North Compound, outranking Lieutenant Colonel Clark, who had been serving as SAO. Goodrich was consulted in matters of camp policy, which was extensive as the Americans participated in every camp activity and organization. Directly under him were the members of the Executive Staff and the barracks chiefs or block commanders. He was a taciturn man who had little use for the Germans and his camp reflected his attitude. He was highly respected and used his staff well. One of his oft-heard and most recognizable admonitions was 'Things will get worse before they get better.'

After the war, he married and had a daughter. Colonel Goodrich made a career in the US Air Force and retired in 1955. He died on 29 November 1987.

First Lieutenant Raymond Kite Grim,
Olympia, Washington, USA

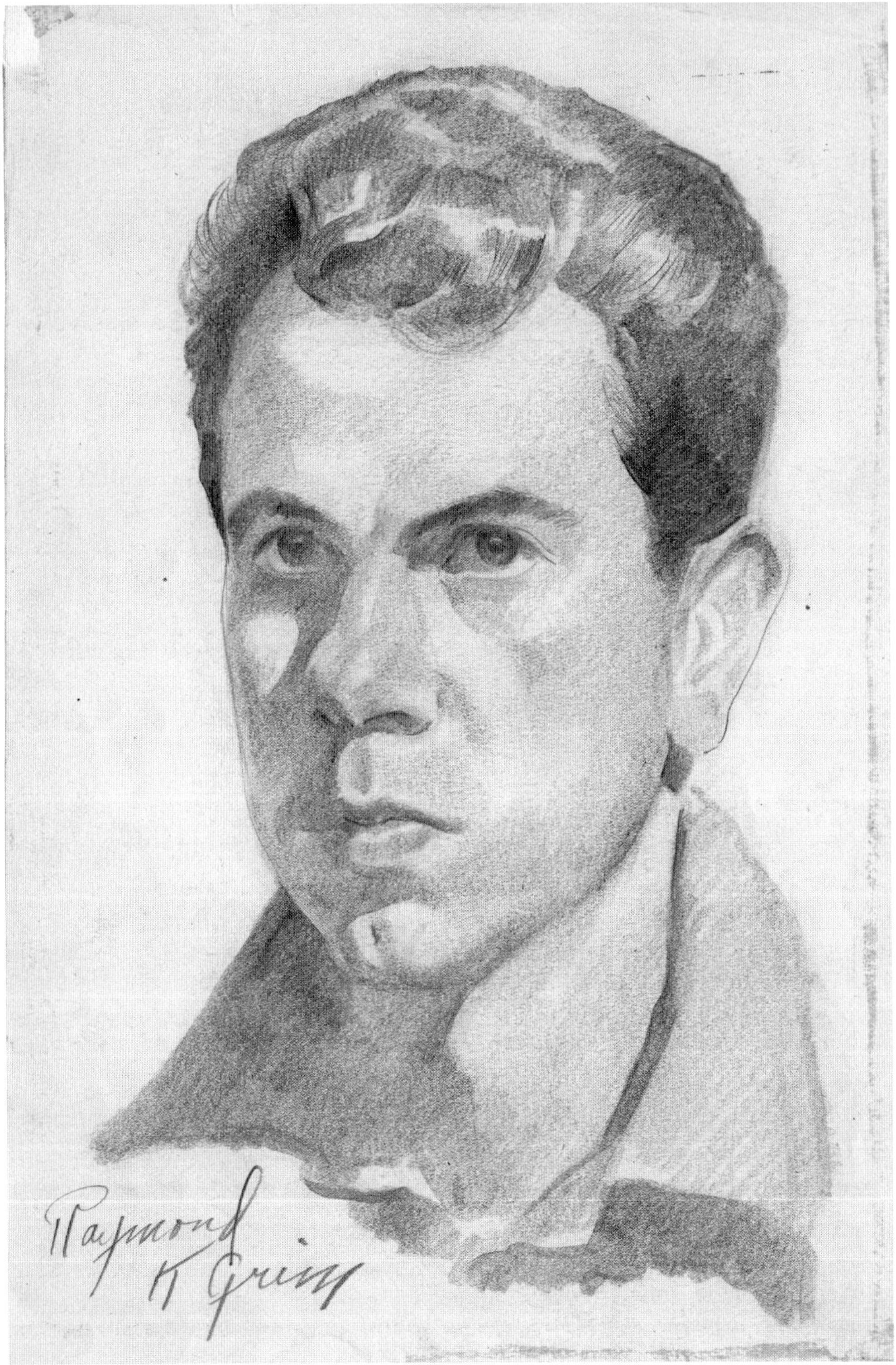

First Lieutenant Raymond Kite 'Ray' Grim from Olympia, Washington, was a B-17 pilot. He was on his twenty-second mission when he was shot down in January 1943 by flak midway between Sousse and Sfax, Tunis. He was captured immediately by Italians assisted by Arabs, interrogated at Dulag Luft and transferred to Oflag XXI-B before going to Stalag Luft III, South Compound, barracks 129, room 11 on 15 April 1943.

While in the service of the US Army Air Force, he was awarded the Purple Heart. He died on 23 October 1990.

Major 'Hal' Houston, Dundalk, Maryland, USA

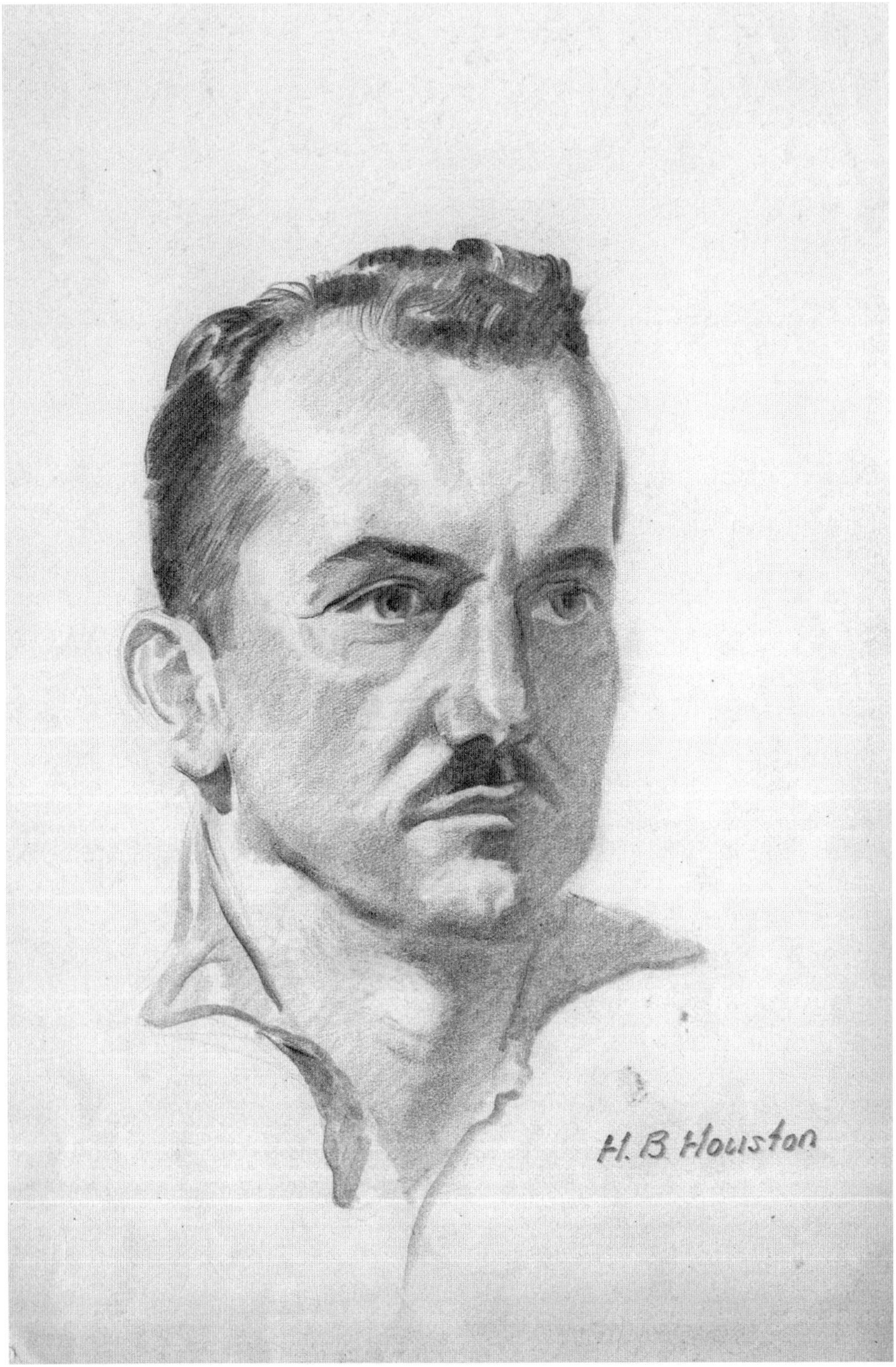

Major 'Hal' Houston from Dundalk, Maryland, was a Group Intelligence Officer who had 'gone along for the ride' on a night raid in the aircraft of his Group Commander, Colonel Charles 'Rojo' Goodrich, based in Egypt. They were shot down by flak over Sidi Haneish, Egypt, and Houston was injured. He went to Dulag Luft from 21 September to 1 October 1942. When he arrived at Stalag Luft III, he was hospitalized until 17 November 1942. Houston was one of the earliest American PoWs to arrive at Stalag Luft III.

After time in the hospital, he roomed with Lieutenant Colonel Clark for the remainder of their stay in East Compound. Houston proved to be a skilled administrative officer and help to the adjutants for the rest of the war. He died on 26 February 2011.

Captain Bill 'Casey' Jones, Parkton, Maryland, USA

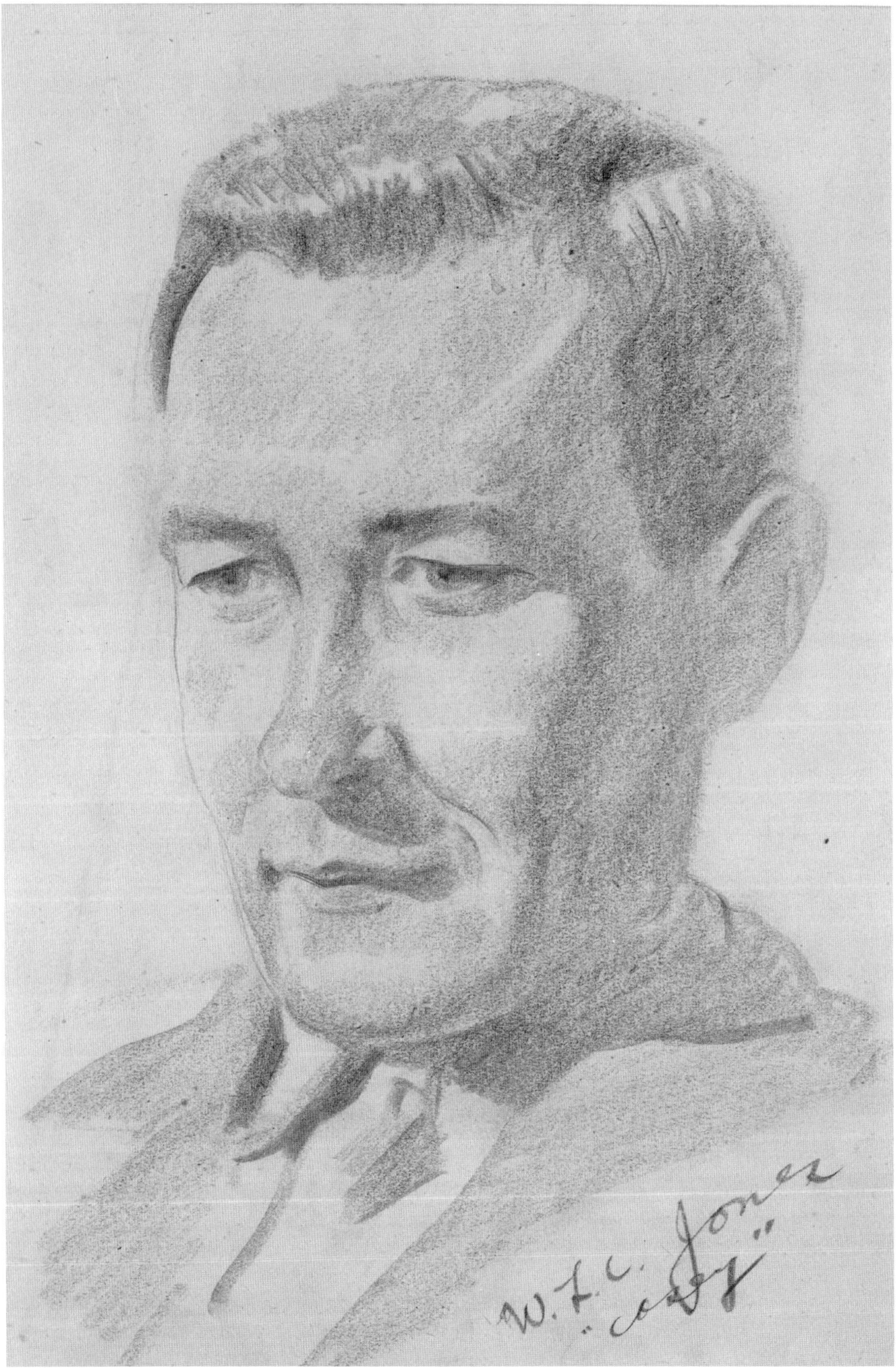

Captain Bill 'Casey' Jones from Parkton, Maryland, was a fighter pilot transferred to England as part of the Second Eagle Squadron of the Royal Air Force (RAF) comprising American flyers who had volunteered to fight for England against Germany early in the war. He had made thirty combat missions and reached the rank of captain before being shot down in March 1942 over St. Omer, France by Messerschmitt 109s as a sweep escort to Lille, France. He spent twenty-two days in the cooler at Dulag Luft and after interrogation was sent to Oflag XXI-B and Stalag Luft III.

During the planning of the Great Escape, Jones was 'on the list to go' when he was sent to a new compound. He was never put on a list again, for it was decided that because he was an American RAF pilot, his knowledge made him more valuable inside the prison than out.

Second Lieutenant Henry H. 'Hank' Keller, New Kensington, Pennsylvania, USA

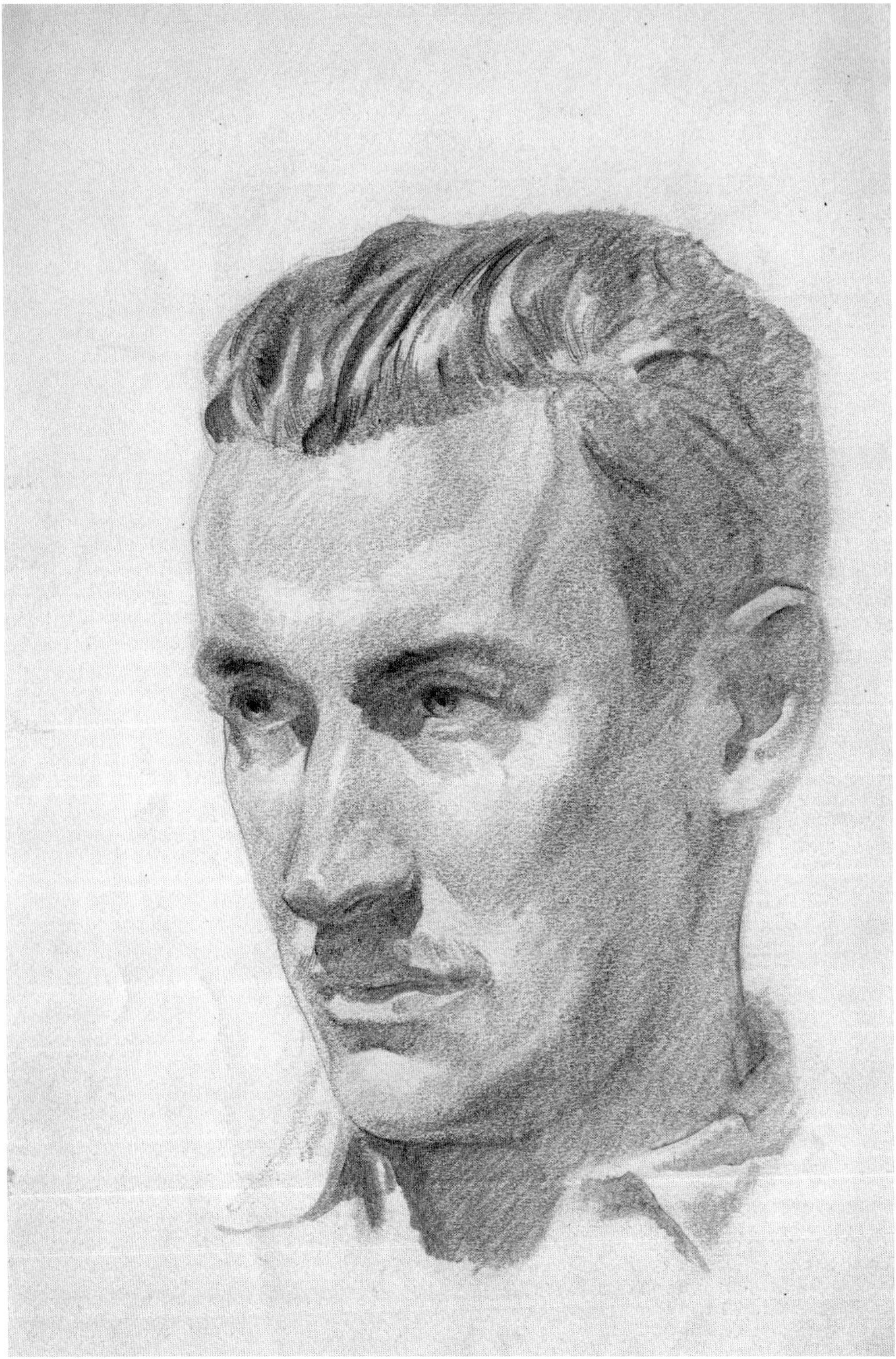

Second Lieutenant Henry H. 'Hank' Keller from New Kensington, Pennsylvania, was a B-17 navigator. He was shot down on 4 January 1943, making an emergency landing behind enemy lines 30 miles north-west of Gabes, Tunisia. He was captured the next day and interrogated at Dulag Luft, went to Oflag XXI-B and then to Stalag Luft III, arriving on 16 April 1943 in South Compound, barracks 136, room 9.

First Lieutenant Harold Korger, Eau Claire, Wisconsin, USA

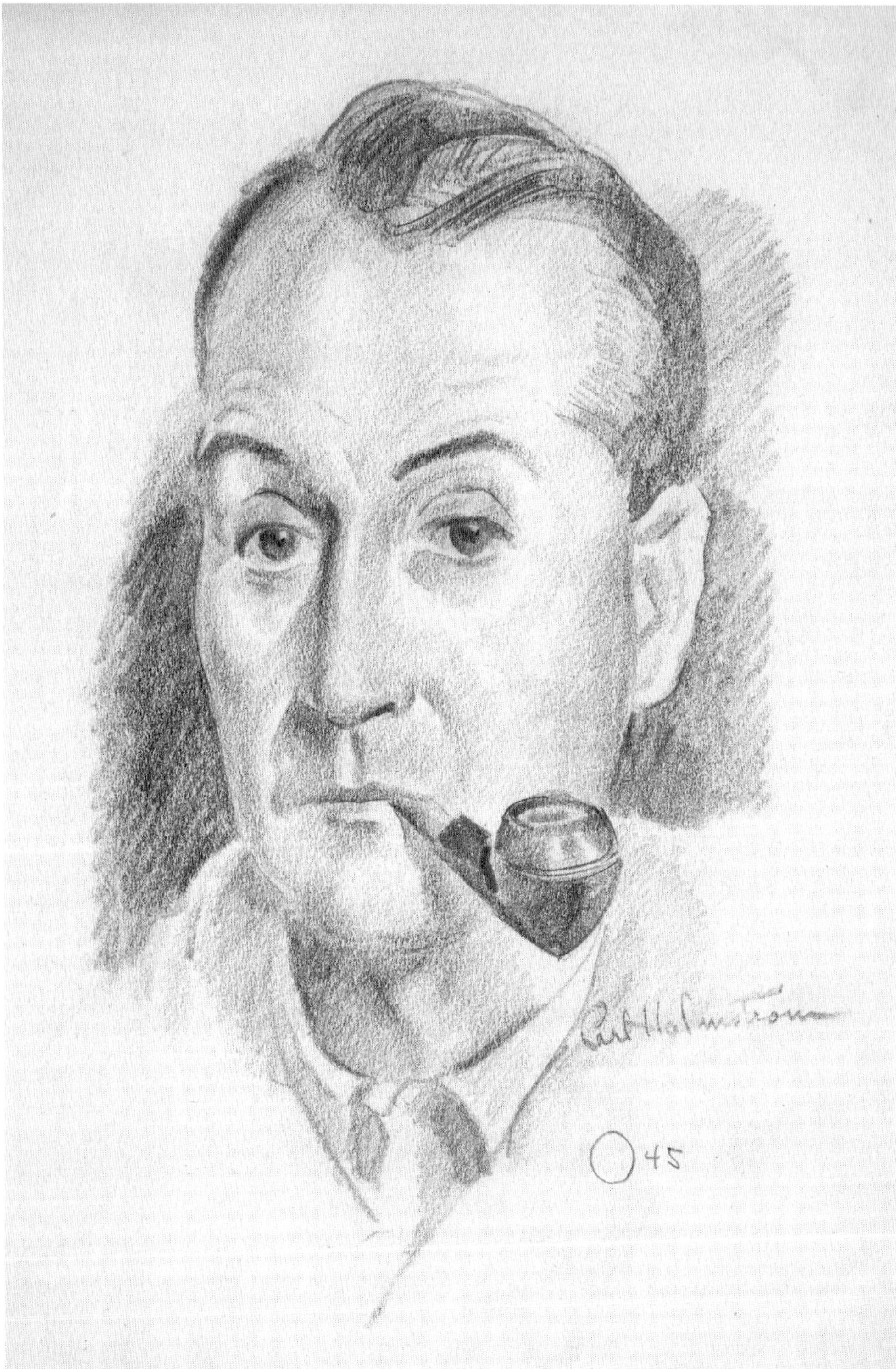

First Lieutenant Harold Korger from Eau Claire, Wisconsin, graduated from Eau Claire State Teachers College and the University of Wisconsin. He enlisted in the Army Air Corps and was a B-24 bombardier with the 98th Bomber Group. In August 1943, he flew on the Ploesti Raid to Romania to bomb the oil refineries. He was on the crew of the lead ship of legendary Colonel John 'Killer' Kane who was a recipient of the Congressional Medal of Honor. The battle lasted twenty minutes. 'We muddled through the fighter attack and staggered away from the target on two and a half engines.' On the return trip, the plane, 'Hail Columbia', was forced to make a crash-landing in the Mediterranean near the island of Cyprus.

On 3 September 1943, Harry flew his thirtieth mission, which he thought would be his last before going home. Korger was given the option of flying home and doing a war bond tour, but he decided that he should finish his missions. On the way to the target, his B-24 plane 'Big Operator' was attacked by Messerschmitt 110s and Junkers 88s. They were hit several times and went into a flat spin. Korger was shot down over Sulmona, Italy. Four of the crew were killed. Harry was injured.

In a letter he sent home, he wrote:

> I saw old friends crash to a flaming death before my eyes. The Jerries were throwing up everything at us. Our plane was shot to shreds but, by sheer flying skill, Col. Kane got us out.... My bombs hit dead center on my target and we wiped the place out. Then the fighters jumped us and more of our friends went down, but they took at least four or five Jerries down with them for every one of us.

In other letters, he told of the raids on Rome and on the Messerschmitt aircraft factory near Vienna, Austria, in which he participated.

Harry was awarded two Distinguished Flying Crosses with one Oak Leaf Cluster, the Air Medal with four Oak Leaf Clusters and the Purple Heart. One of his DFCs was earned for Ploesti. In the next few months, Harry was transferred by the Italians and spent time in Stalag VII-A, Oflag 64 and Stalag Luft I at Barth, Germany, where he was choir director of the Kriegie Glee Club, one of the most important entertainment and morale-boosting factors in camp. It was thirty-six men strong and put on five king-size shows.

Later, an orchestra was added to the Glee Club. It consisted of twelve pieces: four saxes/clarinets, three trumpets, guitar, bass fiddle, piano, drums and a trombone. Several of the members had played with big name bands in the United States. Korger felt that the biggest drawback was the lack of music. He had to arrange most of his own music and did all the arrangements from memory as he had been a high school band director before the war. He wrote a ballad *All Through the Night* and a march *Kriegies on Parade*. Korger was liberated from Stalag Luft I by the Russians on 1 May 1945.

After the war, he married and had three children. He continued his career in the military and was assigned commander of the 725th Strategic Missile Squadron at Lowry Air Force Base, Colorado. The squadron was a unit of the Strategic Air Command's 451st Strategic Missile Wing.

Second Lieutenant Alexander Kramarinko,
Chicago, Illinois, USA

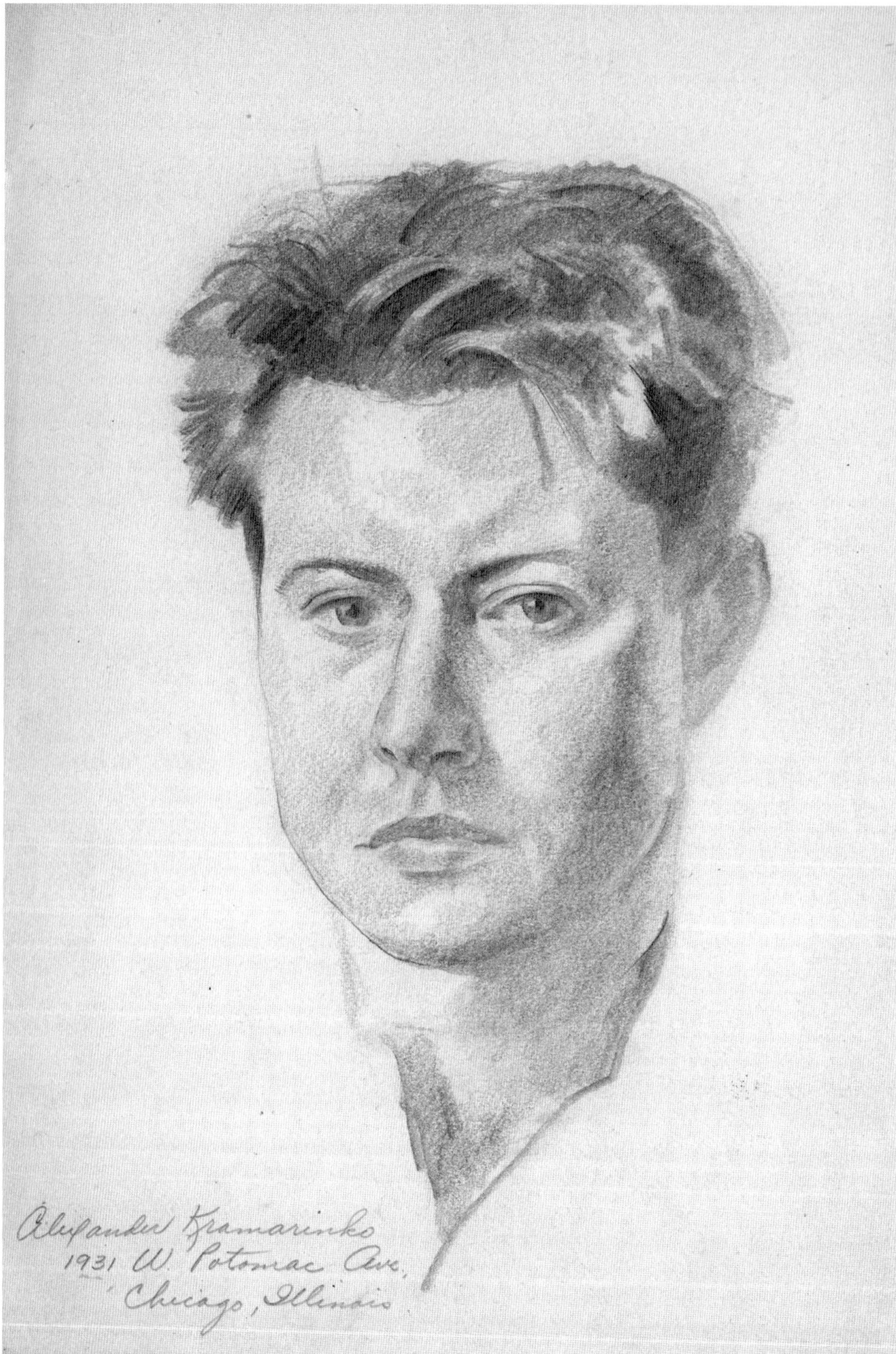

Second Lieutenant Alexander Kramarinko from Chicago, Illinois, was nicknamed 'Russ' and 'Rush' because he was of Russian descent. He was co-pilot of the B-17 'Meltin' Pot', 306th Bomber Group/368th Bomb Squadron. While flying from the US to the UK, mechanical problems forced the plane down, and it crashed on 12 September 1942 into the Irish Sea off the coast of Scotland.

On 5 April 1943, he was co-pilot of B-17 'Montana Power' shot down on his eighth mission by Focke-Wulf 190s on a mission to bomb the ERLA Works in Antwerp, Belgium. The plane crashed near de Klein Schietveld, just south of the Heikantstraat, Belgium. Kramarinko bailed out over Loenhout, Belgium, with fellow crew member, left waist gunner, Staff Sergeant William E. Baker. They were helped all the way to Bordeaux by 17-year-old Henri Kuypers of Loenhout.

About seven weeks after bailing out, both men, while evading, were 2 miles across the Spanish border when they were captured. Kramarinko was held in the notorious Fresnes Prison in Paris, sent to Dulag Luft and later to Stalag Luft III, arriving on 13 June 1943, where he was very ill for weeks. He was held in South Compound, barracks 132, room 7.

After liberation from Stalag VII-A, he travelled east to contact his Russian general father. Kramarinko changed his name after the war and lived in the United States. He was an Air Medal recipient.

First Lieutenant Thomas E. Logan, Wichita, Kansas, USA

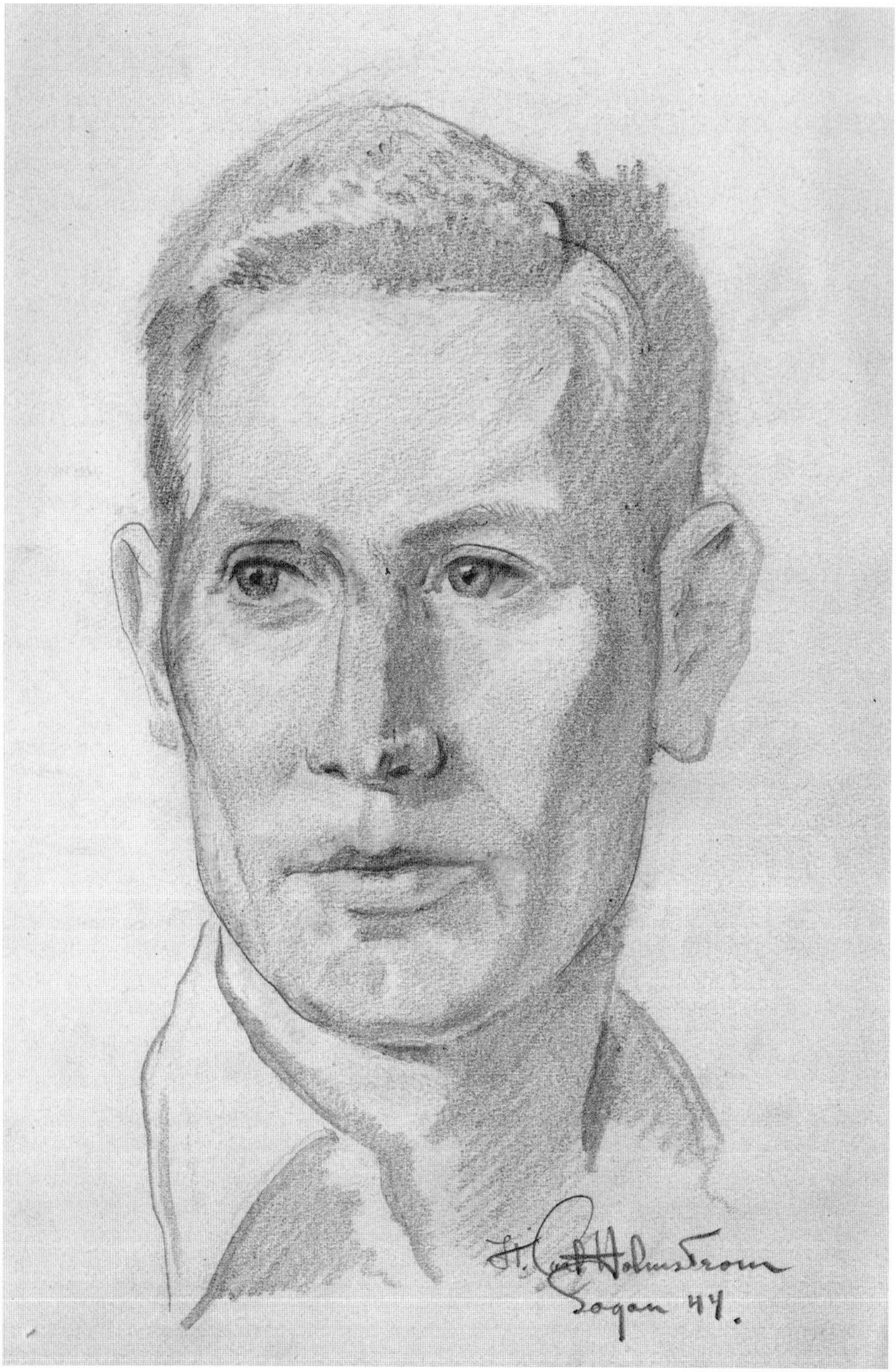

First Lieutenant Thomas E. Logan from Wichita, Kansas, was a B-17 pilot shot down on 25 June 1943 by Focke-Wulf 190s on his eleventh mission bombing the docks in Hamburg. Flak was heavy at Bremen. Lieutenant Logan's plane was hit hard before reaching his target, with the No. 3 engine taking the most punishment. His controls were destroyed and he bailed out, landing 40 miles south-west of Oldenburg, Germany.

Logan was captured immediately by the Home Guard and taken to Dulag Luft and Stalag Luft III on 3 July 1943, where he lived in South Compound. He was an Air Medal recipient.

First Lieutenant Russell K. Lyons, Beverly Hills, California, USA

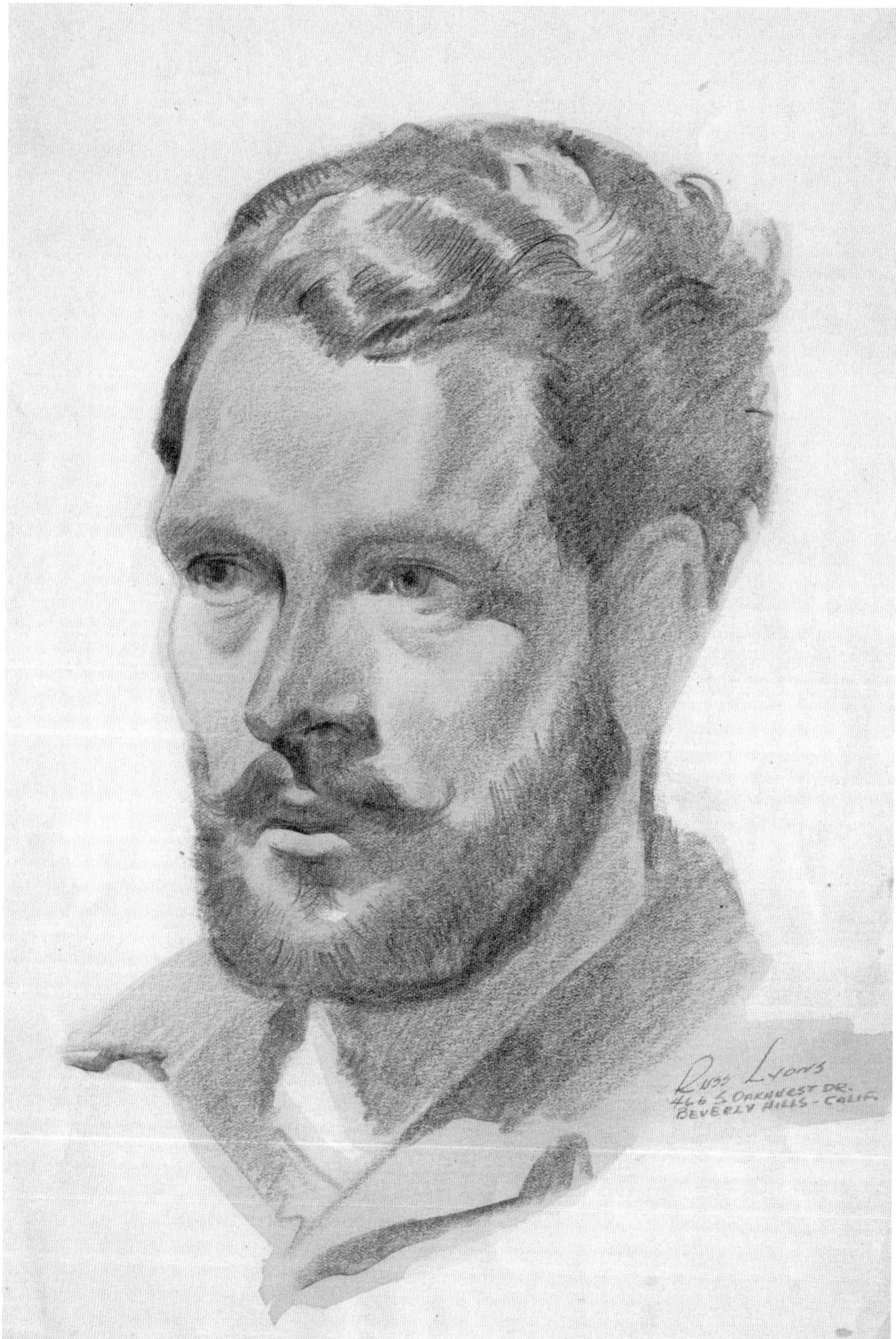

First Lieutenant Russell K. 'Russ' Lyons from Beverly Hills, California, was a P-39 pilot. He was shot down on 13 March 1943 over North Africa and taken to 'the cooler' in Tunis. He had been downed by Messerschmitt 109s 15 miles north of Sidi Bou Said, Tunisia. He crash-landed among hostile Arabs and was captured by the Germans on 14 March 1943. Lyons had been bombing the aerodrome near Mazzouna, Tunisia, on his fifteenth mission.

Lyons was interrogated at Dulag Luft, transferred to Stalag Luft III and placed in South Compound, barracks 133, room 1, becoming a roommate of Carl's. Lyons' image was used for several of the drawings in the section on 'Camp Life' in this book.

Pilot Officer Irven Granger McDaniel, Hot Springs, Arkansas, USA

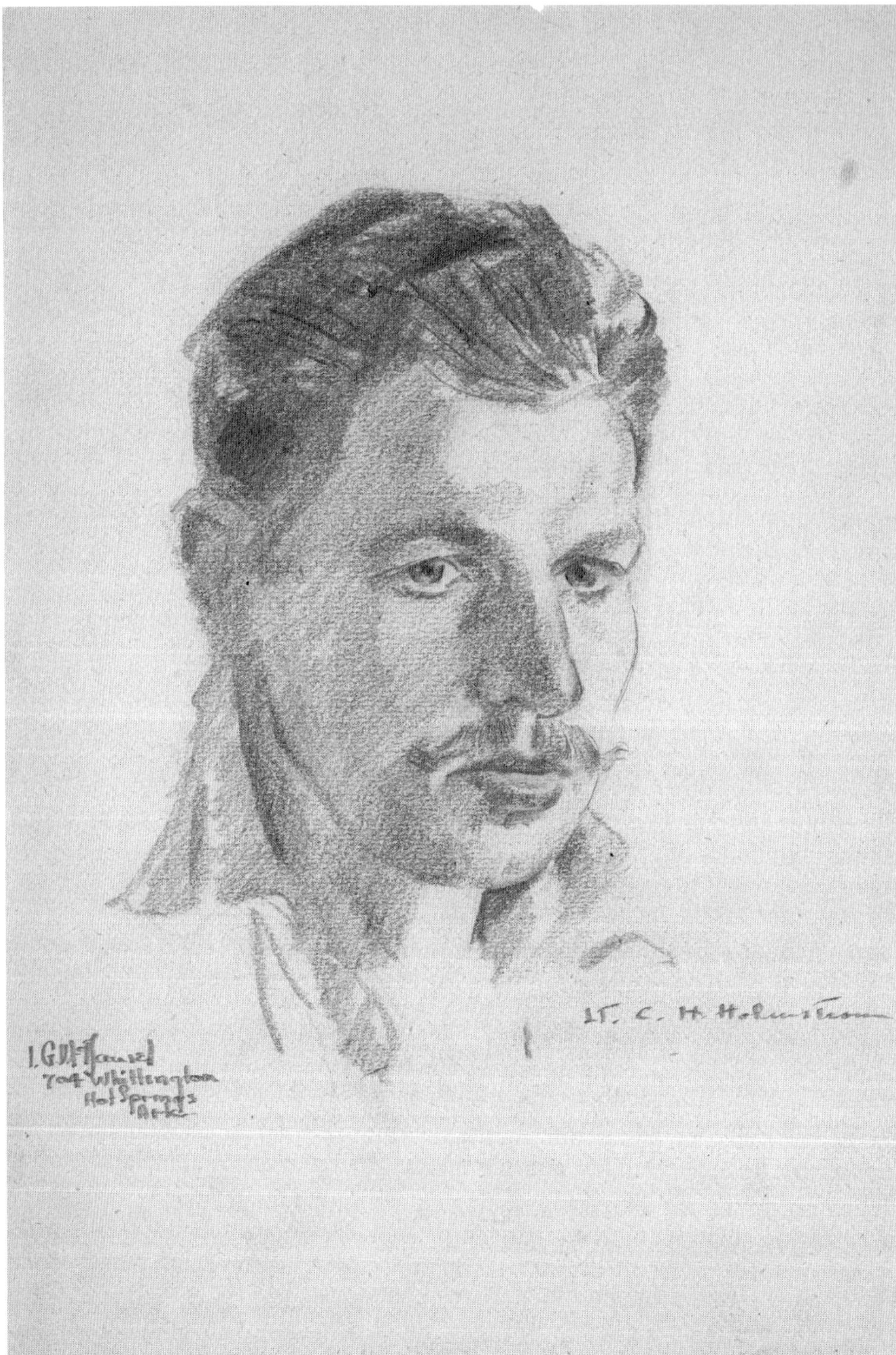

Irven Granger McDaniel from Hot Springs, Arkansas, was a pilot officer for the RAF VR (Volunteer Reserve). At age 17, it is believed he left high school in order to study architecture, but ended up joining the Royal Canadian Air Force. He trained on Vickers Wellingtons at No. 12 Operational Training Unit based at RAF Chipping Warden before posting to No. 1651 Conversion Unit at RAF Waterbeach on 23 June 1942.

McDaniel's first operation on 13 July 1942 was in the second pilot role to Sergeant Sidney Falconer DFM (Distinguished Flying Medal). The crew was briefed to attack Duisburg. They successfully bombed the target, dropping their bomb load with the aid of illuminating flares. Weather conditions were fine, giving the crew the opportunity to view a number of fires in the target area.

McDaniel's first and last operation was undertaken on 18 August 1942. The target was the important coastal port of Flensburg. After a night bombing mission, the crew was attacked by German pilot *Unteroffizier* Friedel Krause over the North Sea west of Esbjerg. Such was the damage to the aircraft that he was forced to ditch the plane. McDaniel, air bomber Sergeant Carly Arthur Powell RNZAF and mid-upper gunner Sergeant William managed to enter the Stirling's dinghy.

After four days afloat in the dinghy, the Danish fishing boat E28 *Dania* out of Esbjerg chanced upon the crew about 40 miles out to sea off the coast of Denmark. The *Dania*'s skipper, Marinus Christensen, pulled alongside the dinghy and took the bedraggled airmen aboard. When the *Dania* reached the German *Vorpostenboot* (VP-boat), her home port in the shipping route off Skallingen, a German patrol launch met the vessel and three German Kriegsmarines boarded and kept guard until the ship had entered Esbjerg's harbour. The German sailors handed the men over to the Luftwaffe.

McDaniel was interrogated at Dulag Luft and then sent to Stalag Luft III on 10 September 1942. He spent four years in various PoW camps. In the camp he was an accomplished forger and was an expert at making stamps out of rubber boot heels to print German insignia on forged documents. He received the nickname 'The Cooler King' for his ongoing escape attempts and was the model for the Steve McQueen character in the 1963 film *The Great Escape*. McDaniel finally made a successful escape in 1943, making his way to the Russian lines and eventually linking up with American forces.

After the war, Granger returned to Hot Springs, Arkansas, married and had three children. He took up design with his father and returned to architecture. His daughter said: 'My father was determined to continue the family business of architecture while in the PoW camp where he had gotten lucky and met a famous old Polish architect. My father went on to become a well-known designer in America and often times credited this man for his influence.' He died on 7 May 1978 in Boca Raton, Florida.

First Lieutenant Robert C. Miller, Chicago, Illinois, USA

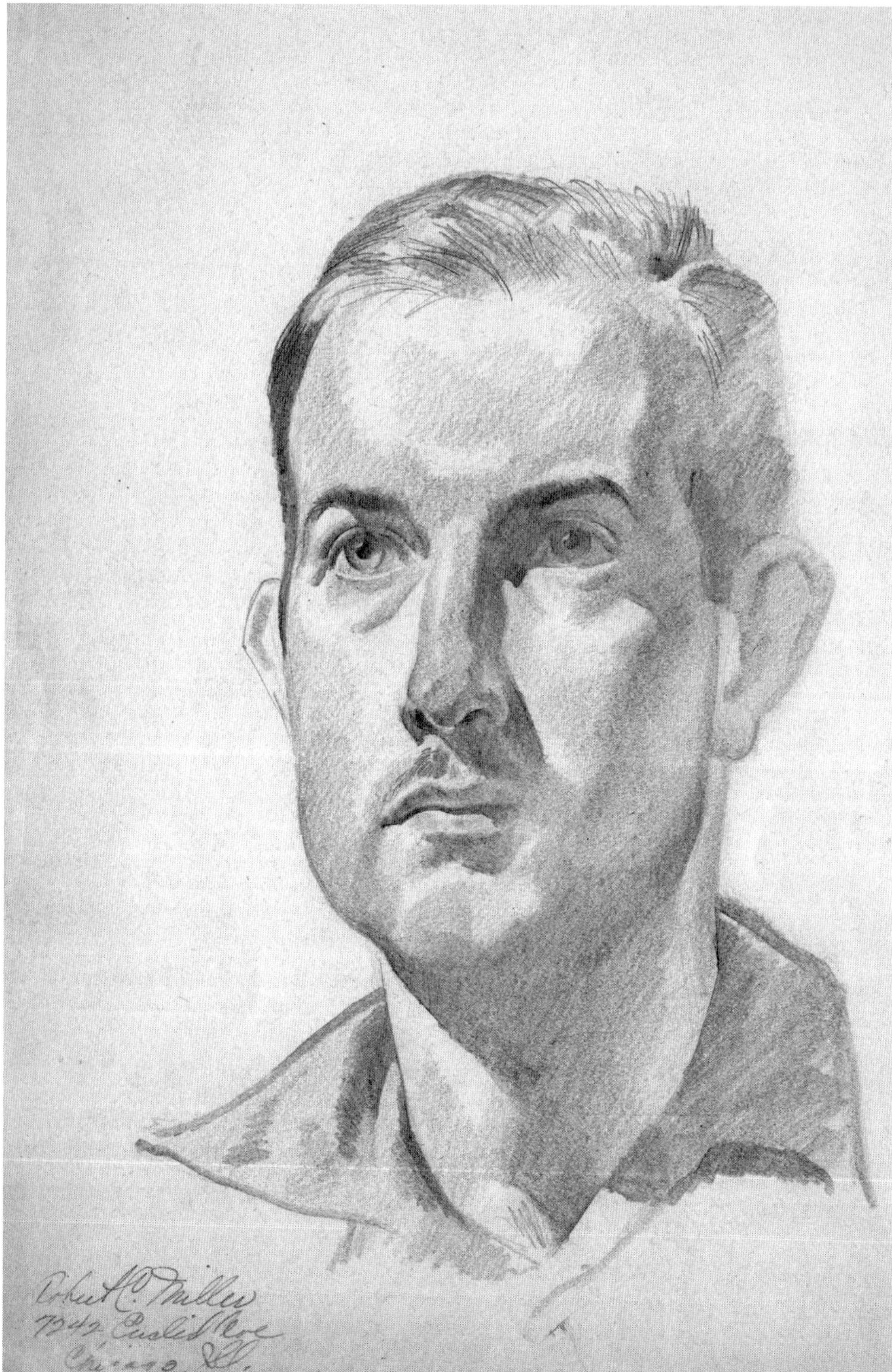

First Lieutenant Robert C. Miller from Chicago, Illinois, was a B-17 pilot. He was shot down on 17 April 1943 by flak and Focke-Wulf 190s and was the sole survivor of his crew. It was his twenty-third mission.

He bailed out and landed 20 miles from Oldenburg, Germany, and was captured immediately. Miller had been bombing a Focke-Wulf factory in Bremen. After interrogation at Dulag Luft, he was transferred to Stalag Luft III on 2 May 1943 and lived in South Compound, barracks 136, room 1.

He received the Air Medal with two Oak Leaf Clusters.

Second Lieutenant Woodrow 'Woodie' Moore, Baltimore, Maryland, USA

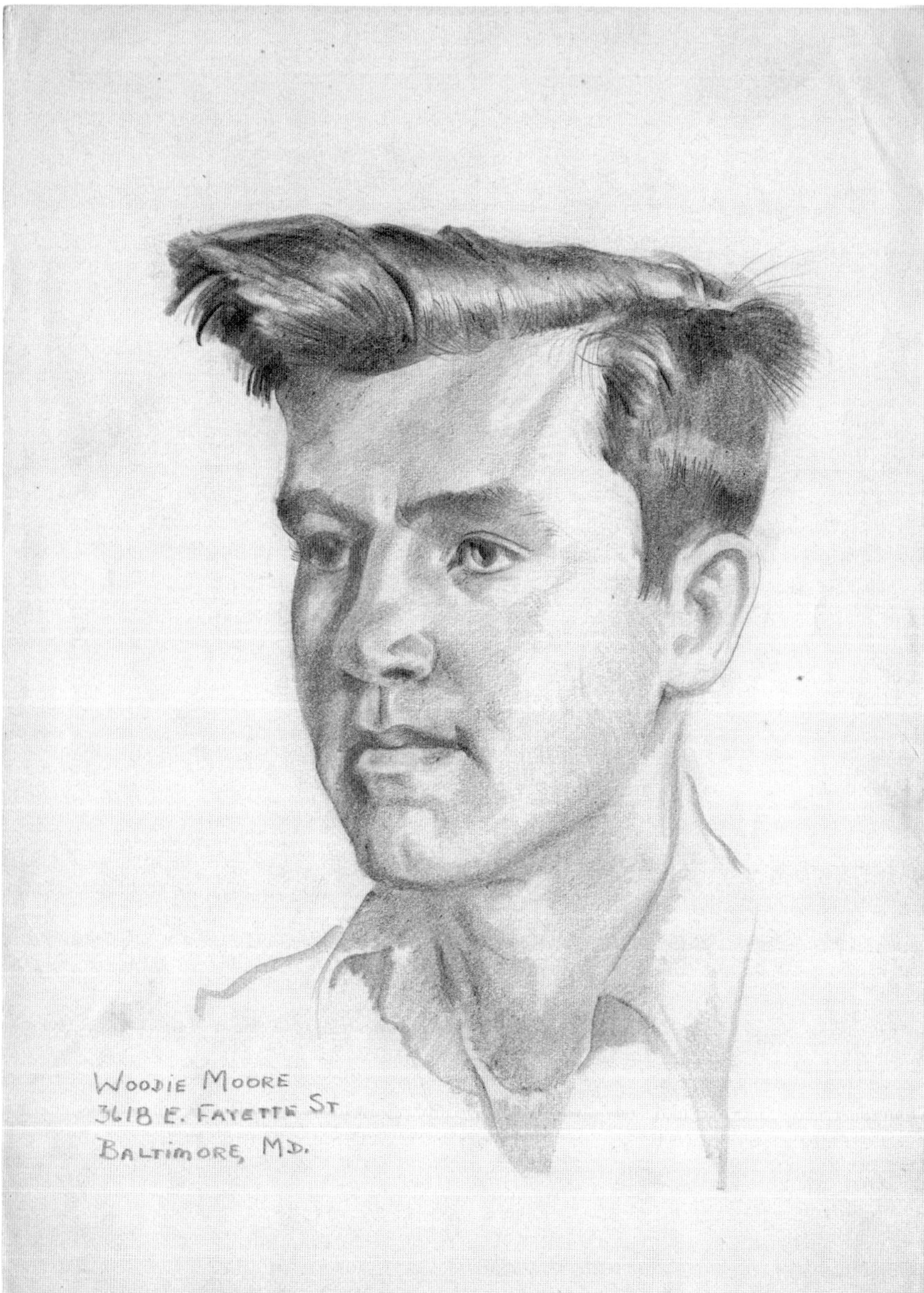

Second Lieutenant Woodrow 'Woodie' Moore from Baltimore, Maryland, was a B-17 navigator shot down on 29 May 1943 by flak and Focke-Wulf 190s while bombing the submarine pens at St. Nazaire, France on his first mission. He bailed out and landed 30 miles north-west of Rennes, France. His tail gunner shot down one of the Focke-Wulf 190s. Moore injured his left knee and was treated at a Luftwaffe *Lazarett* at Clichy Hospital in Paris. He was held in South Compound at Stalag Luft III.

> Lieutenant 'Woodie' P. Moore and Lieutenant Marsten were the officers in charge of the physiotherapy room. They put heat to Kriegies' aching backs. 'Woodie' learned the business while taking treatments for an injured leg. A Kriegie could get on his list and onto one of his tables only by appointment.
>
> Quote from *Clipped Wings*

After returning from the war, Moore earned a degree in mathematics from Loyola College and a law degree from the University of Baltimore. He married and had two sons. He worked for the federal government for thirty-two years. He died on 1 November 2015 in St. Augustine, Florida, at 97 years of age.

First Lieutenant Frank M. 'Tex'/'Hoss' Newton, Cleveland, Ohio, USA

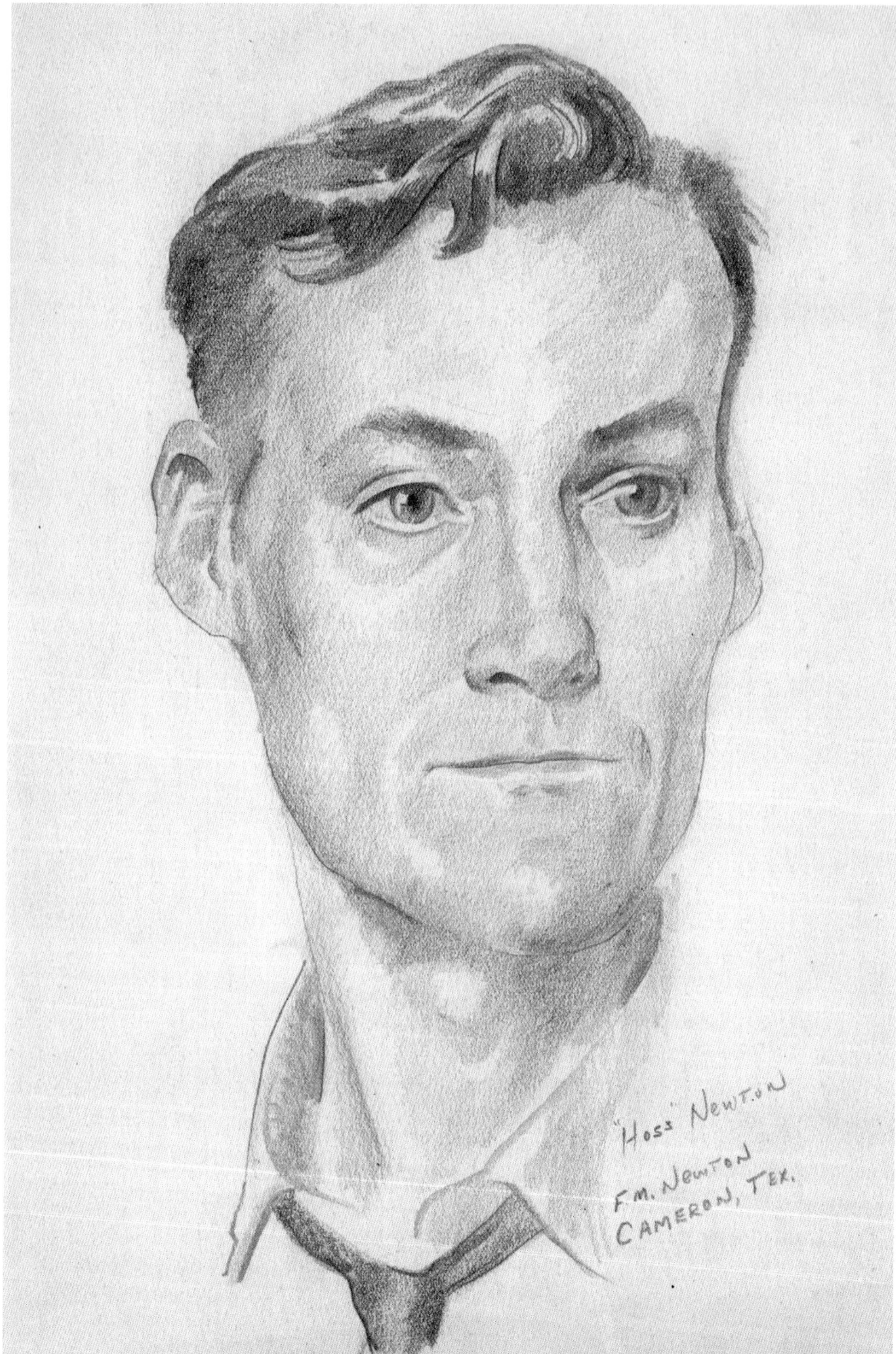

First Lieutenant Frank M. 'Tex'/'Hoss' Newton from Cleveland, Ohio, was the nineteenth PoW to be sent to Stalag Luft III, North Compound on 9 November 1942. He was a pilot shot down by Messerschmitt 110 fighter planes off Gavdos, Crete, in the Mediterranean. He had ditched his aircraft in the sea and lost half his crew and then swam to shore. He went to Dulag Luft from 9 March to 9 August 1942 and arrived at Stalag Luft III from the hospital on 9 October 1942. He was a Purple Heart recipient.

He was also a talented country music fiddler and throughout the war he made important contributions to the morale of the camp. As an early PoW, he was sent to West Compound to help get it organized when it opened in April 1944. He served thirty-two months as a prisoner of war.

After the war, he married and had two children. Following his discharge from the Air Corps, he received his BA at Baylor University, his BD at Southwestern Seminary and went on to become a minister of the gospel. He was a pastor of churches in California, Texas and Heidelberg, Germany. Frank's greatest joy was nurturing a small 'mission' into a full church family. He died on 25 September 2007 at 91 years of age.

Second Lieutenant Clifford H. Pearson,
Cleveland, Ohio, USA

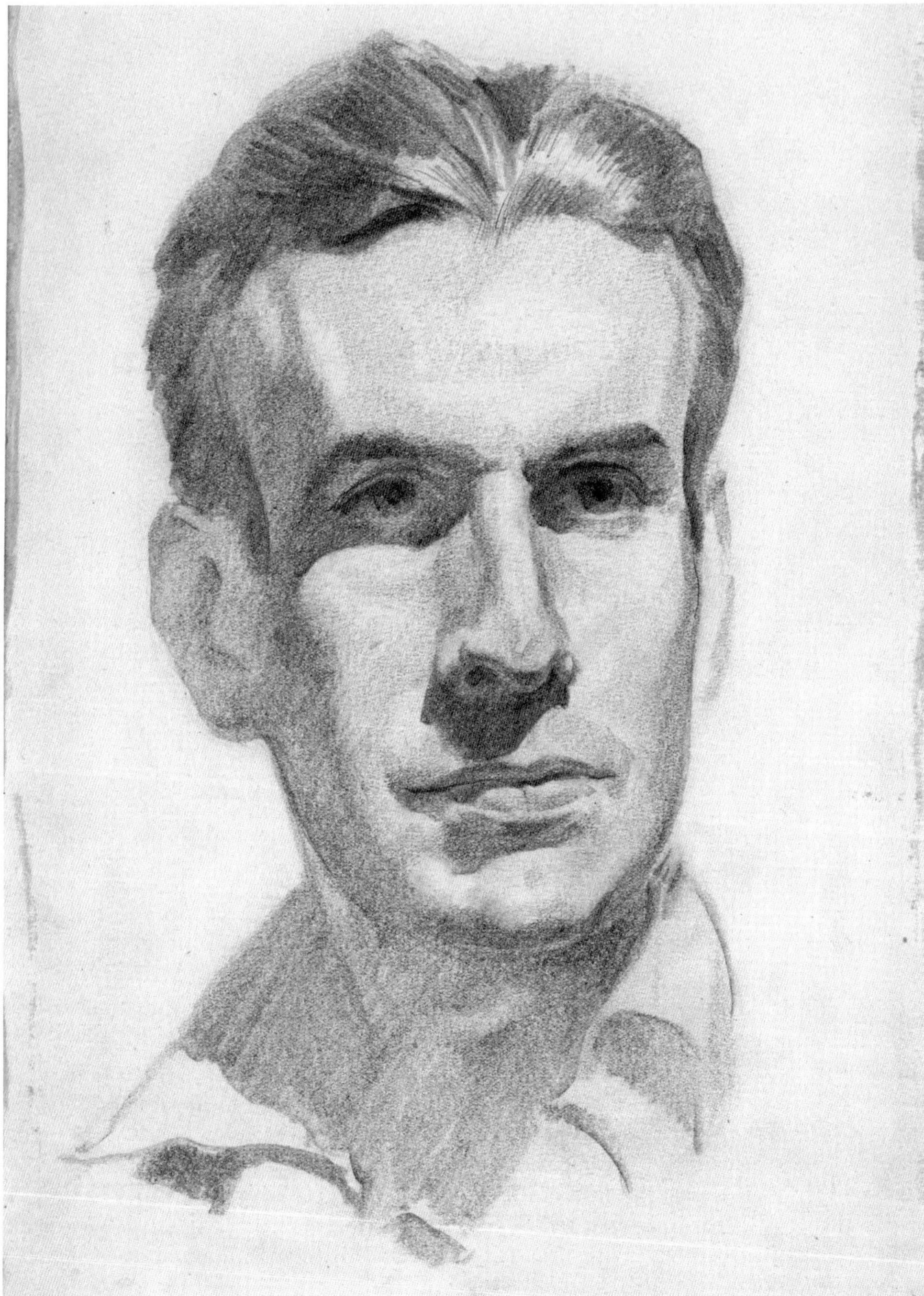

Second Lieutenant Clifford H. Pearson, a member of Carl's crew, was from Cleveland, Ohio. He originally joined the 753rd Tank Battalion, US Army, but re-enlisted in the Army Air Corps as an aviation cadet. As a B-17 Flying Fortress pilot, he was shot down over Africa, landing in a Tunisian desert on 3 January 1943 after making an emergency landing behind enemy lines 30 miles north-west of Gabes. The crew was captured the next day and they were transported through Rome to Bolzano, Italy, Florence and the Brenner Pass, finally passing into Germany to Dulag Luft where they were interrogated. From there, the officers on the plane were moved to Oflag XXI-B and eventually transferred to Stalag Luft III, North Compound, barracks 106. Clifford was later moved to South Compound, barracks 135, room 14.

With the rest of the 10,000 PoWs from Stalag Luft III, he was evacuated in January 1945, walking 52 miles to Spremberg, Germany, and he later arrived at Stalag XIII-D in Nuremberg. Clifford endured a second forced march when he and the prisoners from the camp walked for a week to get to Stalag VII-A in Moosburg, where they were liberated by General Patton's Third Army.

Sergeant Angelo Spinelli,
The Bronx, New York City, New York, USA

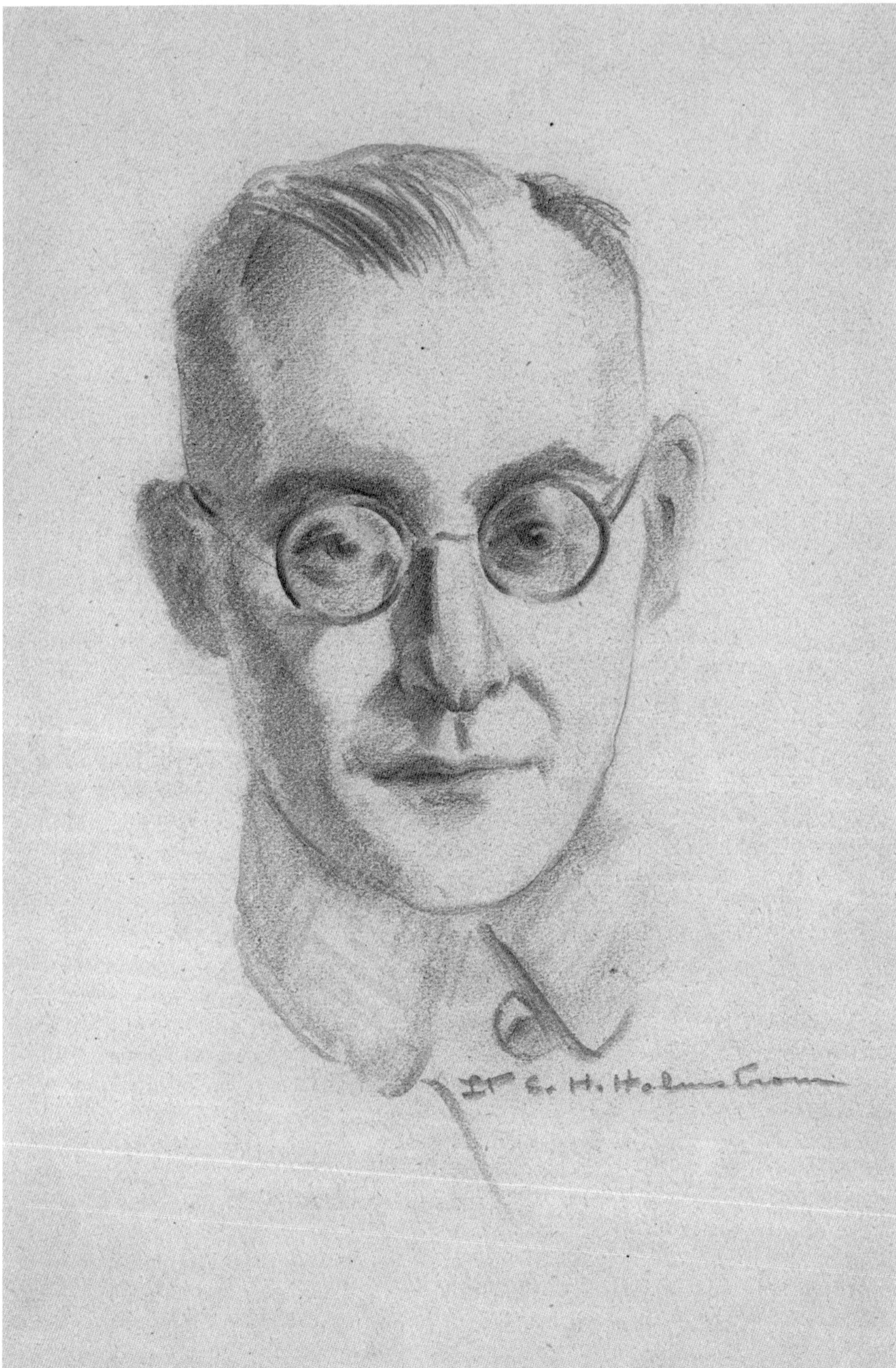

Sergeant Angelo Spinelli, an Italian-American from the Bronx in New York City, was drafted in 1941 and served with the 162nd Signal Photo Company as a combat photographer. He was captured in North Africa by the Germans on Valentine's Day 1943. Sergeant Spinelli spent twenty-seven months in PoW camps, mainly Stalag III-B near Furstenberg, Germany, where he learned the art of bribing and bartering with prison guards using chocolate bars and cigarettes sent by the American Red Cross and in care packages from his family. Spinelli bribed a camp guard to procure a Voitlander camera, tripod and film and then had the film developed while he was still a PoW. He hid the camera in his pants and used it to secretly take 1,200 photographs of the camp's activities and life as a Kriegie, risking his life by doing so.

He undoubtedly would have been severely punished if his activities had been discovered, as evidenced by the photo he took of a Russian prisoner who was shot dead for picking up a cigarette an American tossed over to him. The remarkable photograph later appeared in the book *Life Behind Barbed Wire: the Secret World War II Photographs of POW Angelo M. Spinelli*, which was published in 2004. The photos were enhanced by his co-author Lewis H. Carlson's commentary. The book contained ninety-two photographs. Carlson's explanatory text described prisoners trading with the guards, combating ticks, lice and other vermin, preparing meagre rations on ingenious cooking contraptions, fighting off boredom by playing baseball, soccer and football, putting on musical and dramatic theatre presentations and worshipping in a chapel built by the prisoners themselves, giving a window into camp life where catastrophe was normal and normalcy was often catastrophic. In addition, there are dramatic shots of liberation from Stalag III-A, Luckenwald, Germany, at the end of the war where Spinelli and some 38,000 other Allied prisoners had been moved during the final months. They were liberated by the Russian Red Army in April 1945. The photos are held at the National Historic Site in Andersonville, Georgia.

In 1946, the National Council of the YMCA published a booklet featuring Spinelli's photographs and the PoW paintings by Colonel C. Ross Greening entitled *The Yankee Kriegies*. His photos were then kept in a closet for thirty-three years. Spinelli's pictures have been displayed in many publications and exhibitions, and he received numerous veterans, fraternal, religious and civic awards and honours post-war.

After the war, he married his childhood sweetheart and had a son. Spinelli went into the jewellery manufacturing business with his brother Joseph in Yonkers, New York, where he worked for thirty-eight years.

First Lieutenant Alvin 'Sammy from Alabamy' Vogtle, Alabama, USA

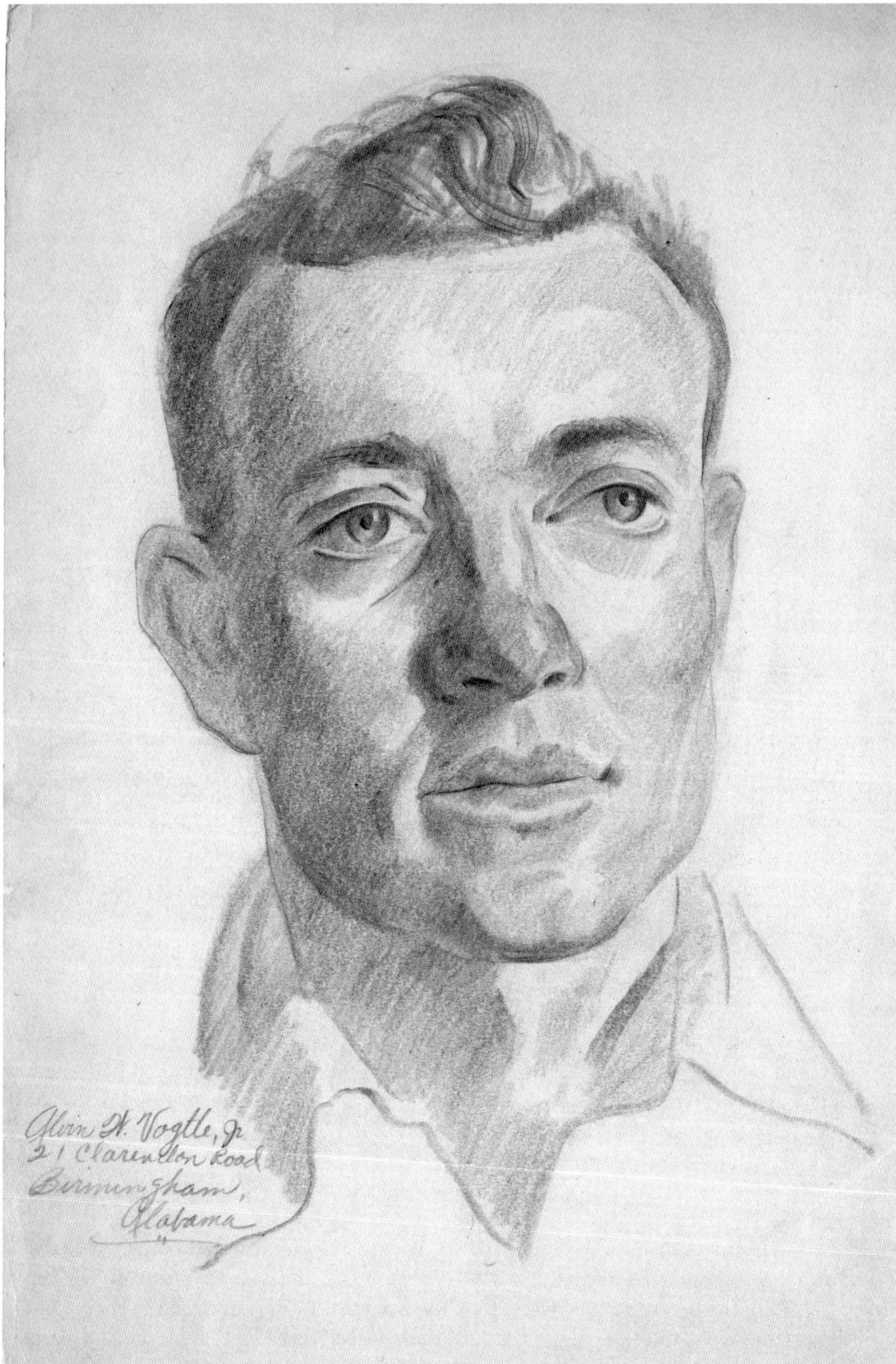

First Lieutenant Alvin 'Sammy from Alabamy' Vogtle was nicknamed with reference to his home state of Alabama. He was awarded a Bachelor's Degree in Science and Literature from Auburn University in 1939 and studied law at the University of Alabama and the University of Virginia.

Immediately after graduating from the University of Alabama Law School, he enlisted in the United States Army where he became a fighter pilot. He flew more than thirty missions before he ran out of fuel over Algeria, Africa. He was sent to Dulag Luft, Oflag XXI- B and then to Stalag Luft III. Vogtle became the designated head of the 'Procurement Committee' as he excelled in stealing tunnel-building materials and bribing guards with Red Cross chocolate and home-made booze. Vogtle was the inspiration for the PoW character portrayed by Steve McQueen, 'The Cooler King', in the movie *The Great Escape*.

> Vogtle and a colleague once managed to hide in a trash wagon in the camp, and he avoided the probing of the ferrets at the gate, while his buddy was found and pulled out. In due course, Sammy jumped out and ran, but he was seen by the old German driver of the horse and wagon, so he didn't have much of a head start.
>
> Quote from granddaughter Katie Kirtley

After the war, he married and had seven children. He was employed as legal counsel at Alabama Power and later became president and chairman of the Board of Southern Company, one of the largest electric utility holding companies in the nation. Southern Company named a nuclear power plant in eastern Georgia the 'Alvin W. Vogtle Electric Generating Plant' in his honour. He died in 1994.

Second Lieutenant Alfred G. Wade, Crofton, Kentucky, USA

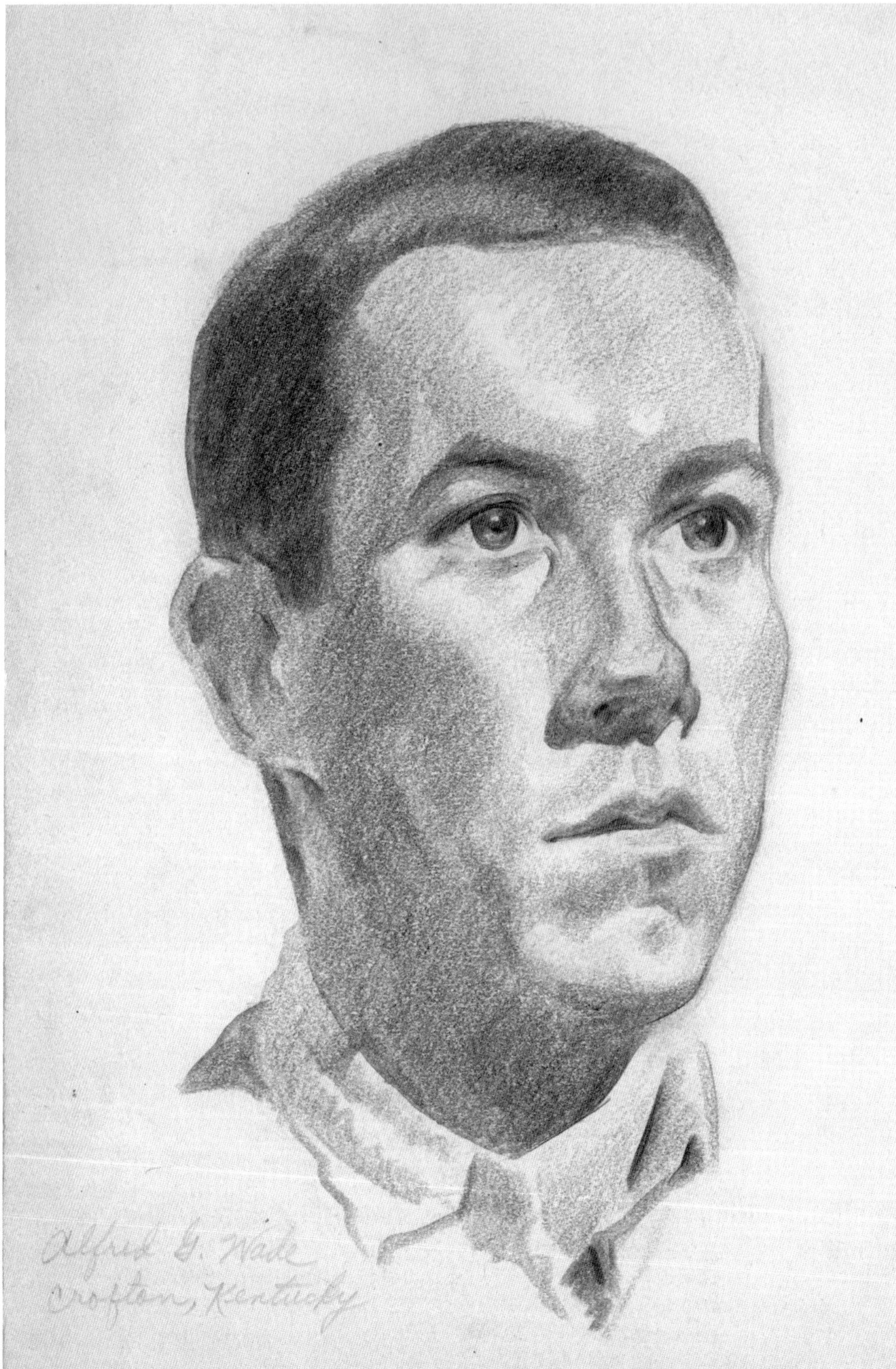

Second Lieutenant Alfred G. Wade was a navigator from Crofton, Kentucky, and was part of the 305th Bomber Group nicknamed 'Can Do' and the 366th Bomber Squadron. On his eighth mission, he was bombing submarine pens in Wilhelmshaven, Germany, and was shot down on 27 January 1943 by flak and Focke-Wulf 190s. He bailed out and landed 120 miles south-east of Wilhelmshaven, Germany and was captured immediately.

After his capture, he was taken to Dulag Luft for interrogation and then transferred to Oflag XXI-B. His final transfer was to Stalag Luft III, arriving on 11 April 1943, where he was assigned to South Compound, barracks 135.

Sergeant Jack Godding Cameron, Toronto, Canada

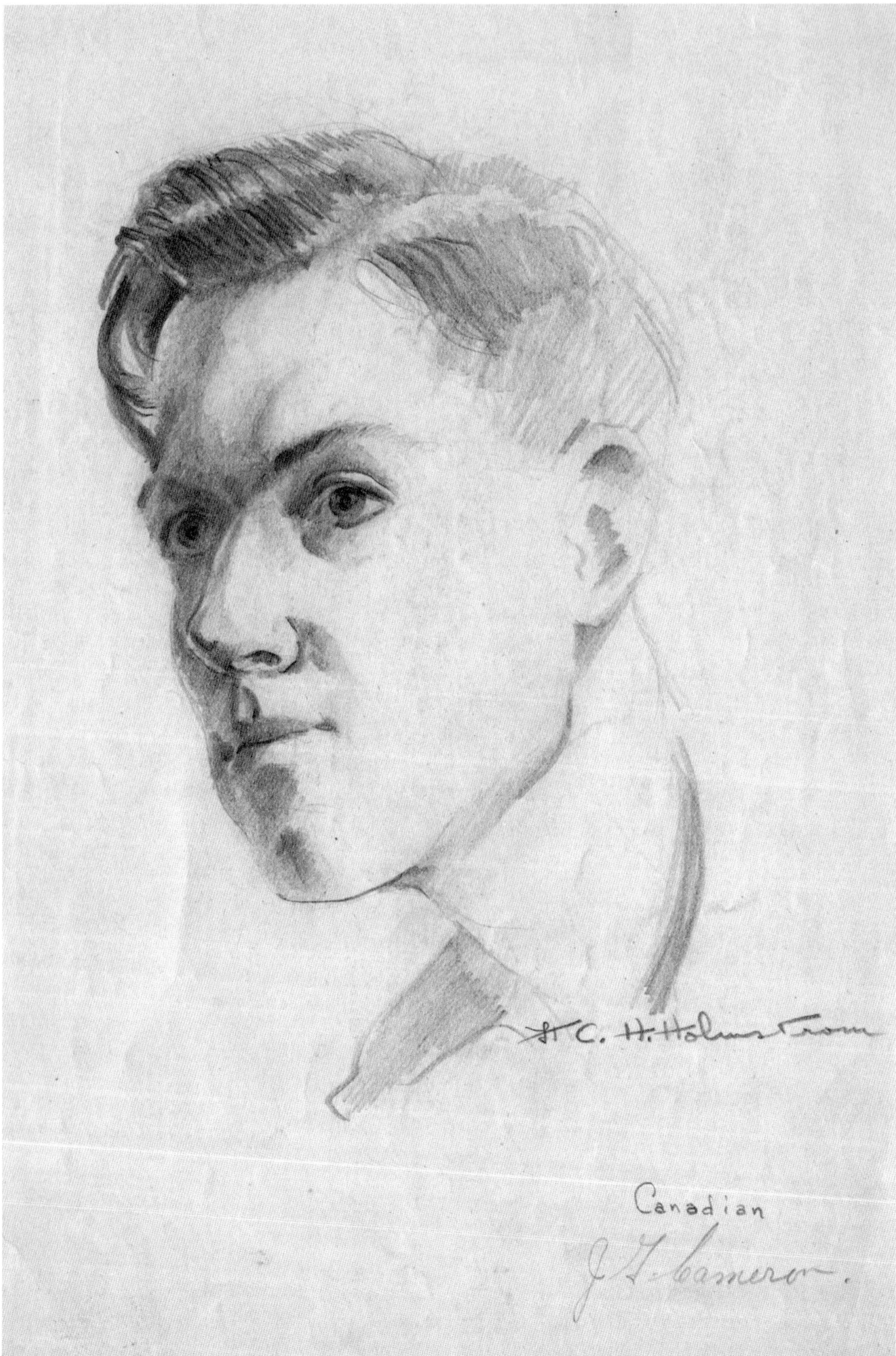

Sergeant Jack Godding 'J.G.' Cameron, PoW #42710, was an airman aboard a Stirling BK599 from 214 Squadron. His plane was lost on operations to Kiel, Germany, on 13 October 1942. He was sent to Stalag 9-C, Stalag Luft VI (also called Heydekrug) and Stalag 357.

He was the son of John Cameron, Toronto, Canada.

Rhys 'Taffy' Jenkins, Wales

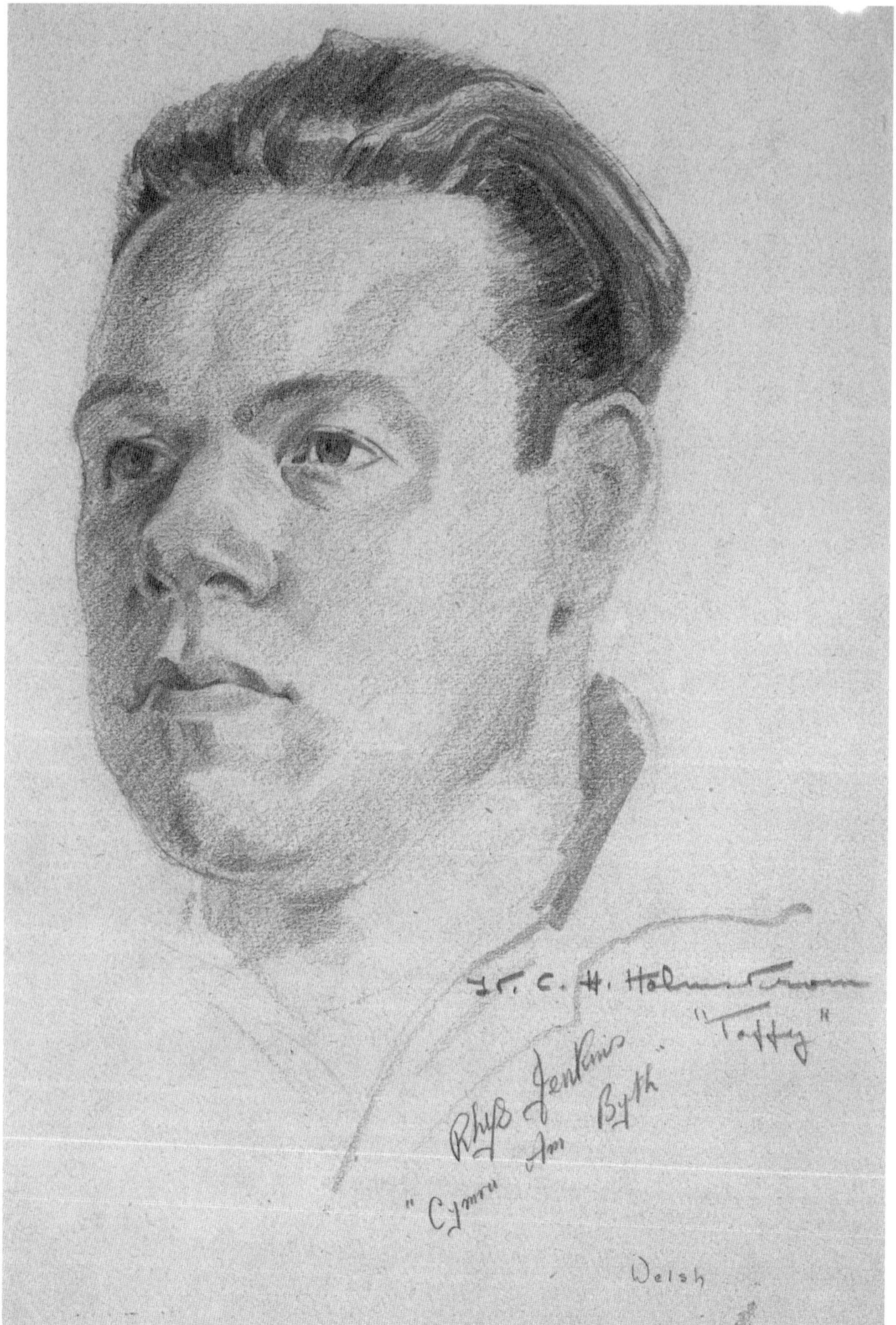

Rhys 'Taffy' Jenkins' sketch has 'Welsh' written on it. No other background details are known.

Unknown PoW

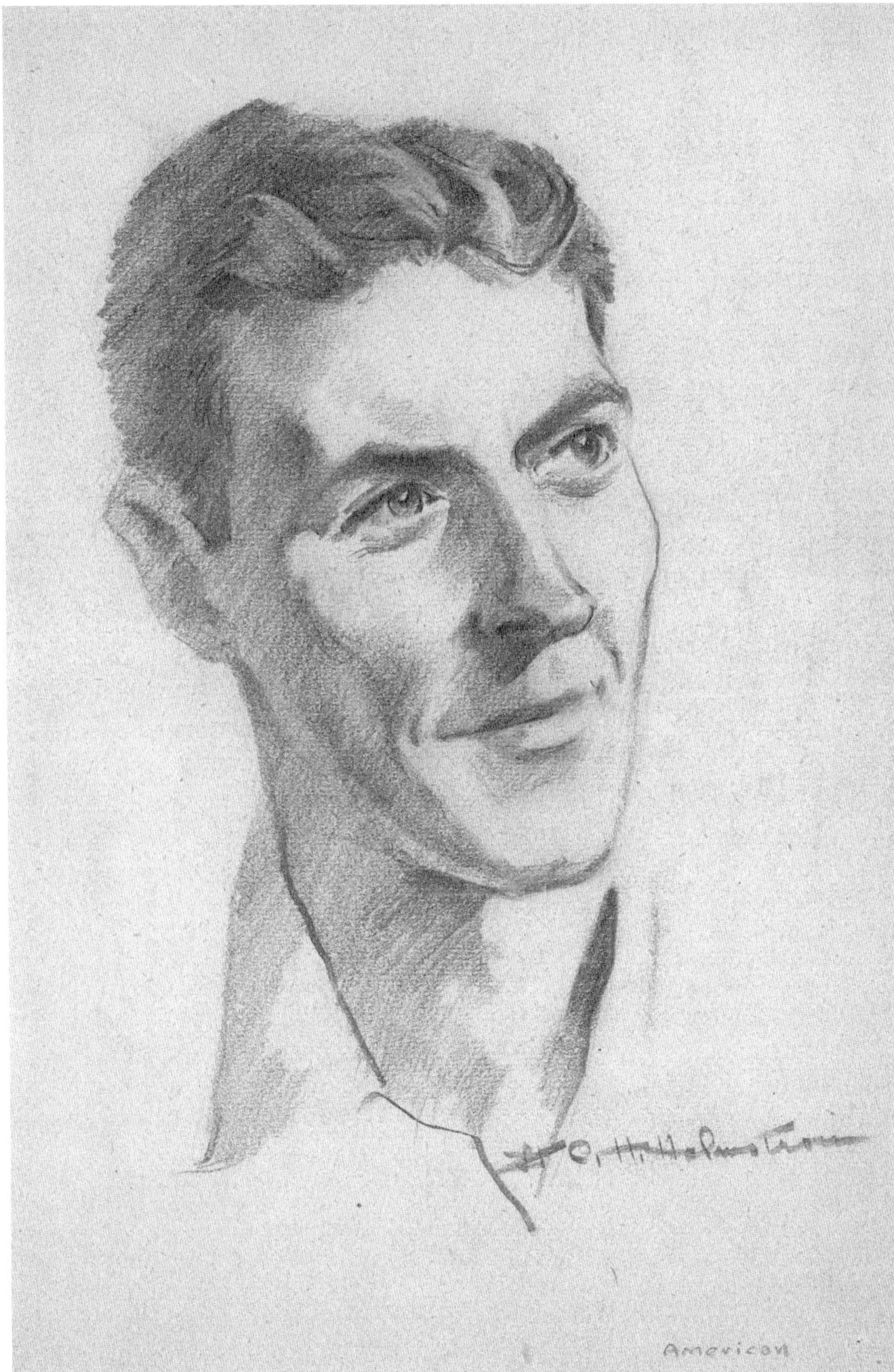

Pilot Officer John B. Locke, Middlesex, England

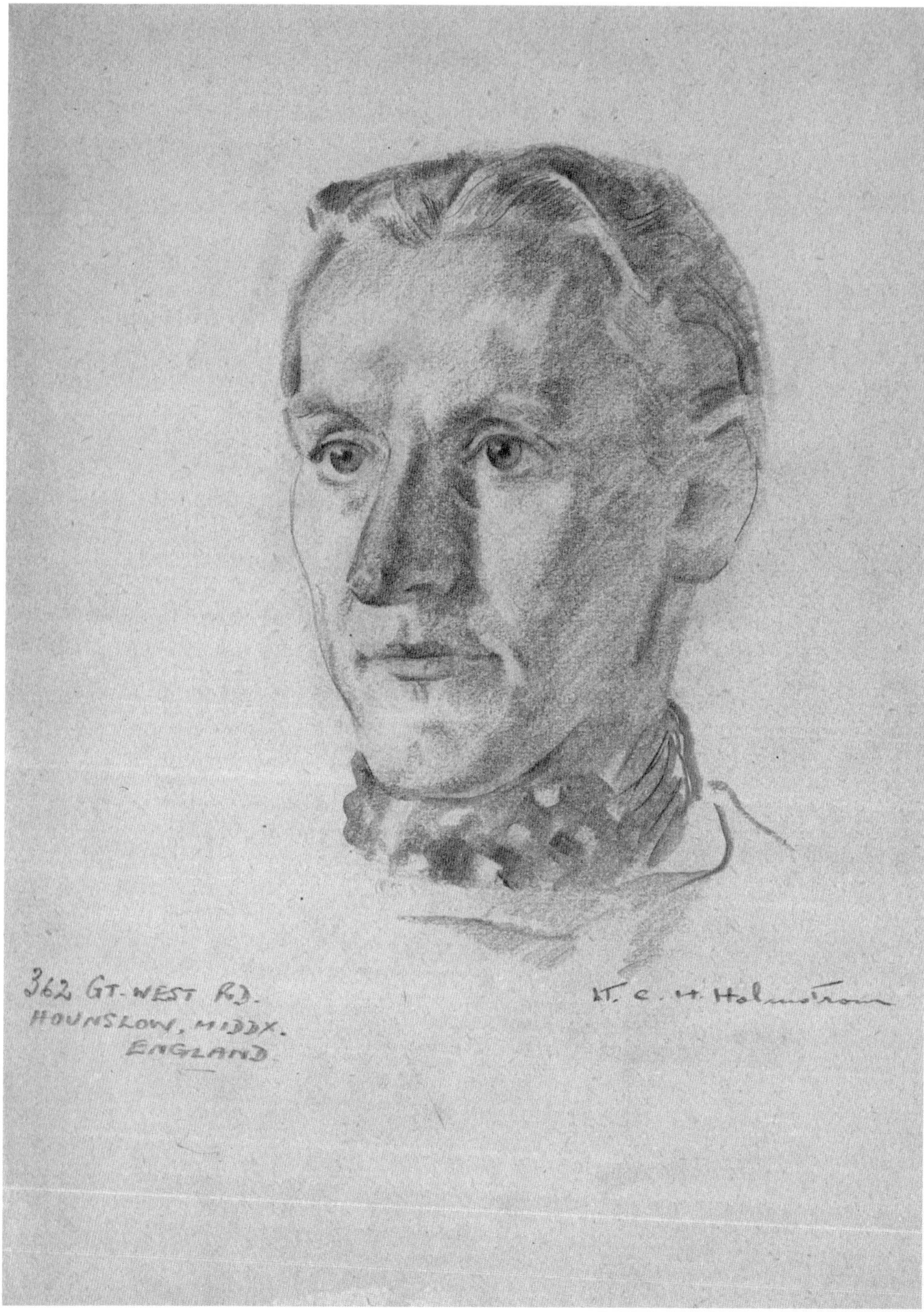

Pilot Officer John B. Locke from Middlesex was a pilot with the RAF. He flew a Halifax DT751 from 76 Squadron and was shot down by a night fighter on the Essex raid on 12 March 1943. The aircraft was hit by flak at a reported height of 100ft over Kiel, Germany. The aircraft crash-landed west/north-west of Venlo, Holland. He was captured and held at Stalag Luft III.

Sergeant Eric N. Neilson, England

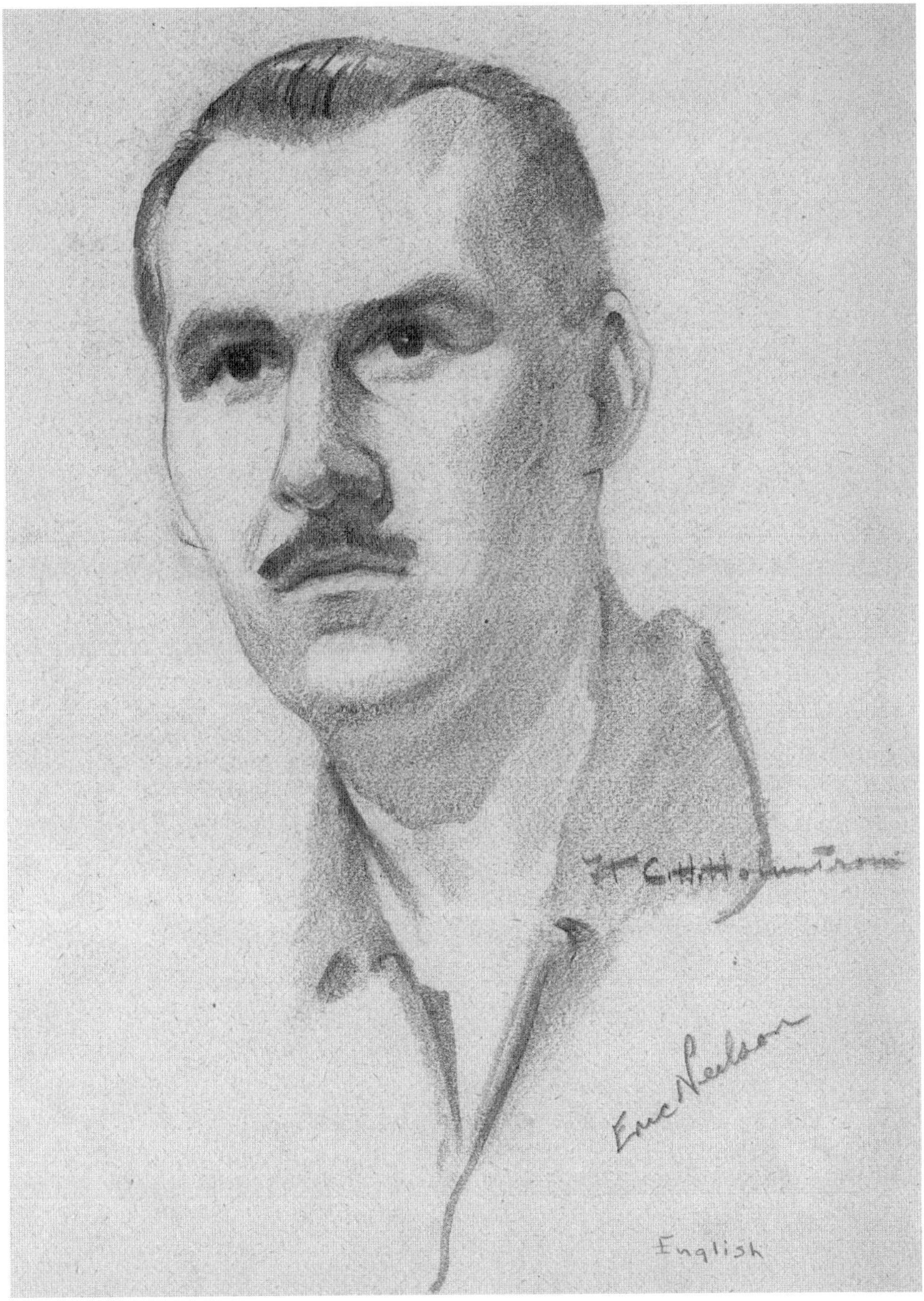

Sergeant Eric N. Neilson was the flight engineer on a Handley Page Halifax II from 102 Squadron on a raid on Frankfurt on 2 December 1942. His plane crashed near Laumersheim on the west/north-west outskirts of Mannheim. He was captured and spent time in Stalag Luft VI, Stalag Luft IV and Stalag Luft I.

Earle Milton Nelson, Australia

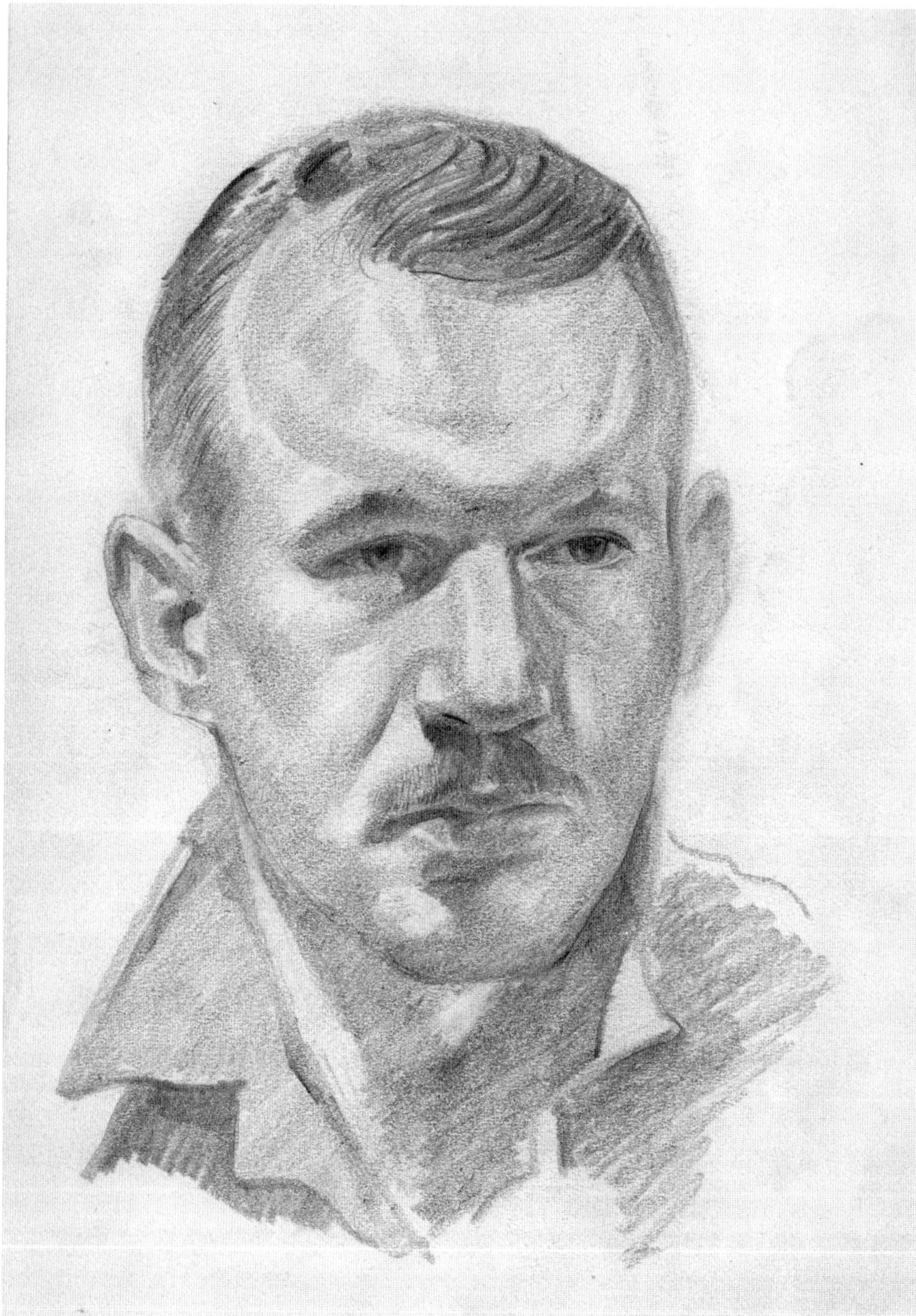

Sergeant Earle Milton 'Eric' Nelson was an Australian PoW from 101 Squadron. He was lost on operations to Duisburg on 9 April 1943 and later held at Stalag Luft III. He was the author of *If Winter Comes*, published in 1989.

Frank Sasling

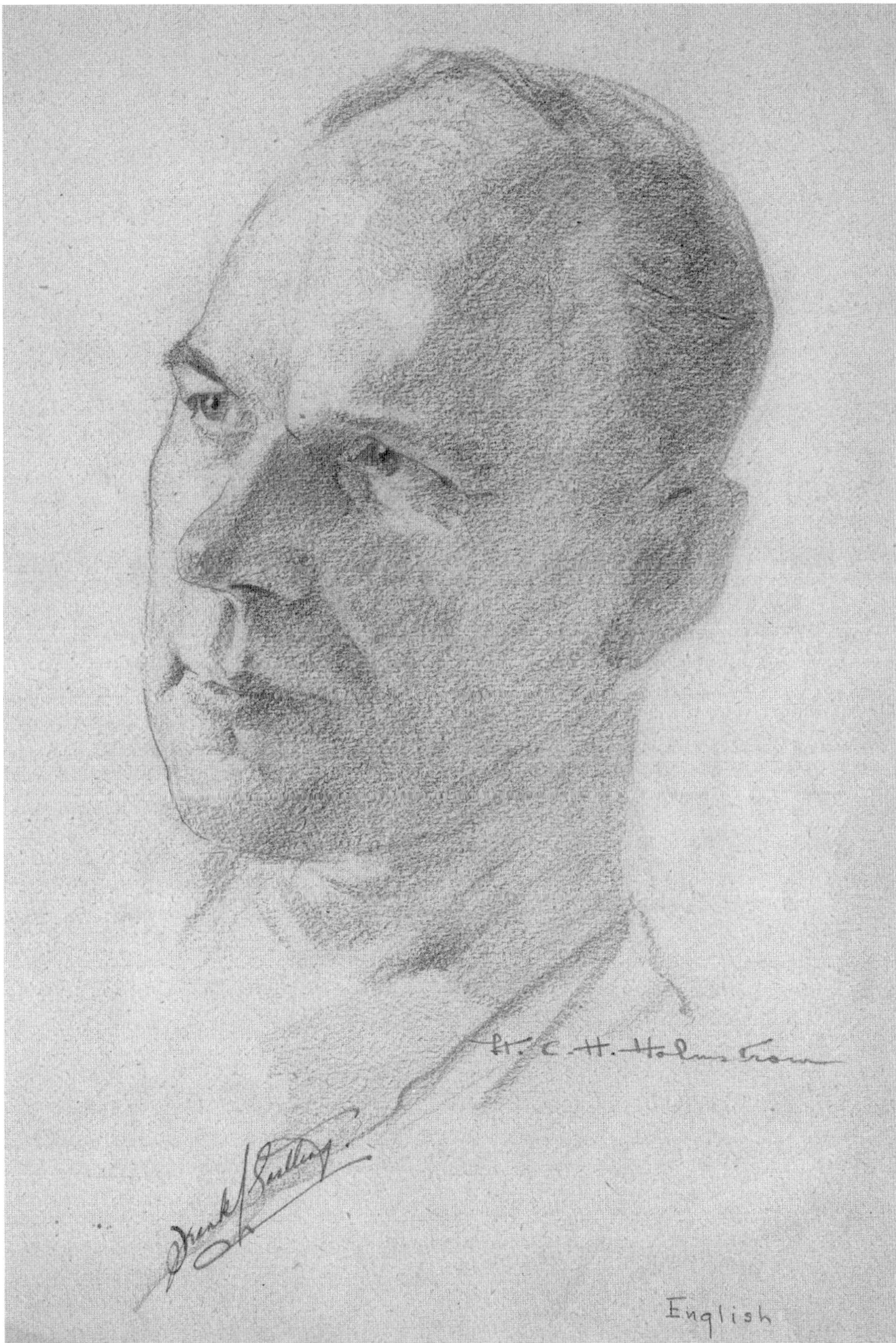

No further information available.

First Lieutenant Ayton Richardson 'A.R.' Whitaker, Maidenhead, Berkshire, England

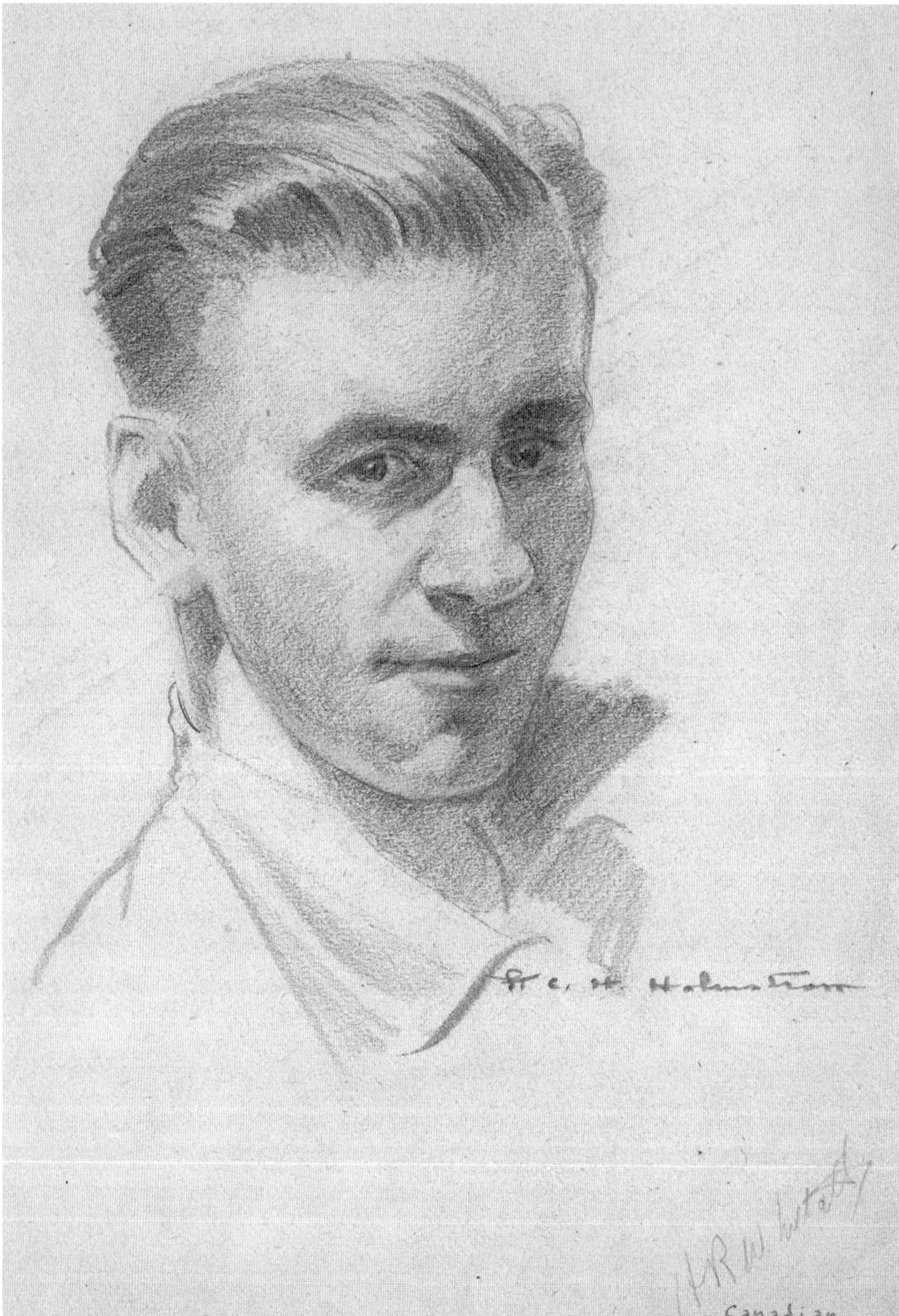

First Lieutenant Ayton Richardson 'A.R.' Whitaker from Maidenhead was an officer in the Royal Air Force. He was the bomb-aimer on an Avro Lancaster III PB523 from No. 582 Pathfinder Squadron. He was shot down on 23 December 1944. The plane was lost on operations to Cologne, one of five such Lancasters lost that night. His plane crashed at Opitter south-east of Bree, Belgium. After his capture, he was sent to Stalag Luft III.

After the war, he was a producer for radio programmes on the BBC Home Service and the Light Programme, a BBC radio station that broadcast chiefly mainstream light entertainment and music from 1945 until 1967. In 1953 he began producing television dramas and concentrated on producing and directing for television. He was involved in the creation of the popular *Doctor Who* TV series. He died in 1999.

Kazimierz 'Kazik' Zakrzewski-Rucinski, Jabłonna, Poland

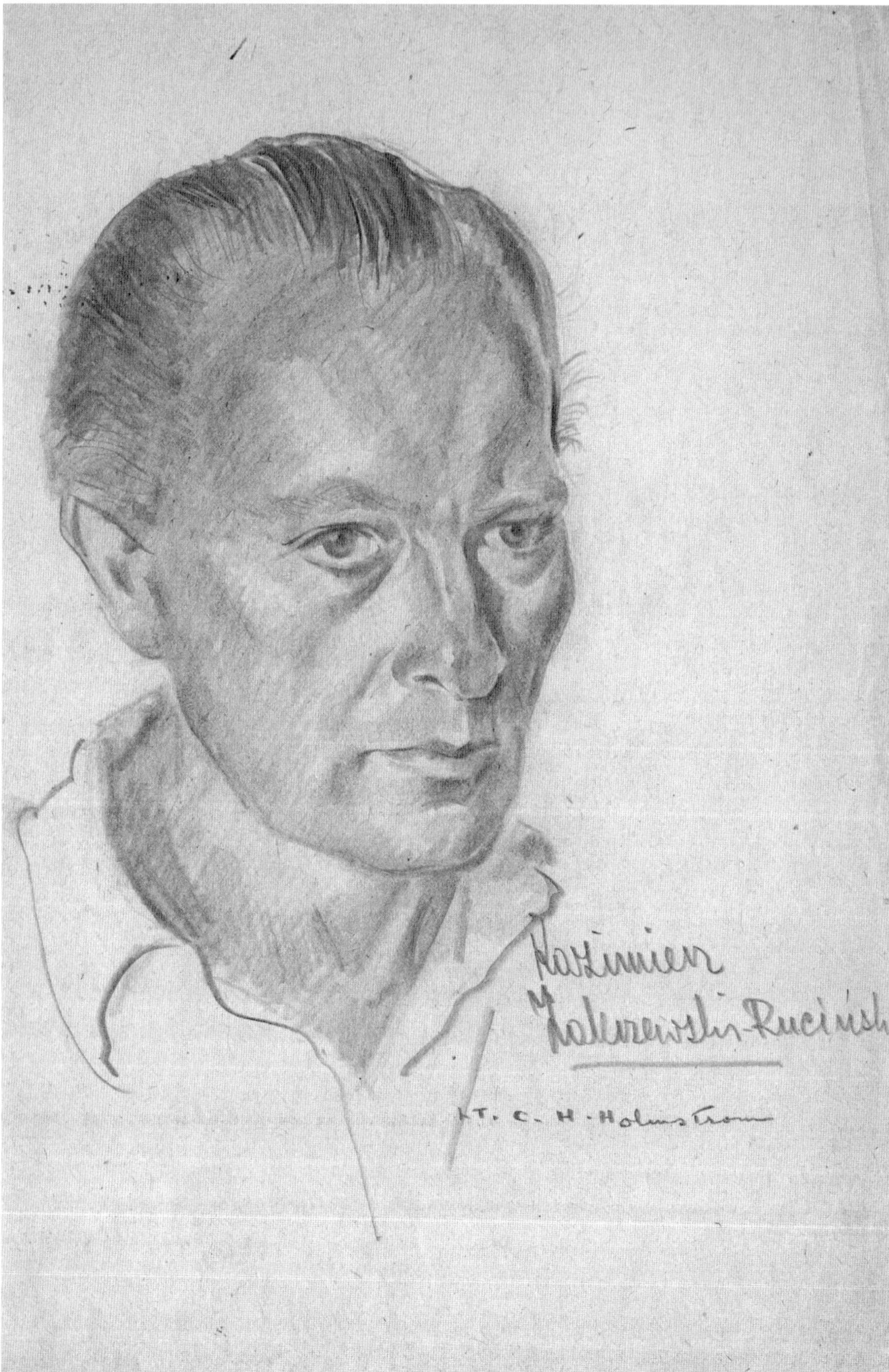

Kazimierz 'Kazik' Zakrzewski-Rucinski from Poland worked as a professional illustrator before the Second World War. In 1940, he travelled from his occupied homeland south through Eastern Europe into Syria via Greece and Turkey, across North Africa, and then caught a boat from Gibraltar to join the Royal Air Force in the UK.

He was shot down over Germany in 1942 in a Wellington bomber during a night mission on the Dutch border. He spent the rest of the war in Stalag Luft III and produced many portraits of his fellow PoWs. He hauled the portraits through the snow in an improvised trolley during the infamous 52-mile Forced March at the end of the war.

He came back to England to remain in the UK after the war, married and had a daughter. He worked as an architect producing a modernist proposal for an RAF Memorial Chapel at Biggin Hill in England, working again with PoW Wylton Todd who Kazik had met in Stalag Luft III. He died in 1982.

Kazik was part of the Free Polish Air Force and received the Polish Cross of Merit, Third Class, Bronze; Polska Swemu Obrońcy Medal; Medal for Victory and Freedom 1945; Great Britain, 1939–45 Star; Air Crew Europe Star; and War Medal 1939–45.

Polish PoWs at Stalag Luft III

The Polish Air Force was destroyed when the Germans struck Poland by surprise in September 1939. Many of the captured fliers escaped within a year. Enduring incredible hardship, they travelled in large groups to the eastern Mediterranean, took ships to France, arriving in England, integrating into the RAF as Polish units flying with No. 303 Squadron. They became some of the most aggressive and daring pilots with one of the best records during the Battle of Britain.

All the fliers were fighting under assumed names to protect their families, who, in some cases, lived within a few miles of the prison camps. Lieutenant Colonel Clark stated in his book, *33 Months as a POW in Stalag Luft III*, 'More than 120 Polish officers were held in the North Camp at Stalag Luft III by the end of the war.' Block #107 was the 'Polish block' in North Compound where the largest group of Poles lived with Czechoslovakian airmen.

Many Polish airmen were involved in the Great Escape. Fighter pilot, Flight Lieutenant Mieczyslaw Wyszkowski, was flying with the RAF and was shot down in North Africa. Flight Lieutenant Bronislaw Mickiewicz became the tunnel trap genius due to his ingenuity in creating traps to block the tunnel entrances from scrutiny of German ferrets, designing trap doors for tunnels Tom, Dick, and Harry, and working closely with Polish 'Big X' Stefan Janus.

Pilot Officer 'Danny' Król, one of the best diggers on Flight Lieutenant Wally Floody's team, became one of the fifty murdered by the Gestapo after the 'Great Escape'. Flight Officer Pawel Tobloski, captured and murdered at Stettin, was fluent in German and travelled with British 'Wings' Day as his German NCO escort after the escape. Flight Officer Jerzy Reichenberg was at the head of a party of train travelers.

Near the end of the war, the Polish PoWs endured the Forced March with the rest of the PoWs at the camp, marching away from their homeland, and after liberation they returned to finally reunite with their families, if any of their families remained.

(Courtesy Marilyn Jeffers Walton and Michael C. Eberhardt – *From Interrogation to Liberation*)

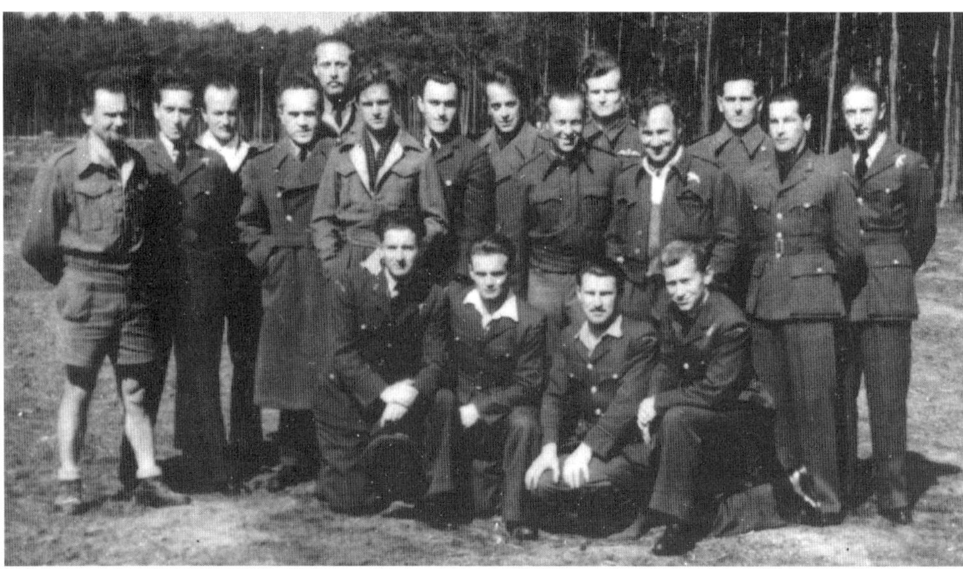

Standing from left: F/Lt Bronisław Mickiewicz, S/Ldr Władysław Szczesniewski, P/O Zbigniew Gutowski, F/Lt Stefan Kolodynski, F/Lt Zbigniew Kustrzynski, F/Lt Witold Lokuciewski, P/O Eugeniusz Nowakiewicz, S/Ldr Wacław Wilczewski, S/Ldr Stefan Janus, F/O Leszek Xiezopolski, S/Ldr Stanisław Pietraszkiewicz, P/O Roman Pentz, F/O Emil Landsman, P/O Czesław Daszuta. Kneeling from left: F/O Bernard Buchwald, P/O Stanisław "Danny" Król, F/O Jerzy Zbierzchowski, P/O Stefan Maciejewski.

(Courtesy of Marek Lazarz)

Portraits of the Staff

Koziol Juliusz, Honey Wagon Man, Poland

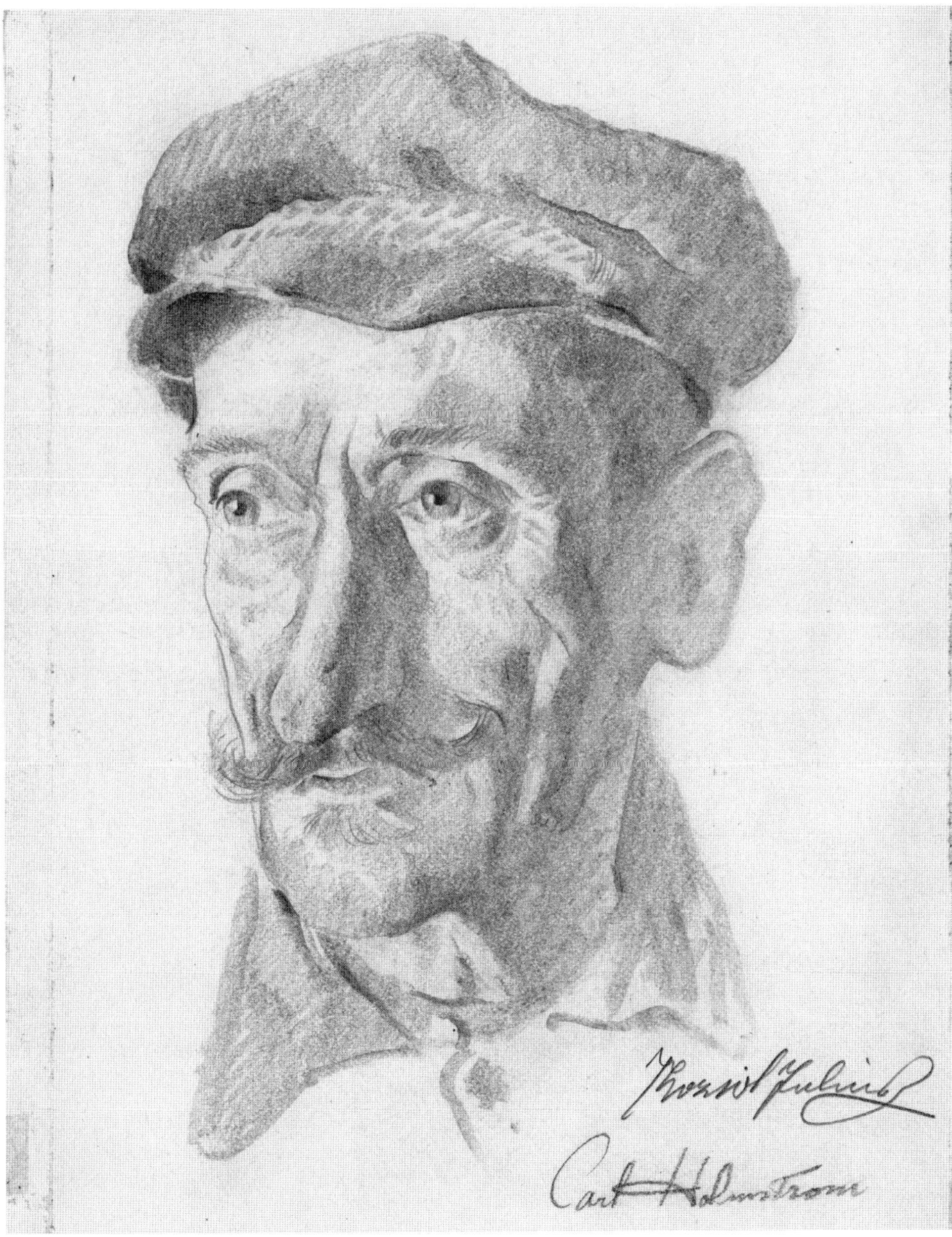

Koziol Juliusz from Poland worked in the camp as the sanitation worker, also known as the 'Honey Wagon Man'. No other information is known about him.

Oberfeldwebel Guard F.E. Eidmann: Guard, Germany

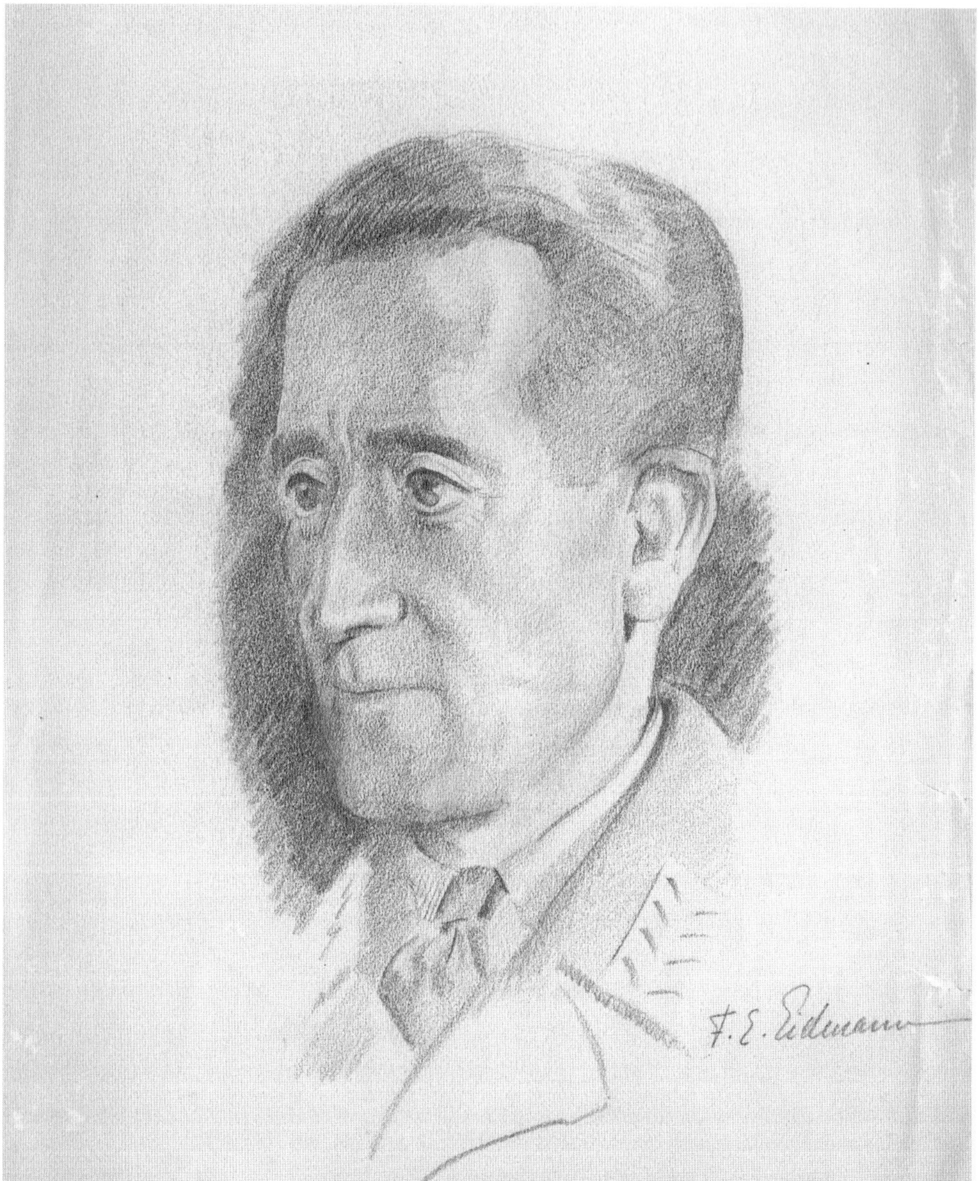

F.E. Eidmann from Germany was an Oberfeldwebel at Stalag Luft III.

> …an obviously well-educated and decent man. I engaged him in a serious conversation about the situation in Normandy. He recognized the significance of the forthcoming battle of St. Lo and expressed confidence that we would be stopped. He grudgingly acknowledged that if we broke through, it meant we were on the Continent to stay and that he believed portended the ultimate defeat of Germany. After St. Lo, I never could make eye contact with this man again.
>
> General A.P. Clark, *33 Months as a Prisoner of War in Stalag Luft III*

Obergefreiter Dufour: Guard, Germany

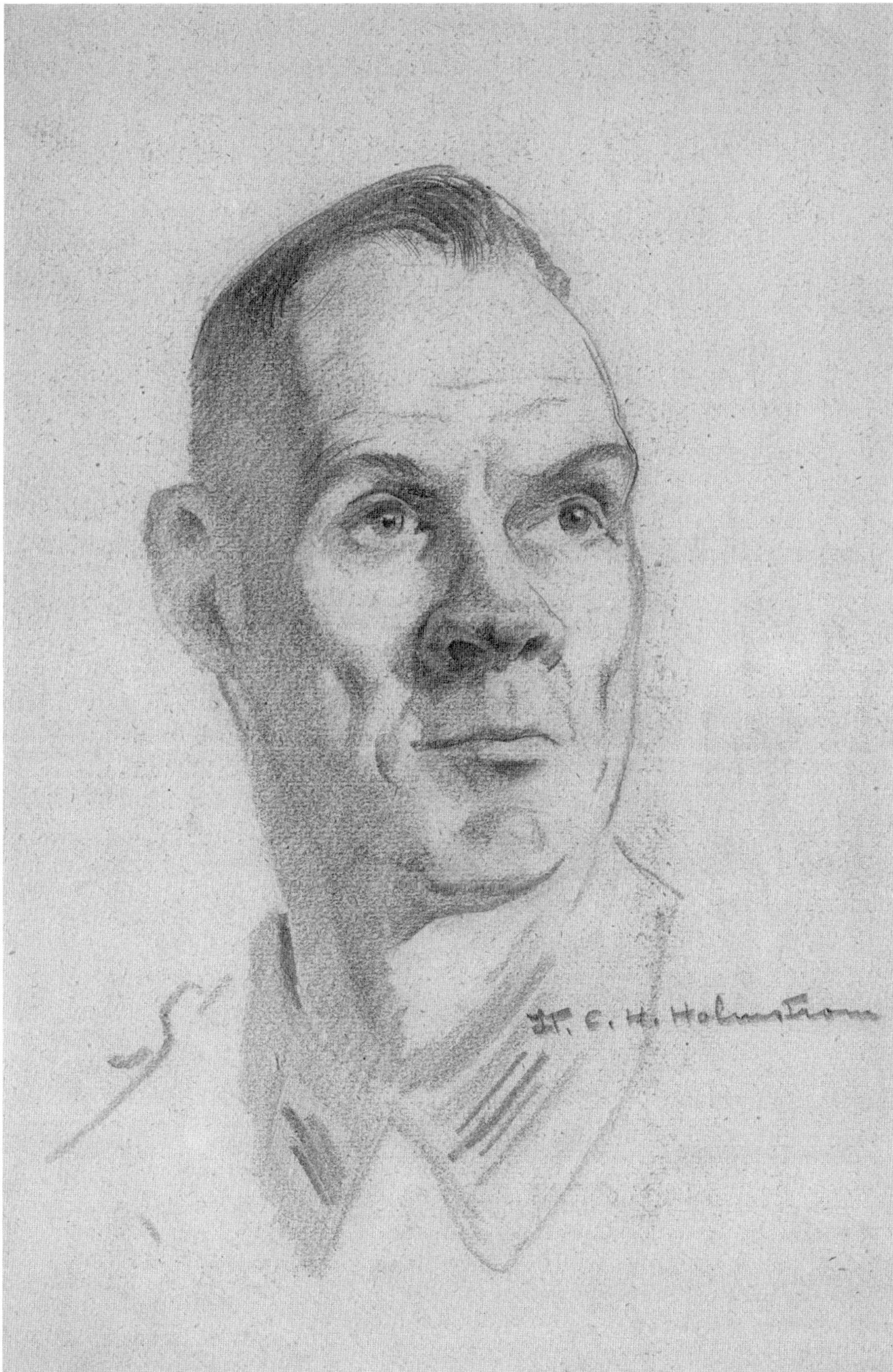

Obergefreiter Dufour: Guard, Germany

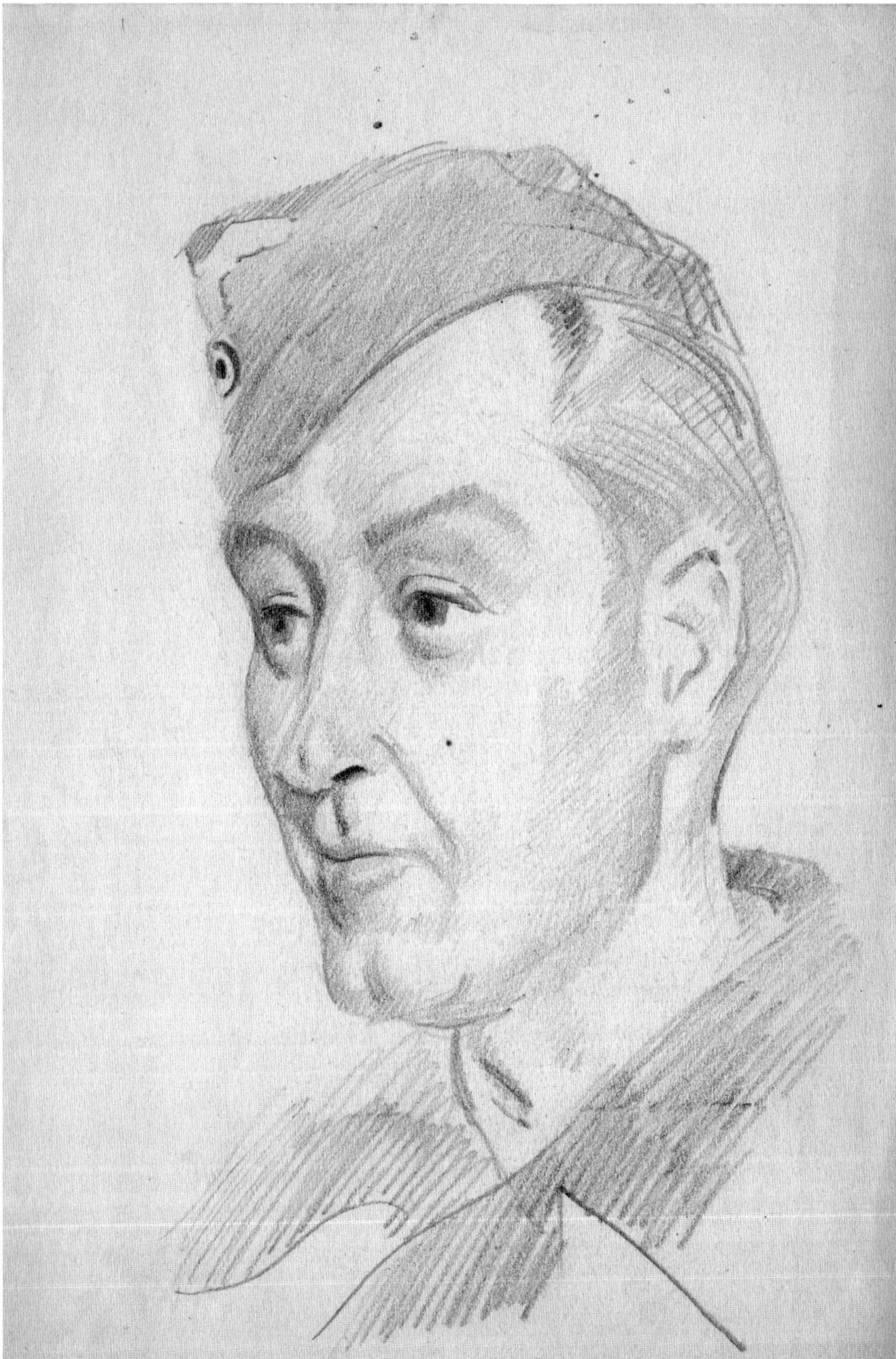

Unknown Obergefreiter: Guard, Germany

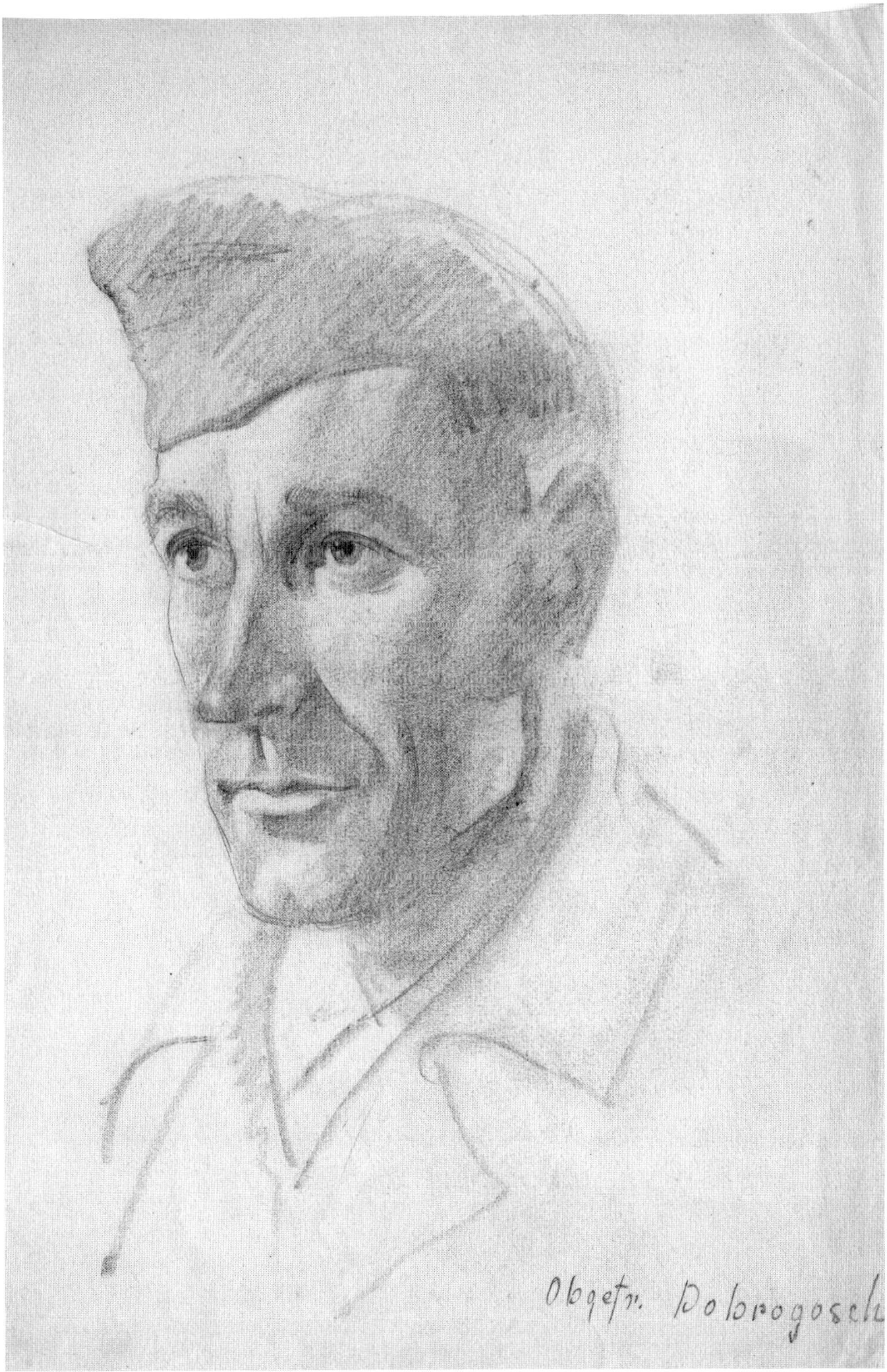

Unknown Portrait

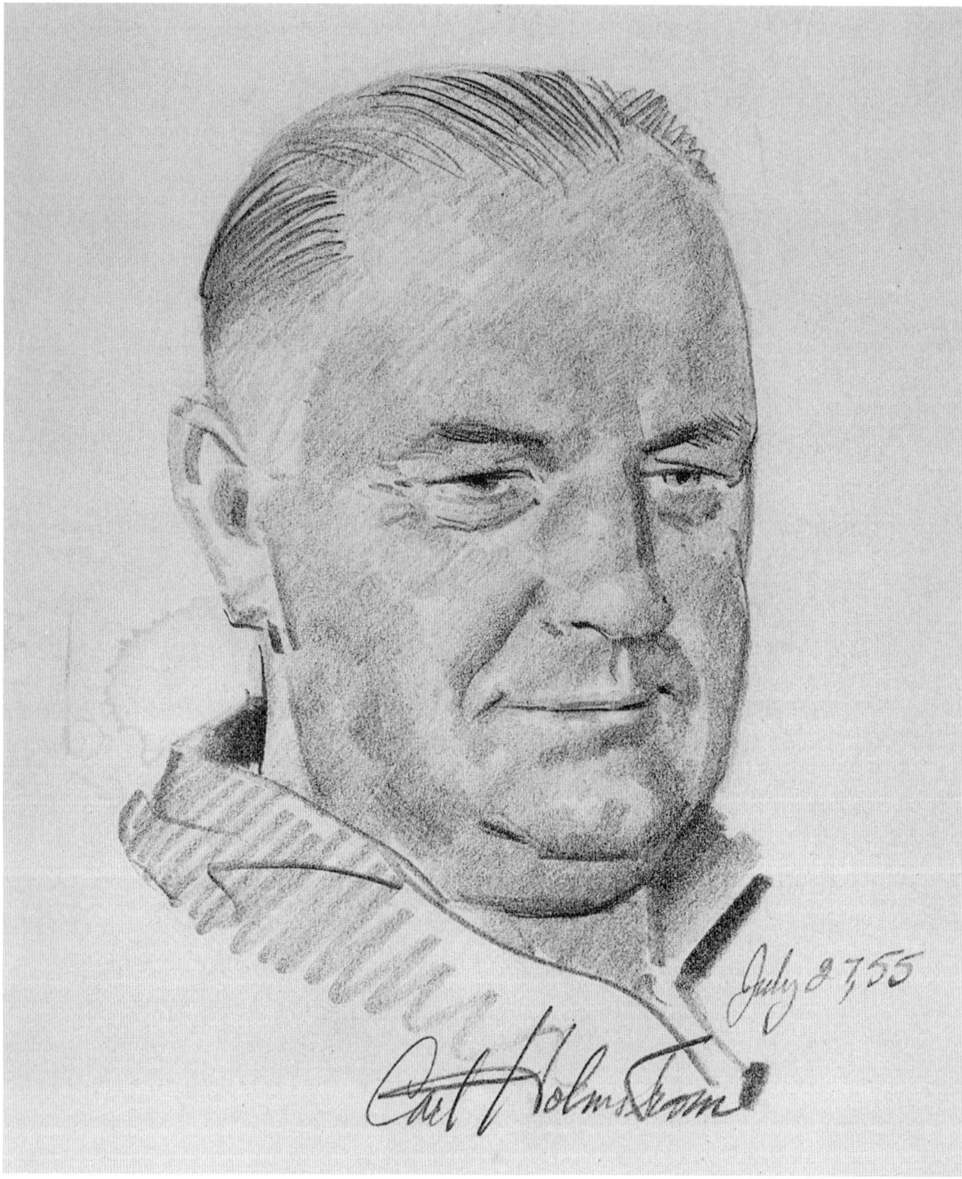

Glossary

Abort – prison camp latrine
Appel – roll call where all prisoners were counted by the Germans
AWOL – Absent Without Leave – military term indicating absence without permission
B–17 bomber – nicknamed 'Flying Fortress' – four-engine heavy bomber
Bash – an all-out culinary celebration or feast, or to eat a large amount
Black bread – dark German bread provided for the military and Allied PoWS noted for its long shelf life
Camp Lucky Strike – one of a number of temporary US Army tent cities situated near Le Havre, France, to process liberated American PoWs back to the US – named after cigarette brands to keep the locations secret
Chlorical – chlorine cleaner used to clean barracks
Clogs – shoes made of wood
Combine – collective name indicating number of men in a room
Condendo – sweetened condensed milk from Red Cross parcels
Dean & Dawson – London Travel Agency and nickname of forgery group at Stalag Luft III
'Dear Lieutenant letters' – letters to PoWs from wives or girlfriends who chose to leave them
Dobie stick – improvised implement used to wash clothes in a jam bucket
Dulag – from *Durchgangslager* – camps that served as a collection point for PoWs prior to reassignment
Ersatz tea – German imitation tea made of burned acorns and other unknown ingredients
Evacuation March – 1945 forced march of PoWs from Stalag Luft III across Germany
Ferret – guard assigned to look for escape activities
Flak – anti-aircraft fire
Focke-Wulf 190 – a German single-seat, single-engine fighter plane
Foodacco – Kriegie-run canteen for barter or exchange
40 & 8 boxcars – 40 men or 8 horses – railroad cars that transported PoWs
Geneva Conventions – a series of agreements accepted by most nations concerning the treatment of prisoners of war and of the sick, wounded, and dead in battle – first made at Geneva, Switzerland in 1864

'Go around the bend' – exhibit signs of mental illness due to incarceration
Goon – nickname for German guard after a popular comic strip character, 'Alice the Goon'
Goon baiting – harassing or teasing the German guards
Goon box – German watch tower manned by guard and equipped with search lights
'Green Death soup' – thin, watery dehydrated vegetable soup containing bugs and grass
Honey wagon – sanitation wagon that came to clean latrines (aborts)
Hundeführer – German sentry dog-handler
Jam bucket – large pail originally containing jam improvised to use to clean clothes with dobie sticks
Jagdgeschwader – German Second World War fighter which used the Messerschmitt Bf 109 and Focke-Wulf 190 aircraft
Junkers 88 – Second World War Luftwaffe twin-engine multirole combat aircraft
Keintrinkwasser – German lead container used to carry water for bathing and cleaning, never drinking water
KLIM – milk spelled backwards – dense powdered milk in Red Cross parcels
Kohlrabi – also called German turnip – tough, fibrous vegetable fed to PoWs
Kommandant – German commanding officer
Kommandantur – German compound
Kriegie – short for *kriegsgefangen*, or prisoner of war
Kriegsmarine – German Navy
Logging sack time – sleeping or staying in bed
Long March – British name for 52-mile evacuation march from Stalag Luft III in 1945
Luft – German word for 'air'
Luftwaffe – German Air Force
Mauldin, Bill – American editorial cartoonist who won a Pulitzer Prize for his satirical drawings of the life of the Second World War combat soldier
Moosburg – German town where Stalag VIIA was located
NCO – non-commissioned officer
Nuremberg – German town where Stalag XIIID was located
Oflag – German term for 'Offizierslager'– prisoner of war camp for officers
Oflag XXI-B – PoW camp for officers and enlisted men in Schubin, Poland
Palliasse – a mattress cover that held the wood shavings or excelsior
Parcel day – delivery of Red Cross food parcels and mail
PoW – prisoner of war
Pranger – a British multi-functional improvised tool
RAF – The United Kingdom's Royal Air Force

Raisin brew – homemade alcoholic beverage made from raisins
Red Cross parcels – Boxes of essential food and personal necessities sent by many countries through Switzerland to sustain PoWs
RNZAF – Royal New Zealand Air Force
Road apples – American slang term for horse dung or droppings
Sack – slang name of a bed for prisoners of war
Sack artist – habitual sleeper
SAO – Senior American Officer
SBO – Senior British Officer
Silent treatment – not communicating with new PoWs until it was determined they were not a German plant
Spremberg – German town where evacuated Stalag Luft III PoWs boarded 40&8 boxcars
SS – 'Schutzstaffel' – major paramilitary organization under Adolf Hitler and the Nazi Party
Stalag – German from *stammlager* – a prison for the 'common stock' of the army or servicemen below officer grade ranks
Stalag Luft III – One of two PoW camps for Allied flying officers – located in Sagan, Germany
Stooge – person elected to do chores and to monitor whereabouts of Germans
SPAM – (SPiced hAM) a brand of canned, cooked pig meat included in Red Cross parcels
Stroller – a guard that patrolled the barbed wire around the PoW camp
Submarine pen – a type of submarine base with bunkers to protect submarines from air attack
'There I Was' Stories – stories detailing all aspects of one's shoot down and capture
Third United States Army – American Army Unit that directed the American 14th Armored Infantry Division which liberated Allied PoWS at Stalag VIIA in Moosburg, Germany
USAAF – The United States Army Air Forces
V-E Day – Tuesday, 8 May 1945 – to mark the formal acceptance by the Allies of Germany's surrender of its armed forces
Verboten – German for forbidden
Vorlager – Stalag Luft III German compound which contained administrative buildings, a small hospital, and cooler at the front of the camp
Wachhunds – German sentry dogs used in camp
Wartime Logs – diary-style books issued by the YMCA to each prisoner
WAVE – women's branch of the United States Naval Reserve during the Second World War
Wehrmacht – German Army

Weasel – assistant to guard assigned to look for any escape activities

White House – highest building at Oflag XXI–B that contained offices, hospital, and library for the camp

Winchell, Walter – most powerful columnist and radio commentator in America in the 1930s and 1940s

YMCA –Young Men's Christian Association